DWIGHT D.
EISENHOWER

Hero and Politician

TWAYNE'S TWENTIETH-CENTURY AMERICAN BIOGRAPHY SERIES

John Milton Cooper, Jr., General Editor

DWIGHT D. EISENHOWER

Hero and Politician

Robert F. Burk

TWAYNE PUBLISHERS • BOSTON
A Division of G. K. Hall & Co.

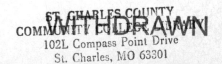

Copyright © 1986 by G. K. Hall & Co.
All Rights Reserved
Published by Twayne Publishers
A Division of G. K. Hall & Co.
70 Lincoln Street, Boston, Massachusetts 02111

Twayne's Twentieth-Century
American Biography Series No. 2

Photographs courtesy of the Dwight D. Eisenhower
Library unless otherwise noted.

Designed and produced by Marne B. Sultz
Copyediting supervised by Lewis DeSimone
Typeset in 11/13 Goudy by Compset, Inc.

Printed on permanent/durable acid-free paper
and bound in the United States of America

First Printing

Library of Congress Cataloging in Publication Data

Burk, Robert Fredrick, 1955–
Dwight D. Eisenhower, hero and politician.

(Twayne's twentieth-century American biography series ; no. 2)
Bibliography: p. 191
1. Eisenhower, Dwight D. (Dwight David), 1890–1969. 2. Presidents—United States—
Biography. 3. Generals—United States. I. Title. II. Title: Dwight D. Eisenhower, hero
and politician. III. Series.
E836.B87   1986   973.921'092'4   [B]   86-7693
ISBN 0-8057-7752-0
ISBN 0-8057-7773-3 (pbk.)

CONTENTS

FOREWORD

Dwight David Eisenhower identified himself with George Washington. As Robert Burk shows in this incisive biography, Eisenhower strove to be for twentieth-century America what Washington had been almost two centuries before—"Father of his Country"—and in many ways he succeeded. Other generals besides Eisenhower and Washington have become president, but only these two have made equally great marks in military and civilian life. Both men led armies to triumph in the field and became overwhelmingly popular heads of state, but it was more than their successful leadership that gave them an enduring hold on people's imaginations and affections. Eisenhower, like Washington, became a paragon of patriotic devotion and a symbol of imposing dignity.

Yet how different this humbly born man from the nation's heartland was from the Virginia aristocrat on whom he modeled himself. Son of an unsuccessful small Kansas businessman, the young Eisenhower rose in the world initially through his athletic prowess. He chose a military career in order to acquire a free college education. Throughout his early years in the army he remained inwardly detached from its institutional traditions and taboos, and he later likened himself to Mark Twain's Huckleberry Finn in uniform. Yet, as Robert Burk demonstrates, this seemingly unassuming officer, who had long since acquired his folksy nickname, "Ike," was consummately ambitious, and he manipulated connections and assignments to bring off his phenomenal ascent through the ranks when World War II began. The stage was set for the emergence of the greatest single American reputation from that global conflict, the plainspoken, supremely competent, yet unwarriorlike supreme commander of Allied forces in Europe—Ike.

Eisenhower's military career alone would have earned him a major place in American history, although hardly an uncontroversial one. His brief experience as field commander raised many questions about his generalship, and as this biography also shows, his managerial and diplomatic methods had their sour as well as sweet sides. One of the advantages of this book's approach to Eisenhower is that it considers his military and political careers as part of a whole life. The young officer who became the general-diplomat laid down the patterns for the civilian statesman who became president from 1953 to 1961

Eisenhower's presidency has remained curiously paradoxical. This enormously popular, venerated public figure, with his winning grin, came to be regarded by some critics as a bumbler and temporizer, whereas others have lauded him as a model of restraint and circumspection. Robert Burk penetrates this paradox with sympathy and sense. Ike's shortcomings and virtues receive thorough, evenhanded exposition, and they are placed in the context of the man's whole life and character. Given the significance of his careers and of the events through which he moved as a military and civilian leader, perhaps no American of the twentieth century needs to be understood more clearly than Eisenhower. Robert Burk's biography brings this understanding by bringing Ike to life again.

John Milton Cooper, Jr.

PREFACE

Dwight D. Eisenhower remains perhaps the greatest American hero of the twentieth century. His fame as a national soldier-statesman is exceeded only by that of his personal role model, George Washington. But Eisenhower was a distinctly twentieth-century version of the martial national hero. He grew up in the late nineteenth century when images of flamboyant individual valor still prevailed, although those images were bearing a steadily decreasing resemblance to reality. Born in the year labeled by Frederick Jackson Turner as the end of the frontier in American life, he would live until the year in which Americans traveled the new frontier of space to land on the moon. His life and career paralleled the rise of national and international bureaucratic institutions in business, labor, the military, and politics. By its end America had become a global colossus, but with its power to impose its will on world events proven limited in Southeast Asia and its future haunted by the risk of nuclear war.

As a major figure in both the military and politics during this extended period of national transformation, Eisenhower, like others of his generation, would attempt to preserve the opportunities for, and the values of, individual initiative within the changed institutional setting of the twentieth century. In so doing he would become a symbol both of traditional individualist values and of the newly acquired global power of the United States. His career would be that of the adaptive hero, not seeking to dramatically alter the direction and goals of modern America, but instead attempting to preserve individual avenues of success within powerful national bureaucracies for himself and others.

In his own case, Eisenhower would prove strikingly successful, rising from relatively humble origins to become supreme Allied commander in Europe in World War II, army chief of staff, Columbia University president, supreme commander of NATO, and president of the United States. In order to achieve such success in the bureaucratic world of the twentieth century, to become an American hero, Eisenhower would learn, sometimes painfully, the necessity of being the politician. Personal advance depended no longer upon theatrical individual valor but upon the success of the institutional "team," combined with the public relations skills to translate it into the traditional imagery of individual heroism. Heroic lives were not forged so much as careers were managed. And perhaps more successfully than any other man of his generation, Eisenhower adapted himself to the managerial techniques of the modern state. He managed his own personality and temperament, restraining his more intemperate impulses. He managed men and resources effectively as a military commander and politician. Most skillfully of all, he managed his image and standing with the American public through nearly thirty years as a prominent national figure. In short, Dwight D. Eisenhower became the manager of the modern American national security state. This is his story.

ACKNOWLEDGMENTS

Dwight D. Eisenhower has been a regular companion of mine for over a half-dozen years now—alternately a source of frustration, curiosity, and joy. Fortunately, in my attempts to wrestle with the man and the legend that is Ike, I have been aided by many fine individuals and institutions. Special thanks go to the staff of the Eisenhower Library in Abilene, Kansas, the source of most of the manuscript material and photographs used for this study. Other photographic sources include the Republican National Committee and the John F. Kennedy Library in Boston, Massachusetts. My appreciation also is extended to the State Historical Society of Wisconsin, the University of Cincinnati Library, and the Muskingum College Library for their help in unearthing secondary source materials.

One of the rewards of working on a manuscript is the opportunity to share ideas with and benefit from the criticism of able colleagues in the historical community. My thanks to Dr. Lorle Porter for reviewing the complete manuscript, and to Dr. David Sturtevant for helping me avoid errors of fact and interpretation regarding Eisenhower's war record. Most of all, I owe a special debt of gratitude to Professor John M. Cooper, Jr., of the University of Wisconsin, who has on this occasion and before demonstrated his wisdom and consideration as an editor and friend. My appreciation also goes to managing editors Caroline Birdsall and John LaBine of Twayne Publishers for their faith in me and in the manuscript.

Finally, I would be remiss if I did not acknowledge the debts I owe to my family for years of support and encouragement. To my parents, deep appreciation for showing me the value of a small-town Kansas boyhood. To Mrs. Helen Rutter, thanks for her understanding of my hermitlike isolation at the typewriter during a Philadelphia visit in the summer of 1984. To Tristan and Bruce, gratitude for constantly reminding me that work is not the only item of value in life. And to Patricia, my partner in work and at home and my sincerest critic, the hopes that I may someday repay, at least in part, my obligation for her sacrifices.

I

AMBITION
WITHOUT
ARROGANCE

It is a typical American hero's story, full of images borrowed from a Norman Rockwell painting. It is the log cabin myth and the frontier thesis adapted to the environment of the Great Plains at the turn of the century. The hero's origins are ordinary but in their plainness contain the stuff of greatness. As a boy he is raised in a small-town setting free of artificial distinctions and barriers. His parents are humble, hard-working, God-fearing folk. Rural life provides ample opportunities for testing himself against the natural environment and for building his physical strength. His family and neighbors have imbued him with the proper values of self-reliance, thrift, hard work, and a cooperative spirit. Nurtured in this midwestern small-town setting, the young man is hesitant to leave it, but leave it he must. But his youthful memories and values never leave him. Instead they supply the foundations of character that, when tested in dramatic and dangerous new settings, lead to fame, glory, and heroism. The small-town boy becomes an American hero, and the Americanness is contained in the notion that save for chance and circumstances, it could have happened to any of thousands in a land where "anyone can grow up to be president."

In such a fashion biographers have narrated the life of Dwight David Eisenhower, arguably America's greatest popular hero of the twentieth century. With allowances for personal modesty, this rural version of the Horatio Alger tale also is the way in which Eisenhower himself accounted for his rise to greatness. Boyhood in the midwestern hamlet of Abilene, Kansas, he wrote, had "provided both a healthy outdoor existence and a need to work. These same conditions were responsible for the existence of a society which, more nearly than any other I have encountered, eliminated prejudices based upon wealth, race, or creed, and maintained a standard of values that placed a premium upon integrity, decency, and consideration for others." For Eisenhower the roots of greatness were simple and straightforward: "Any youngster who has had the opportunity to spend his early youth in an enlightened rural area has been favored by fortune."[1]

But the making of a hero, even an American one, is seldom such a neat and tidy matter. If small-town life was so idyllic, why would anyone ever leave it for the dangers and challenges of a larger world? Where did the driving ambition come from, the determination to make a name outside the seclusion of Abilene? Closer inspection of the details of Dwight D. Eisenhower's early life reveals significant variations from the romanticized, Rockwell-style portrait of small-town life. It was those differences, as well as the positive features of an Abilene boyhood and the factors of chance and circumstance, that propelled the young boy on his path to fame.

Dwight Eisenhower was born in 1890, the year that historian Frederick Jackson Turner cited as the end of the frontier era in America. If late nineteenth-century Abilene, Kansas, was any indication, Turner was right. Despite the prevailing dime-novel image of the town, by the time young Dwight arrived there at the age of two Abilene already had been transformed from a wild cattle town into a sedate midwestern community. Although dubbed the "Gem on the Plains" by town boosters anxious to drum up settlers and customers, Abilene found it difficult to live up to the slogan. Except for the occasional excitement stirred by such events as the Spanish-American War, news of the world beyond seldom upset the town's tranquility. Owing to their unusual positions as conduits to the outside world, the town telegrapher and newspaper editor possessed a special status in the community. Neither a boomtown nor a cattle town, Abilene was settling into a sleepy existence with a small but reasonably stable population.

For a brief time Abilene had been more exciting. In the early 1870s, the town had been the terminus for longhorn cattle drives from Texas. The turbulent cow-town days had been followed by a short-lived population boom, but by the 1890s only a few illegal liquor establishments marred the community's new image of dull respectability. Instead of cleaning up after, or shooting down, carousing cowboys, Abilene's police force of one officer and a daytime marshal devoted their main attentions to rounding up truant schoolchildren. Residents in search of the "strenuous life" found it less often in real-life adventures and more frequently in social and club activities such as boxing, skating, and sledding. Late nineteenth-century Abilene was a town of modest-sized businesses—groceries, meat markets, drugstores, notions stores, and barbershops—each reliant in turn upon the prosperity of the surrounding agricultural economy. The town's churches were the heart of community values, social life, and cultural enrichment, supplemented occasionally by the traveling chautauqua. Not surprisingly, Abilene was cautious and conservative in its outlook, its religion, and its politics. Everyone was either formally or informally Christian in upbringing and of European origins, and a strong majority voted Republican.

On occasion modern improvements and social frictions tempered and challenged the town's bedrock conservatism. A new sewer system elicited admiration in 1903, a new high school was constructed in 1905, and paved streets followed in 1910. Cement sidewalks replaced wooden planks. Acquisition of an electrical generator and a telephone system further signaled the arrival of twentieth-century ways. Modernization also brought with it an expanding professional elite of doctors, lawyers, and bankers, and tensions simmered between the town's more affluent North Siders and the poorer South Side, located literally on the "wrong side of the tracks." But despite the changes and the conflicts, Abilene's basic character remained close-knit, protective, and provincial. Eisenhower's younger brother Milton recalled, "The isolation was political and economic, as well as just a prevailing state of mind. Self-sufficiency was the watchword; personal initiative and responsibility were prized; radicalism was unheard of."[2]

Yet in ways that few townspeople recognized or understood, Abilene

3

was part of, and affected by, the larger world outside. In spite of the homilies to self-sufficiency, the town's economic lifeline was the railroad, which carried in finished goods from the East and hauled out wheat. The unseen fluctuations of supply and demand on the international agricultural markets had a direct impact on the lives of farmers and town merchants alike. Even the most self-reliant of farmers could do little about the vagaries of weather, blight, or pests. Despite the town's political conservatism, the national government that seemed so remote and irrelevant had been, and remained, crucial to the community's very existence. Without the government's forced evacuation of the Indian from the Great Plains, Jacob Eisenhower and his band of Pennsylvania River Brethren would have found the area far less hospitable. Without government land grants to the Kansas–Pacific Railroad, the town would have had little or no economic base. Without agricultural policies promoting farm exports, Abilene might have gone the way of other boom-and-bust towns. Although Abilene's citizens liked to think of their community as a sheltered oasis on the plains, they were not without their prejudices, their fears, and most bothersome, their own forms of dependency.

If turn-of-the-century Abilene was not quite the exemplar of rugged midwestern self-sufficiency it made itself out to be, neither was Dwight Eisenhower's family quite so idyllic as the small-town myth predicted. It was easier for both Eisenhower and his later biographers to accept a simplified and idealized version of Dwight's boyhood years than to examine them in their full complexity. About his own father, David Eisenhower, it is fair to say that Dwight held ambiguous feelings at best. In later life he said very little about his father in public or in his writings, and such silence always was his most sincere form of criticism. Dwight ascribed few of the personal qualities he sought to develop in himself and others to his father. Nor was he the only Eisenhower sibling to criticize, albeit softly, David's actions. The portrait of David Eisenhower that surfaces from the personal accounts of his sons is that of a frustrated man, alternately subdued and embittered; a man more often feared than loved by his children. Dwight, for example, described his father as the "breadwinner, Supreme Court, and Lord High Executioner." Holding the commanding voice in a traditional German household, David insisted that the family's routine accommodate his daily schedule, and accordingly the boys were awakened at 5:00 A.M. to fix his breakfast before he left for work at a

4

six-day-a-week, 6:30 to 5:00 job. During the school term or not, one of the boys was expected to take him his lunch at work, and negligence sometimes resulted in whippings.[3]

David Eisenhower's violent outbursts and his stern demeanor toward his children might have been more excusable had he proven himself more successful to them as the family breadwinner. But he spent a large part of his adult life struggling to overcome early financial mistakes and failures. His parents, members of the River Brethren, or Plain People, had brought him to Kansas at the age of fourteen from Pennsylvania, the family home since the 1740s. Both parents claimed colorful backgrounds and were distinguished citizens of their devout, simple religious community. David's mother was the great-granddaughter of a Revolutionary War soldier and granddaughter of a War of 1812 captain, and his father, Jacob, had combined his talents as a successful farmer and minister. Not being one to refuse a shrewd business deal, David's father had sold the family property in Pennsylvania for $175 an acre and had purchased a new homestead in the Abilene area for $7.50 an acre. Within a year the new holdings of 160 acres had included a dairy herd, and Jacob Eisenhower had been able to offer each of his children a wedding dowry of a quarter-section of land and $2,000 in cash.[4]

David had never liked the farming life, however, and he was determined to make a living some other way. Aspiring to an engineering career, he attended Lane University in Lecompton, Kansas, where he met and fell in love with his future wife, Ida Stover. Upon his return to the family homestead, he mortgaged away his dowry for $2,000 in order to start up a general store partnership in the nearby town of Hope. Owing to irregular farm prices, a grasshopper invasion, overextended credit, and what neighbors rumored to be an overindulgent life-style, David's business went bankrupt. The children were told later by Ida that the store's failure had been due primarily to the chicanery and poor management of their father's business partner. The story of the partner's dishonesty was at least partly true, but the choice of such an associate nevertheless reflected poorly on David's business judgment.[5]

It was because of David Eisenhower's financial difficulties that Dwight, the family's third child, was born in Denison, Texas, rather than in Abilene. The first child, Arthur, had been born in Hope in 1886, but after the store's collapse David had left the family and migrated to Texas to work as an engine wiper for the Cotton Belt Railroad. For ten dollars a week he rented a small room in a frame house near the tracks in Denison. Ida had remained back in Kansas, pregnant with a second child whom she delivered in January 1889 and named Edgar. Following the birth, Ida joined her husband in Denison, where on 14 October 1890 she delivered a third son, named initially David Dwight Eisenhower. In an unusual twist, Ida insisted that her new son be called Dwight rather than David, so as to "avoid confusion" with his father. Later the official order of names was reversed to Dwight David Eisenhower.[6]

With three young children and a wife to support on a meager income, David found it necessary to swallow his pride and accept the assistance of relatives when they offered it in 1891. The River Brethren had opened a new cooperative creamery in Abilene, and its foreman was Chris Musser, David Eisenhower's brother-in-law. Musser also was the man who had overseen the foreclosure of David's farm in order to pay off some of the remaining debts from the general store failure. The creamery needed a mechanic, and in addition Jacob Eisenhower, now an elderly widower, wanted his son to rejoin the rest of the family in Kansas. Offered the job of mechanical engineer at the creamery for fifty dollars a month, David brought his growing family back to Abilene with only twenty-four dollars in his pocket.[7]

When visitors travel to Abilene today to visit Dwight Eisenhower's boyhood home, they see a modest but comfortable two-story structure that reinforces the idyllic images of his boyhood. But it was not until seven years after the return to Kansas that the family moved into the famous house on Fourth Street. From the ages of two to eight, Ike spent his childhood south of the railroad tracks in a structure not much larger than a shack. When the family did move to the larger house in 1898, again it owed more to the generosity of relatives than to any dramatic improvement in David Eisenhower's financial fortunes. David's brother Abraham, an amateur veterinarian, suddenly decided to become an itinerant preacher and offered to sell his residence on Fourth Street to his brother at a large discount. Even the Fourth Street house claimed a checkered heritage, for it was located on the general site of Abilene's former red-light district, the Devil's Addition. Although the new home was a definite improvement, its 818 square feet of space still had to accommodate a family that eventually numbered ten members, including seven children and the elderly Jacob Eisenhower.[8]

The Eisenhower family did not become financially secure for many years. As a result, the children were expected from an early age to contribute in whatever financial ways possible. Some of the boys ran errands for neighbors; others ran small vegetable stands with produce from the Eisenhower garden. David, in turn, took a correspondence course in engineering in his continuing hope of self-improvement. In his later years, he did obtain better-paying jobs, first as a gas plant manager and then as director of employee savings for a public utility. But for over twenty years his workplace remained the Belle Springs Creamery, and at the end of that time his salary was still only a hundred dollars a month. Constantly haunted by his early failures, David often withdrew into a brooding shell of pessimism and dread of debt. By the time Dwight himself reached adulthood, he understood better the tribulations of his father, and his sympathy for him grew accordingly. But even after the passage of many years, his father remained a distant figure to him.[9]

Despite his father's moodiness, the adult Dwight later recalled his adolescent years with affection. Never were the memories happier than when reminiscing about his mother. In his book, *At Ease: Stories I Tell to Friends,* he dedicated an entire chapter, entitled "Life with Mother," to Ida Stover Eisenhower's influence on him. In Ida, Dwight found the sources of character and values he prized in others and sought to develop in himself. Bearing a remarkable physical resemblance to him that merely underscored the closeness of their relationship, Ida was his and the other children's tutor, manager, and rock of stability. If David unknowingly proved the basis for Dwight's later dread of "paternalism," Ida was the model of leadership by example and cooperation, sprinkled with a firm sense of duty. With David gone from the home much of the time, Ida became both the chief organizer of family life and the most reliable presence in the children's lives.[10]

If her other qualities were not sufficient, Ida in many ways also cut a more inspirational figure than her husband. She had been born in Mt. Sidney, Virginia, in the Shenandoah Valley country, only to lose both of her parents by the time she reached age twelve. Along with ten other children, Ida had been raised by her maternal grandfather. When the children reached adulthood the entire family moved to

Kansas. After teaching school briefly in order to raise the necessary tuition, Ida enrolled at Lane University, where she met David Eisenhower. She married him two years later. When David was forced to leave Kansas in search of work, she stayed behind to care for their infant son and to prepare for the birth of another. Throughout their marriage she willingly shared the hard times, and she defended her husband's name and character to the children whenever it was hinted that their hardships might be his fault. She even read law books, telling the children that she intended to restore David's good name from the ravages of his former partner and the settlement lawyers.[11]

Among Ida's great gifts was her skill at keeping the family running efficiently from day to day while treating each child as a unique personality. She rotated family chores and bed assignments to relieve boredom and to reduce quarreling. When food disputes arose, she selected one contending faction to divide the food, the other to choose the first portion. A person of good humor, she nevertheless carried with her a streak of fatalism and a strong sense of duty. She was given to quoting homilies, one of her favorites being "The Lord deals the cards, you play them." She also instilled in her sons a burning drive to succeed, tempered by a sense of moral responsibility—an "ambition without arrogance," as she put it. Although she and David both resorted to corporal punishment on occasion, Ida apparently administered it with a greater sense of fairness. Dwight himself never recalled being whipped by his mother, although the memories of his brothers disagreed.[12]

If Dwight idolized his mother, in fairness it should be noted that Ida possessed her own eccentricities and could be as stern a taskmaster in her own way as David was. Both parents stressed the values of honesty, self-reliance, and godliness in a very strict home setting. Every morning and evening the family prayed together, and members took turns reading the Bible aloud. Neither parent smoked, drank, swore, or gambled, and Dwight's minor acts of adolescent rebellion against their authority accordingly took exactly those forms. If David ran a stern German household, he did so with Ida's blessing and cooperation. If David's unorthodox private beliefs included a faith in the prophetic content of the Pyramids' measurements, in later years Ida organized and held meetings of the Watchtower Society in the family parlor. If David impressed the children as a dark, unyielding father, he did so with the acquiescence of Ida, who catered to his moods and soothed the children's hurt feelings. In short, Ida's personality complemented David's, while at the same time she created an idealized role model of patience and perseverance for Dwight and the other children to follow.[13]

Life in Abilene had its rewards for the Eisenhower children, but it also had its dangers. Although Abilene was no longer the wild cattle town, it still offered a boy the chance to go camping, hunting, or fishing. If he was especially daring, he might try negotiating a flatboat down the Smoky Hill River. School took up valuable adventure time, but it was geared toward immediate outside employment. Even so, many schoolboys were either truant, dropped out of school entirely to go to work, or at the least worked at summer jobs on nearby farms, on newspaper routes, or at businesses like the creamery. This immediate introduction into the adult world of work and saving provided a sense of maturity and accomplishment that partly ameliorated the economic necessities that lay behind it for many families. But adventure was accompanied by dangers in a turn-of-the-century childhood, and the Eisenhowers experienced their share of adversity. One of David and Ida's sons, Paul, died of diphtheria at the age of two. Another, Earl, lost his sight in one eye from a knife accident. Dwight nearly died of blood poisoning. Milton, one of Dwight's younger brothers, contracted scarlet fever at age four and remained the weakest physically of the surviving sons, though perhaps intellectually the brightest. Dwight and Edgar even managed nearly to drown themselves in the Smoky Hill River while clowning around in a leaky boat during a flash flood.[14]

Accordingly it was the frustrations of hard times, the strictness of family life, and the relative quiet of Abilene as much as the positive features of small-town life that provided the basis for a strong but unfocused ambition in Dwight Eisenhower and his brothers. As an adult Dwight would recount with understandable pride the brothers' successful careers. But success was not the inevitable product of the small town; rather, it was noteworthy for its very exceptionality. In 1897, Dwight's first year of school, two hundred students entered the town's two elementary schools. By 1909, his senior year of high school, only thirty four (twenty nine of them girls) graduated. But of the Eisenhower brothers, Arthur, the eldest, later became a banker and grain marketing authority in Kansas City; Edgar attended the University of Michigan and became a lawyer and corporate director;

Roy owned a drugstore in Junction City; Earl attended the University of Washington, owned a radio station, and became a public relations director for a newspaper; and Milton worked his way through Kansas State University, served in a number of federal government posts, and became a college president. Even excluding Dwight's own sparkling record of national service, in other words, something clearly was present that set the Eisenhower siblings apart from the small-town norm.[15]

For Dwight himself, the fires of ambition burned no less brightly than in his brothers, but Abilene provided few role models for that ambition. Bob Davis, an uneducated guide and outdoorsman, taught Ike shooting, fishing tricks, and cardplaying skills, but such was not the stuff of modern legends. *Dickinson County News* publisher Joe Howe allowed him to read newspapers from afar full of exciting deeds, but the activity provided only a limited, vicarious satisfaction. To the romantic Dwight's regret, the raucous gunfighter days of Abilene were long past. Even further back in history lay the valorious deeds of the Civil War. For a boy in a turn-of-the-century town, it was hard to picture great feats of heroism emanating from the dwindling ranks of aged veterans who were passing their remaining days in quiet contemplation. Seeking fresh sources of inspiration and escape, Ike avidly devoured colorful books about military heroes and statesmen. Hannibal and Caesar fascinated him, but his special hero was George Washington, whose "stamina and patience in adversity" and "indomitable courage, daring, and capacity for self-sacrifice" won his heart. But if Dwight dared to dream great dreams, the most attainable "heroic" careers appeared to be those of a railroad engineer or a baseball star.[16]

Although he hated to admit it, Dwight's future offered as its likely best prospect his becoming a big fish in a small pond. Ironically, his chief competition as a teenager in making a name for himself in Abilene came from his own brothers, especially his older brother Edgar. Throughout their young lives the two maintained a highly competitive, love–hate relationship frequently punctuated by fights. At the time, Edgar seemed more likely than Ike to convert small-town dreams of glory into reality. It was Edgar who in high school won the highest accolades as an athlete, while Dwight had to settle for being the best history student and mathematician. The high school yearbook predicted that Edgar, not Ike, would be president of the United States "in 1940 or 1944." Ike, it claimed, would have to settle for professor of history at Yale. But if Dwight appeared to come out second best, it was never for lack of effort. In his freshman year, Dwight's face was beaten to a pulp by a bigger Wesley Merrifield in the annual North Side versus South Side challenge fight, but he managed to obtain a draw. He could not allow himself to do less, for Edgar had won the fight for the South Side the previous year. Later in that same year, Ike contracted blood poisoning from a leg injury, but he refused to allow an amputation even though he risked death by doing so. Dwight's determination to match and exceed the exploits of his brother even extended to the senior play, a slapstick version of Shakespeare's *The Merchant of Venice.* Although Edgar, owing to the fact that he had dropped out of school for two years and was therefore in Ike's class, got to play Shylock, Ike took pride in the local paper's rave reviews of his performance as Gobbo.[17]

Given Dwight's determination to match his brother's feats of physical valor, it is not surprising that athletics became his consuming passion for years. Because Abilene's school system lacked the funds to cover the costs of equipment for its athletic teams or for their transportation, Dwight and his school friends formed the Abilene High School Athletic Association. It was a valuable early education for him in the problems and possibilities of group endeavor. Dues to the organization were twenty-five cents a month, and the money went directly for bats, balls, and uniforms. Most other equipment was homemade, and the teams improvised transportation by such means as hitching rides on freight trains to nearby towns. In the games against teams from surrounding schools, Dwight acquitted himself well. More important, he learned to value the individual contributions he could make within a team setting toward the common objectives of financial solvency and victory on the playing field.[18]

Even though both brothers graduated from high school in May 1909, the older Edgar was given the first opportunity to escape Abilene for greener pastures. Defying his father, Edgar refused to go to the University of Kansas to study medicine but instead insisted on attending the University of Michigan to study law. Given David Eisenhower's hatred of lawyers, Edgar's decision meant the father's refusal to offer any financial support for his schooling. Fortunately for Edgar, Uncle Chris Musser again intervened, agreeing to guarantee a two-hundred-dollar loan for his initial tuition. Edgar and Dwight in turn arranged for Dwight to work in Abilene to pay for the rest of

Edgar's first year at Michigan. In exchange, at the end of the first year he would return to Kansas and do the same for Dwight. During the intervening summer of 1909, both sons worked to save money for college—Edgar at the creamery, Dwight as a galvanized sheet metal loader for another local business. When the older brother left for Ann Arbor in September, Dwight took his place at the creamery, first as an iceman and later as a furnace operator. Finally he was promoted to night manager, and the result was that within a matter of months his take-home pay of ninety dollars a month nearly equaled his father's. Since his job as night manager ran from 6:00 P.M. to 6:00 A.M., he continued his habit of spending afternoons in Joe Howe's newspaper office reading dailies and debating current topics.[19]

But disappointment soon arrived with the end of the first school year. Edgar insisted on pushing back his return to Abilene for another year, and he remained at Michigan during the summer of 1910. Dwight was left in Abilene to continue his job at the creamery, disappointed but publicly reconciled to the decision. He was not one to bemoan his fate in front of others, but Edgar's choice imposed an indefinite hold on his own career ambitions. He dreamed of broader horizons, of escape from the confines of Abilene and of parental controls. He yearned for adventure, for the chance to experience new and exciting things. But the chance appeared to be fading for lack of money and an avenue of escape.

Fortunately for Ike, during that disappointing summer of 1910 he had developed a strong friendship with Everett "Swede" Hazlett, the son of one of the town's doctors. Because Swede had attended a military school in Wisconsin, Dwight had not known him very well until then. At first glance it was an odd pairing, for Swede did not share Ike's passion for sports and had a schoolboy reputation as something of a sissy. In June 1910 he had returned to Abilene after having received a preliminary appointment to the United States Naval Academy at Annapolis but having failed the mathematics section of the written entrance exam. Swede intended to retake the test the following year, and his descriptions of the Naval Academy and the possibilities it offered of adventure and a free college education gave Ike new hope. Reluctant to give up on the old bargain with Edgar, and hoping to try out for one of the athletic teams at Michigan, Ike required persuasion from Hazlett to consider going to a military academy. But Swede pointed out that the Naval Academy also had football and baseball teams, and it offered the additional advantages of a cheap education and an interesting postgraduate career.[20]

Dwight jumped at the chance. Learning from Swede that appointments to the service academies were made by a state's congressmen or senators, he recruited Abilene's leading citizens to write recommendation letters to Sen. Joseph Bristow of nearby Salina. In his application letter he tried to enhance his chances of selection by indicating a willingness to attend either Annapolis or the United States Military Academy at West Point. At the time, however, his clear preference was to join Swede at the Naval Academy. Ike's drive to be accepted was so strong that he even listed his age on the application form as a year younger than it was in order to meet academy entrance requirements. To his disappointment, he learned that Senator Bristow had many more applicants than appointments to fill and had opted to hold an open competitive written examination to determine his appointees.[21]

Ike crammed feverishly for the special examination, with Swede initially serving as a tutor; the student eventually exceeded the teacher in several subjects, however. In early October 1910, Dwight and eight other candidates gathered in Topeka, the state capital, for a two-day battery of tests. He proved most capable in grammar, scoring 99, algebra, 94, and arithmetic, 96. His marks of 90 in geography and spelling were nearly as good. To his surprise, he did least well in geometry, 77, American history, 73, and general history, 79. His low marks in history derived from his reading habits in the subject, which had steered him more in the direction of battles and military heroes than toward the political and economic topics the examinations stressed. His overall score of 87.5, however, placed him second among the contestants. Since the first-place finisher had insisted on attending Annapolis, Bristow tabbed Dwight for the available slot at West Point instead of the Naval Academy.[22]

Although Swede Hazlett was disappointed at this turn of events, Ike was noticeably less concerned. He had hoped to attend the Naval Academy with Swede, but at twenty years of age he was too old to meet the entrance requirements there and would have had to continue deceiving the navy to gain admission. West Point would provide him with an equally good and inexpensive college education, the prospect of an adventurous career, and escape from the confinements of Abilene. There were, however, two remaining obstacles—obtaining his pacifist parents' approval to attend West Point and passing a formal entrance examination similar to the one Swede had failed. The first task, obtaining his parents' permission, turned out to be easier than Dwight might have expected. David Eisenhower typically maintained a cold detachment from the decision, and in any event, since a cadet's tuition at West Point was free, any attempt by him to prevent Ike's departure by withholding money would have been wasted. For her part, Ida, although clearly unhappy at her son's choice of a military education and tour of duty, could not bring herself to stop him, for she knew how much it meant to him. In sharp contrast to his parents' reluctance, Dwight's brothers could not contain their excitement at the prospect of a soldier in the family.[23]

The formal entrance examination proved to be a more difficult hurdle, not because the test itself was difficult, but because Ike nearly failed to show up for it. Through the fall he prepared diligently, even returning to Abilene High School for review courses in chemistry, mathematics, and physics. Because no athletic eligibility limits were yet in effect, he even played an additional year of football. The examination itself was scheduled for January 1911 in St. Louis, Missouri, the farthest from home he had ever been in his life. Anxious to see the sights of the city, he nearly threw away his chance for admission to West Point by larking about the night before the test, missing the last streetcar back to his barracks, and having to sneak back into his lodgings after curfew without being discovered. After the adventures of the previous night and his narrow escape, the examination itself proved an anticlimax. It turned out to be very similar to the Topeka tests, and he passed it easily.[24]

He had cleared the last remaining hurdle to West Point, and he made his preparations to leave his home and family for the life of a military cadet. In other ways, he had already traveled a long personal road. Physically he had matured into a handsome, athletic young man with genuine pretensions of becoming a sports star in college. He still retained the expressive face he had inherited from his mother, the boyish grin, and the spirit of youthful rebelliousness. He had made his choice of a military education and career in that same adventurous, even haphazard spirit, for he had as yet no knowledge of how monotonous, oppressive, and disciplined the life of a West Pointer could be. But if he had chosen West Point as an afterthought, he did know that ambition burned within him—an ambition tempered by an outward, self-effacing modesty. His drive to succeed in the world beyond Abilene had not yet focused on specific career objectives, but presumably it soon would. And at the very least, West Point would help him make the right choices.

WEST POINT, WAR, AND FRUSTRATION

From the very outset, West Point proved to be a great shock to Dwight Eisenhower's romantic dreams of military adventure. Almost as if to heighten his shock, on his trip eastward he included such pleasant diversions as spending a day in Ann Arbor with Edgar, canoeing with double dates down the Huron River, and enjoying the sights from his train to New York. From the opening moments of his arrival at the academy, West Point was a different story. During the course of his four-year stay on the banks of the Hudson, he would develop sharply contrasting impressions of the ideal of military service versus the harsh realities of the Point.

One of the earliest impressions Eisenhower formed of the academy hearkened back to the less appealing aspects of life in Abilene; rather than being an escape from a regimen of dull routine, intrusive discipline, and arbitrary brutality, West Point offered an exaggerated form of it. Cadets were physically isolated from the world outside. The academy was arbitrary and capricious in its rules and their administration. Once a cadet arrived, most of the trappings of individual choice and freedom, even his clothes and his pocket money, were confiscated. With only brief furloughs to break the monotony, West Point became for the cadet more a military monastery than a place of intellectual stimulation.

Making matters worse for a cadet of Eisenhower's generation, the academy's practice of hazing was at its peak in the early twentieth century. The plebes were subjected immediately to verbal abuse, including being assigned insulting names by which upperclassmen constantly addressed them. Plebes were conspicuous targets, and even more so because of their traditional housing assignment at "Beast Barracks." Superiors ordered new cadets to perform "bracing" (the act of standing at exaggerated attention for long periods), to pick up ants from anthills one at a time, to hold Indian clubs at arm's length for hours, to perform push-ups or sit-ups on command until ordered to stop, and, most agonizing, to "swim to Newburgh" (balancing by one's stomach on a pole and performing swimming strokes). Even at meals, plebes were ordered to sit with their feet upraised as high as the underside of the table top. Ike's first roommate, who had left his hometown to the sound of bands blaring and neighbors cheering, could not endure the strain of Beast Barracks and left within weeks. As for Dwight himself, he had been well served by his rough-and-tumble adolescence. Even more important, he was at age twenty-one older and more mature than the typical plebe. He reminded himself at those times when the hazing seemed unbearable that his tormentors had gone through the same process and survived, and that despite the temporary agony, he was receiving a free education.[1]

But what kind of education? Hazing was just an extreme activity of an institution that by all indications placed discipline over creativity, tradition over innovation. Accommodations had scarcely changed at the Point in decades. Rooms were hot in summer, cold in winter; food was plain and unappetizing; activities were dull and repetitious. The academy reeked with a timelessness that discouraged innovative ideas and intellectual exchange in favor of rote memorization and the unquestioning acceptance of accumulated conventional military wisdom. Ideas were not debated—facts were recited. The cadet's duty was to accept what he was told, not to question it. The setting was smug, complacent, and stifling. Despite its shortcomings, the cadets seemed loath to change it. Most came from reasonably comfortable, traditional, white Protestant families in the South or the Midwest. There, Bible study had meant memorizing verses, not discussing theology, and values were transmitted through the vigorous application of rigid rules of conduct. Like its heartland constituency, West Point was certain that it knew the truth, and it felt little need to examine it regularly. The academy's curriculum was more that of a technical school than a university, with an emphasis on military and civil engineering. All the teachers were themselves West Point graduates, and learning consisted of reciting approved answers to standardized questions. English consisted of composition, never the study of literature. History was an accumulated memorization of facts, not an exercise in inquiry.[2]

Dwight's own traditional, small-town education stood him in good stead for the academy's methods. Abilene's schools had stressed rote learning in basic subjects, and Ike's skills in English composition and mathematics were ideally suited for the Point. Neither did his conception of history as the accumulated consequences of battles and wars hurt him at all. While at the Point, classmates marveled at his ability to turn out brief and logically organized, if not brilliant, essays on short notice for classroom assignments. Because Abilene had prepared him well for the academic regimen of the academy, at the end of his plebe year he stood fifty-seventh overall in academics in his class, and tenth in English. The accomplishment was even more impressive in light of the fact that 55 out of the initial class of 267 had chosen to leave the academy by the end of the first year.[3]

If Dwight actually seemed to thrive academically within the restrictive curriculum of the academy, the same could not be said of his experiences with West Point's rules of personal conduct and behavior. As a child he had rebelled against his parents' strictures against smoking, fighting, and contact sports. He was dismayed, therefore, to discover that the academy's system of controls was even more intrusive than that of David and Ida. In its task of molding a young man into an effective officer, West Point was structured to either force conformity of behavior or break the nonconformist or malcontent in the process. The rules prohibited cigarettes. A cadet's room, bed, clothing, and shoes had to be always immaculate. The academy required punctuality and correctness both in appearance and in the observance of military protocol. Individualism was not desirable, though personal initiative and courage within the proper contexts were. The model cadet was compliant, obedient—almost mechanistic—in performing his duties.

At the Point as in Abilene, Ike turned to familiar avenues of individual expression and escape. The most important remained participation in team sports. In his plebe year, he joined the Cullen Hall, or junior varsity, football team as a lineman despite weighing in at barely 150 pounds. The following winter he worked out regularly on the indoor track to improve his speed and in the gymnasium to build up his arm and leg strength. Despite the academy's bland food, he gorged on it in order to increase his weight. In the spring he played baseball, along with another athletically minded member of his class from Missouri, Omar Bradley. By the beginning of the next football season in the fall of 1912, Eisenhower was faster, stronger, and bigger than ever before, now carrying an additional twenty pounds on his nearly six-foot frame.[4]

Ike was determined to make the varsity team as a yearling, or sophomore, and he succeeded beyond even his own expectations. Because of his improved speed, the coaches moved him from the line to the backfield as a reserve. When the first-string halfback was injured, he moved into the starting lineup, and after a series of sparkling performances the *New York Times* carried a two-column photograph of him and heralded him as "one of the most promising backs in Eastern football." He even enjoyed the opportunity of playing that season against the Carlisle Indian School and its great athletic star, Jim Thorpe. But in the next game against Tufts, he injured his knee and had to be removed from the game. The injury was not believed to be serious, and Ike expected to be ready in time for the crucial season finale against Navy. But West Point stubbornness again raised its head, and the result was an abrupt end to his athletic career. Despite his injury, Dwight was forced to participate in a horse-dismounting exercise dubbed the monkey drill. While bounding on and off his mount, he severely tore additional cartilege and tendons in his knee. The leg was placed in a plaster cast, but even after it was removed the doctors informed him that he would never again play football.[5]

Eisenhower was not one to accept such news without an argument. Hoping to prove the doctors wrong, he launched a personal rehabilitation program through distance running. But for the rest of his life, his knee remained subject to sudden dislocation under stress and to periodic swelling and pain. For the young cadet who had placed so many hopes on an athletic career, the injury proved nearly a life-shattering experience. As he later described it, with athletics gone as a proving ground, "life seemed to have little meaning. A need to excel was almost gone." Under the strain of the combined physical and emotional tribulations of the second year, Ike's grades suffered, and he fell to a ranking of 81st out of 177. He did take the opportunity to exercise his right to a ten-week furlough that summer, and the return home to family and friends restored a measure of good spirits and self-confidence. But there was a tinge of sadness in the sight of the young soldier walking the streets of Abilene in his dress uniform, regaling others with stories of the Point and of athletic valor. The past, it seemed, now held greater attraction and promise than did the future.[6]

Ike bounced back, but the revival took time and, more important, the discovery of new avenues of activity. One such avocation was performing as a cheerleader for Army's athletic squads, which provided him a measure of vicarious participation in sports. Because cheerleaders also were expected to exhort the corps of cadets at pep rallies on the eve of games, Dwight had the chance to develop little-used oratorical skills. Cheerleading was not enough, however, for he wanted an even greater measure of athletic participation. Because of his interest and perseverance, he received an appointment as a coach for the junior varsity squad. Within weeks he was a clear success, which should have surprised no one. Besides his obvious love of football, he brought to the job enormous energy and enthusiasm, a high capacity for hard work, and excellent organizational skills. One of history's more intriguing "what if's" is what might have followed had he, as a result of his West Point frustrations, abandoned an army career for service in the coaching ranks. Given his personal attributes, he might have become the Knute Rockne of his day. Instead, the slang of the football coach permeated the later Eisenhower leadership rhetoric. As a supreme commander during World War II, he would regularly employ such phrases as "pull an end run," "hit the line hard," and "get that ball across the goal."[7]

Eisenhower's activities with the football squad as cheerleader and coach made him more popular than before with his fellow cadets. They also strengthened his growing faith in teamwork within a command organization as the path to personal accomplishment. But these new substitutes for the direct personal glory of the athletic star, the Frank Merriwell, were not altogether adequate to temper his impatient, rebellious ways. At the same time that he pursued these new activities, he also violated the academy's rules of personal conduct more frequently than before his injury. He continued to test the outer limits of the army's tolerance of defiance and constantly bent, and occasionally broke, the cadet code. He never went so far as to do anything that would have triggered his immediate dismissal. Instead his flaunting of cadet regulations resembled his defiance of parental rules as an adolescent. Cigarette possession and smoking were barred at the Point, but he smoked anyway, rolling his own Bull Durhams over the objections of his roommate and despite the fears of other cadets. When caught, he cheerfully complied with the punishments of extended marching or room confinement, and then continued his errant ways. He often failed to keep his room neat, was late for formation or guard inspection, and regularly flunked dress inspections.[8]

Not only did punishments fail to reform Ike's behavior; on occasion he even found opportunities to retaliate in his own way. When ordered to appear before a senior cadet along with another rule breaker in full dress coats, Eisenhower and his partner appeared for their inspection wearing their coats, but not a stitch of pants or any other clothing. Nor was he ashamed in any way of his conduct record. Instead he viewed his collection of demerits as a badge of honor, and he scorned those with nearly perfect conduct records as gutless or unimaginative. Accordingly, by the end of his final year at West Point, he stood 95th overall out of 164 in his class in discipline, and an even worse 125th of 164 for the senior year alone, having accumulated one hundred demerits. His total rating for academics and conduct combined was a better 65th out of 170, and if he had concentrated less on his various extracurricular activities, he likely would have finished comfortably in the top third of his class.[9]

Eisenhower's four years at West Point were at best an uneven experience, but he did benefit from them in several specific ways. One of his never-ending sources of enjoyment and inspiration, reflecting his boyhood love of military history and heroism, was the academy's own historic tradition of service to the nation. The ghosts of heroes past seemed everywhere. A cadet walked the halls and even lived in the barracks where Lee, Grant, Sherman, Scott, and Custer had resided in an earlier time. Dwight could sit at the barricades of the old fortress as it overlooked the Hudson River and conjure up vivid images of Benedict Arnold's thwarted attempt at treachery during the Revolution. Such memories impressed upon him constantly, as they did other cadets, the unbreakable links between the past and the present, and the honorable and heroic traditions of the military profession.

In addition to instilling its tradition of national service, West Point also contributed, despite its imperfections, to the skills and values necessary for a twentieth-century American officer. After his academy training, Eisenhower was familiar with army customs and procedures, with the organizational structure and hierarchy of command, and with logistics and military engineering. He also had absorbed, despite his rebellious streak, the basic ideals of the good officer. He was motivated by a sense of duty; he was patriotic and capable of decisive action; and he possessed a high level of physical courage. Building upon his personal characteristics, he was not an arrogant prima donna, but an ambitious man whose goals for himself were channeled by a sense of being a necessary part of a larger military machine. Ambition was acceptable, but only if used in service of the larger military order and the nation. Individual initiative and theatrics were not banned, but they must not be allowed to interfere with the teamwork and efficiency of the army. Success in modern war would not be achieved through reckless personal daring, but through planning, group cooperation, and efficient execution.

A growing deemphasis of the older version of the dashing military hero in favor of the more methodical manager of resources and manpower was not unique to the United States Army. In fact, its most obvious early twentieth-century model was the German General Staff. Modern war was to be rationalized and routinized, to be made ever more "scientific." Along with the development of this new model of military organization came a new breed of officer, presumably with a discipline and efficiency of operation superior to either the civilian or the earlier flamboyant warrior. At West Point this new breed of cadet/officer was encouraged to see itself as an elite, to view itself as the bearer of a special code of professionalism and honor to each other and to the nation, able to rise above the corruptions of grubby individualism. At least in the idealized view of the officer, both the army and the country were seamless webs, not clamoring welters of conflicting special interests to be brokered. In other words, the West Point graduate's basic values, circa 1915, were a martial variant of the broader managerial and nationalistic impulses of the Progressive Era.[10]

The military's adherence to the Progressive ideal of an efficient professionalized bureaucracy carried with it an accompanying devotion in Dwight Eisenhower and other cadets to an apolitical creed. Politics, in the popular sense, was seen by cadets and their superiors as contentious partisanship and special interest clamor, and it was the good officer's duty to avoid its corrupting influence on teamwork and efficiency. In practice the apolitical ideal promoted at West Point led to distinctive patterns of thought and behavior in the political realm among Eisenhower and other officers. It most certainly did not remove politics in the broad sense from the internal deliberations and intergovernmental dealings of the American military. It did, however, encourge a kind of political involvement that was less openly partisan, less public, and that employed the behind-the-scenes methods of the bureaucratic politician rather than those of the elected officeholder. In addition, the military's devotion to the nation, personified in its commander in chief, the president, led to a distinct willingness of officers to separate their veneration for the presidential office from their dislike of the president's electoral role as a partisan leader. Many of Dwight Eisenhower's later hidden-hand techniques of executive leadership, as well as his hatred of politicians and his view of the best president as one above politics, derived from this basic conception of the apolitical creed.

The watchword of the military ideal, the justification for channeled ambition and the preserver of virtue, was the concept of duty. And devotion to duty was about all that Dwight Eisenhower had to cling to for many years in the army. Upon graduation from West Point, he was denied his sought-after commission in the more glamorous cavalry because of his bad knee and found himself assigned instead to the infantry. He hoped at least for an exotic locale for his tour of duty, such as the Argentine or the Philippines, but he found himself dispatched to Fort Sam Houston, on the outskirts of San Antonio, training troops and coaching the camp football team. Despite the growing border troubles between the United States and Mexico and the post's proximity to the fighting, superiors denied his request to serve under

Gen. John J. Pershing in the punitive expedition against the outlaw Pancho Villa. Instead, he remained the mess officer for a prim and fussy commanding officer at the fort.[11]

New hopes of adventure, action, and advancement stirred in April 1917, with news of America's entry into World War I. Eisenhower was relatively unaware of the sequence of international events that had led to the war declaration, but he relished the prospect of an overseas assignment directing troops in battle on the western front. Once again his army superiors viewed matters differently. Eisenhower had developed into a good football coach, and camp COs were more eager to protect their charges' athletic reputations against other outfits than to release their coach for overseas duty. In addition, Ike had proved too good as a trainer of troops and was seen as too valuable in that capacity to be moved to Europe. When new orders arrived in September of 1917, he learned to his dismay that he was being sent not abroad but to Fort Oglethorpe, Georgia, to train officer candidates. From there subsequent orders dispatched him to Fort Leavenworth, Kansas, training provisional second lieutenants in physical conditioning—a spin-off of sorts from his earlier coaching duties. Having been tagged initially at West Point and Fort Sam Houston as a coach and training officer, he could not get the opportunity to shake the label.[12]

Eisenhower refused to take the frustration lying down. Instead, he sought ways to make bureaucratic end runs around his dilemma. At Fort Sam Houston, he had already tried and failed to circumvent his obstacles through proposing a transfer to the army's Aviation Section. At Fort Leavenworth, he enrolled in the army's first tank school in hopes that tank training would place him on the fast track to active duty overseas. In February of 1918, he was ordered to Fort Meade, Maryland, to help develop tank tactics. Once again, however, his very ability at the task led superiors to assign him as a tank tactics trainer for the newly created Tank Corps at Camp Colt, near Gettysburg, Pennsylvania. Instead of acquiring glory in France, he found himself engaged in haggling with uncooperative local civilians and politicians. His spirits revived only upon learning that he would be embarking for France on 18 November 1918 as part of the buildup for a major Allied spring offensive planned for 1919.[13]

Eisenhower never made that passage to France. To his personal dismay, the armistice ending the Great War took effect on 11 November. His inability to secure a combat assignment in World War I proved more than just a temporary personal frustration. For years afterward, his lack of a documented record commanding troops in battle would slow his career advance, and it would restrict superiors' consideration of him to coaching, training, and staff desk jobs. Even when he would attain the rank of theater commander in World War II, his lack of prior battlefield experience would be used as an arguing point against him by contentious colleagues, most notably British field marshal Sir Bernard Law Montgomery.

Instead of martial glory, war's end brought military demobilization, even more unglorious assignments, and tons of paperwork. Eisenhower was reassigned to Camp Meade to oversee the phased dismantling of army units. In 1919 he gained an additional assignment, which he viewed as something of a lark, of accompanying an army truck convoy on a cross-country journey to California. The purposes of the trip included testing the speed and durability of army vehicles (neither of which proved very impressive), "showing the flag" to the American citizenry for public relations purposes, and dramatizing the genuine national need for better roads and bridges. The trip garnered little fanfare from a war-tired public, but it did illustrate the inadequacy of the army's hardware, which constantly broke down, and the poor roads. The average speed achieved by the convoy reached barely five miles an hour. Eisenhower would have occasion to recall the experience years later as president, when, for similar commercial and military reasons, he would sponsor the creation of the Interstate Highway System.[14]

Eisenhower received a brief glimmer of hope upon his return from San Francisco to Camp Meade. He was named as an instructor for a newly created Infantry Tank School at the base, and in contrast to the war years, he now even had actual tanks to practice and train with. But most exciting of all for the young officer, he now had the opportunity to learn from and share ideas with a tank veteran of World War I and a West Pointer five years his senior, Col. George S. Patton. Despite their enormous differences in personality and temperament, the two men quickly became fast friends and maintained their friendship despite numerous emotional trials later during World War II. In 1919 Patton was clearly the senior partner of the two, and they collaborated in teaching tank tactics and testing equipment at the post. Through their experience both men became convinced that conventional army tank doctrine, which employed scattered tanks merely as accompaniment to infantry units, was wrongheaded. Instead, they argued, separate sizable tank units should be organized to provide greater maneuverability and massed firepower in battle. For that purpose, they also concluded that bigger and faster tanks than those presently available would be necessary in any future war. In Great Britain, B. H. Liddell-Hart was reaching similar conclusions on the effective use of armor in modern warfare, and the Nazi use of massed panzer units would revolutionize military doctrine at the outset of World War II. Full of the eagerness and conviction of youth, the two men submitted separate articles for army publications expounding their ideas, Patton in the *Cavalry Journal* and Eisenhower in the *Infantry Journal*.[15]

Eisenhower soon discovered, however, that the army and particularly the infantry, which had designed the conventional use of tanks only as infantry support, was not pleased at being told by an upstart that its tactics were wrong. Not only were his ideas rejected out of hand; the entire episode became an official black mark on his record and a continual impediment to promotion within the infantry. Summoned before the chief of infantry and reprimanded, Eisenhower was warned that if he published any further implicit or explicit criticisms of accepted tactical doctrine he would be court-martialed. Patton, similarly reprimanded, transferred out of the Infantry Tank School to the Cavalry in hopes of better treatment. Having been offered yet another example of army arbitrariness, Eisenhower could only remain silent, agree not to publish additional material on tank doctrine, make no more instructional lectures based upon his ideas, and hope for a new, nontank assignment that might erase some of the bureaucratic damage.[16]

One source of cheer in an otherwise discouraging time was a flourishing family life. While stationed at Fort Sam Houston in 1915, Ike had fallen in love with a young, attractive socialite named Mamie Doud, who had been vacationing with her family in San Antonio. Following a whirlwind courtship, the couple had married in the Doud family home in Denver on 1 July 1916. Although neither the athletic type nor a skilled housewife or cook, in other ways Mamie proved an ideal army wife. She was remarkably tolerant of the constant moves from post to post, proved an excellent hostess to COs and junior colleagues of Ike, and served as a capable instructor in the social graces to a relatively rough-hewn husband. It had been because of objections from Mamie and her parents on safety grounds, which had threatened cancelation of their wedding plans, that Ike had withdrawn his reassignment request to the Aviation Section in 1916. Despite the inherent strains to marital relations of the constant mobility of army life (in their first thirty-five years of marrige they would move thirty-five times), Mamie kept a comfortable home for the young officer and made his professional frustrations more bearable. She also provided him with a son, Doud Dwight Eisenhower, during their brief and otherwise unhappy stay at Fort Oglethorpe in the fall of 1917.[17]

The child, nicknamed "Icky" (Eisenhower himself had been nicknamed "Little Ike" or "Ugly Ike" as a little boy), was Dwight's pride and joy, although army duties unhappily kept him away from his son and Mamie for extended periods. But during that long season of personal and professional disappointments, the cruelest blow of all fell during the Christmas holidays of 1920. While the family was stationed at Camp Meade, only a week before Christmas, three-year-old Icky contracted scarlet fever, apparently from a young maid who had failed to inform Mamie of her exposure to the disease before entering her employ. Mamie herself soon was quarantined by doctors, and Dwight could not even enter either his wife's or his son's room to lend solace. All that the young officer could do was pray and hope that his son would survive, as his younger brother Milton had years earlier. Given the limitations of medical knowledge of the time, prayer was about all that even the doctors, including a specialist from Johns Hopkins University, could prescribe. On 2 January 1921, Icky died.[18]

Of his first child's death, Eisenhower later said, "This was the greatest disappointment and disaster of my life, the one I have never been able to forget completely." Icky's death put a severe strain on Ike and Mamie's young marriage which was slow to recede. If at this time Eisenhower questioned his previous career and personal decisions and contemplated a fresh start, no one could blame him. For all the magnitude of Icky's tragic death, he did not even have the luxury of being able to escape by throwing himself into his work. Once again, his tasks consisted of the same dreary routine of coaching a camp football team and teaching a program of tank tactics he did not believe in. Nor did the immediate future hold out much hope of improvement. The army as a whole was shrinking rapidly in numbers following the armistice. Within six months after the war's end, 2.5 million enlisted men had returned to civilian life, and with the decline in troop strength came an accompanying decline in the need for officers. Already almost

130,000 officers had obtained discharges. By 1920, the army contained only about that same number of enlisted men on active duty. In a shrinking army, promotions would be even harder to come by, especially for an officer who had never made it to France. For Ike the army was rapidly becoming a stagnant social club full of career officers with nowhere else to go. He had become a permanent major in July 1920, and he would remain at that rank for the next sixteen years.[19]

His early dreams of an adventurous career and quick martial glory had faded, and personal tragedy only heightened his sense of loss. With other avenues open to him in private business back in Kansas or in nearby Washington, D.C., it is difficult at first glance to understand why Eisenhower stayed in the army. But certain features of his personality, along with the values of duty and service he had absorbed in the military, kept him from radically recharting his course. Duty called upon him to make the best of his career and to perform his appointed tasks, however mundane, to the best of his ability. There was also the hope, however faint at present, that time and events would revive his career prospects, and the very mobility of army life helped keep such hopes alive. The alternatives presented by private business seemed to offer little escape from the frustrations and dullness of military life, despite their promise of greater material comfort. In any case, his absorption of military ideals had encouraged him to value such rewards less highly. And how would it appear to his family, his colleagues, his neighbors, and, most important, himself if he walked away from his chosen profession now? He had always been a fighter, and he could not allow himself to become a quitter. He would stick it out, while learning better how to control his outward emotions and exuberance. Along with Mamie, he would "play the cards the Lord dealt," and he would make the best of it.

3

APPRENTICESHIP

By the early 1920s, Dwight Eisenhower already had learned that despite the homilies to cooperation and selfless service in the nation's defense, the army was very much a political institution. Rivalries within sections and among service branches over prestige and appropriations, between the services and presidential administrations, and among commanders made the army a political mine field that the young ambitious officer traversed at his peril. The numerous bureaucratic obstacles to advance were even more pronounced in peacetime, when a shrunken, top-heavy service had little else to concentrate on except its Washington turf wars.

The key to successfully negotiating the traps of internal army politics for a young officer was to find a patron with the personal clout and prestige to clear away the obstacles to promotion. But the task of finding and keeping a powerful ally was not an easy one. Mere flattery rarely was sufficient. Instead, the potential protégé had to prove himself valuable and capable as a junior staff officer, had to be willing to submerge his ego in favor of his commander's, had to be able to think and act in anticipation of the demands of his superior, had to be, in short, his commander's alter ego. Choosing such a patron wisely was crucial, but difficult; the trick entailed somehow having the superior find you, and not the other way around. The choice of a patron in the service also required luck, for the winds of political fortune changed rapidly, affecting patron and protégé alike. Even if all went well and the young officer managed to hitch his star to a rising superior, yet another dilemma could emerge. If the young subaltern proved too good a staff man, he might become trapped in the position and never be given the opportunity to test his mettle as an independent commander.

For Dwight Eisenhower the two decades between World War I and World War II were marked by his attempts to escape the fate of stagnation as a training officer by linking his fortunes to the careers of a series of powerful, and sometimes controversial, senior officers. The names read like a who's who of the twentieth-century United States Army—generals Fox Conner, John J. Pershing, Douglas MacArthur, and George C. Marshall. His period of apprenticeship was long and difficult, and until its very end it appeared only to have resulted in a series of dead ends. Nevertheless, Eisenhower's apprenticeship exposed him to, and educated him thoroughly in, the ways of military politics, patronage, and bureaucracy at the highest levels, and it gave him the opportunity to observe the art of command as practiced by a diverse group of superiors.

The first of Eisenhower's important mentors was Gen. Fox Conner, a soft-spoken Mississippian, a West Point graduate of 1898, and General Pershing's former operations officer in France. Conner had gained a deserved reputation during World War I as the brains of the American Expeditionary Force, and appropriately Pershing brought him to Washington with him at war's end to become his chief of staff. By 1920, however, both Pershing and Conner had become controversial figures in War Department circles. It was in that same year that Eisenhower first became acquainted with Conner through George Patton. Unlike Ike's superiors in the Infantry Section, Conner expressed keen interest in the young officer's views on tank warfare and toured Camp Meade. More important, Conner did not forget his initial favorable impression of Eisenhower, but proceeded to use his influence to secure better appointments for him through his personal contact with Pershing. After the Infantry Section thwarted several earlier attempts, Conner secured Ike a temporary reassignment to Pershing's own staff, which cleared the way for a second appointment as Conner's executive officer in Panama in 1922.[1]

Although Panama was Eisenhower's first foreign assignment, at first glance it scarcely merited rating as a glamorous or exciting posting. Nevertheless, it proved just the personal and professional tonic he needed following his frustrations in the states and the death of Icky. Although Conner possessed a reputation among other junior officers as a needlessly hard driver, Eisenhower enjoyed a close, almost father-son relationship with him. Under his tutelage he became a kind of "junior Conner," which irritated his officer colleagues. Ike cared little, however, for in Panama he learned more about military history, tactics, and global issues from Conner than he had in four years of formal education at the Point. Conner broadened his reading habits beyond his usual fare of western pulp fiction and basic training manuals to include classic military memoirs, commentaries, and philosophical treatises on warfare. He learned to appreciate the simple eloquence and accumulated wisdom of Grant and Sherman, and he and Conner would conduct their own Socratic sessions while carrying out post rounds on horseback. Prodded by Conner's demanding questioning, Eisenhower began to understand America's larger strategic position and its military legacy more clearly. He also grasped more deeply than ever before the meaning of the warrior's place in modern society. Inspired by Conner, he read Clausewitz's treatise, *On War*, three times.[2]

Conner's wisdom touched more than just an interest for broader study in his young pupil. It also encouraged him to consider the future role of American military might in the world. Conner warned that officers like Eisenhower should prepare themselves for the new kind of warfare on the horizon, and he predicted that the Treaty of Versailles would last but twenty years at most. Despite his own service in Pershing's independent American command in World War I, he also lamented the complications in planning and execution on the battlefield that such nationalistic considerations had produced. The next war, Conner insisted, would have to be directed by a multinational command, and the skill of individual commanders in overcoming nationalistic rivalries would be essential to success. He even offered Eisenhower his own assessments of the capabilities of other young officers for assuming such future demands and for assisting Eisenhower's own advance. At the top of Conner's list was a fellow protégé of Pershing's, a colonel by the name of George C. Marshall. Conner predicted a prominent role in the "next war" for Marshall, for he knew "more about the techniques of arranging allied commands than any man I know."[3]

Adding to Eisenhower's newfound happiness was the birth of a new son, John Sheldon Doud Eisenhower, in August 1922. While Mamie smothered the infant with affection, Ike, apparently wishing not to become too attached to the child and risk his feelings anew, played the part of the stern, demanding parent in a manner reminiscent of his own father. Although he did not use physical punishment, as his own parents had, he did give John military-style dressings-down for various misdeeds. John later described his father as a "terrifying figure" during his youth, but the discipline was tempered by a clear devotion and an intent to include the boy in as many of Ike's activities as possible. To Eisenhower's great pride, John eventually followed in his father's footsteps by choosing a West Point education and a military career.[4]

Panama, despite its contributions to Dwight's renewed spirits, remained a difficult place to live and raise a family. By the fall of 1924 the Eisenhowers were ready, with the Conners' assent, to seek a new posting. Ike's reassignment orders at first were puzzling, for they stationed him back at Fort Meade. But Conner counseled patience to his disappointed and impatient protégé, hinting mysteriously that matters would be quickly arranged. What Conner orchestrated specifically was a classic bureaucratic shuffle. Under normal conditions, an officer in the infantry could not be assigned to the Command and General Staff School at Fort Leavenworth, considered the fast track of officer training and tactics, without first attending the Infantry School at Fort Benning and then receiving approval from the chief of infantry. Given the infantry's opinion of Eisenhower from the tank article furor, such approval was highly unlikely. But Conner arranged for Ike's temporary transfer out of the infantry's jurisdiction into the adjutant general's office as a recruiting officer. He then used his contacts in the War Department to persuade the adjutant general to assign the young officer to Leavenworth.[5]

Eisenhower was jubilant upon hearing the news. "I was ready to fly," he later noted, "and needed no airplane." But self-doubt soon crept in. Command and General Staff School was a major career test.

Those who performed well under its pressures could expect promotion; those who did not, oblivion. Was he suffiently prepared for the challenge? An aide to the chief of infantry, probably trying to reassert his section's "superior judgment" of Ike's capabilities, advised him not to go because "you will probably fail." But Fox Conner exuded confidence in his protégé's abilities. "You may not know it," he counseled, "but because of your three years' work in Panama, you are far better trained and ready for Leavenworth than anybody I know." Eisenhower had not realized it at the time, but ever since their initial encounter five years earlier at Fort Meade, Conner had been preparing him for just this opportunity.[6]

Command and General Staff School (C&GS) was designed to provide classroom training in the techniques and routine of combat command, including the preparation of battle and logistical plans. The chief teaching tool was war gaming in the classroom, but the army's approach to war gaming again suggested a greater interest in rote learning than creative tactics. For each war situation, or "problem," given to the officers, there was but one "correct" answer. Within the high-pressure setting of the school, 275 young officers gathered to compete against both one another and the standard of perfection set by the instructors. Candidates received particular battlefield scenarios and were assigned the duty of preparing plans for one side or the other. Instructors graded their solutions and then ordered them to work out the tactical movements of the individual combat and supply units needed to carry out the correct overall plan. In this process, with its cut-and-dried answers, the school primarily sought officers capable of recognizing quickly the basics of a battlefield tactical situation according to the book and of performing the detailed staff work necessary to implement a proper response. Independent thought was not being solicited—efficient staff officers were.[7]

Conner's tutoring in battlefield tactics through the study of historical campaigns had already prepared Eisenhower well for the grind of C&GS. To make himself even more ready, however, Ike pored over George Patton's notes taken a year earlier at the school. Once at Leavenworth, he joined forces with a fellow officer, Leonard Gerow, and the two shared lodgings and worked together on their respective war-game assignments. Although some at the school, partly because they had arrived with loftier reputations, were inclined to view selection to C&GS as a reward in itself, Eisenhower knew its importance to his own prospects, and he threw himself into his work accordingly. The course was well suited to his strengths as an officer, which included his capacity to perform well under physical and emotional pressure and his willingness to subordinate individualistic heroics for plans that emphasized effective coordination of units.[8]

When the final rankings were released, Eisenhower and Gerow learned that they had finished first and second in the class. It was a remarkable achievement for Eisenhower, who had graduated in the middle of his West Point class, had not attended Infantry School, and had been discouraged from attending Leavenworth by his own service section. Congratulations poured in from friends and relatives. Brother Arthur Eisenhower even arranged a celebration at Kansas City's Muelbach Hotel complete with bootleg liquor. But from an otherwise congratulatory George Patton came a useful cautionary on the Leavenworth experience. "You know," he wrote, "that we talk a hell of a lot about tactics and such and we never get to brass tacks. Namely what it is that makes the Poor S.O.B. who constitutes the casualtie [sic] lists fight and in what formation is he going to fight. . . . Victory in the next war will depend on EXECUTION not PLANS."[9]

As matters turned out, Ike's exemplary peformance at C&GS did not even guarantee him a quick promotion in the shrunken peacetime United States Army. He found himself immediately reassigned to football coaching duties, this time at Fort Benning. Once again, Fox Conner came to his rescue. Congress had authorized the creation of a Battle Monuments Commission with the responsibility for compiling a guide to American battlesites in the Great War. Because General Pershing headed the new body, Conner managed to wangle Eisenhower an appointment as Pershing's aide in the preparation of the guidebook. As was the custom, such projects primarily entailed staff work, which meant that Eisenhower was more accurately the author of the book than his superior. In any event, the job was not that difficult, for it was less a creative writing assignment than an assemblage of unit histories, maps, and photographs.[10]

Assignment to Washington, D.C., to work on the guidebook had one other advantage, although it did not pay direct dividends until years later. The job gave the young officer the chance to develop early contacts with capital officials, who might at some future time be called upon to boost his career. Providing his services as a conduit to official

Washington was Ike's brother Milton, already a rising bureaucratic star and the number-two official in the Coolidge administration's Department of Agriculture. In the short run, the assignment gave Eisenhower the chance to develop an independent relationship with Pershing. Becoming a confidant of the general was not easy, for he was a cold, aloof man, similar in his personality to a later superior of Ike's, George Marshall. But Pershing developed a deep respect for his aide's diligence and self-effacement as a collaborator on the guide, and he subsequently sought Eisenhower's advice in writing his memoirs. Although the Pershing-Eisenhower relationship did not pay off as handsomely as others later did in career advancement, it lasted until the general's death in 1948. Eisenhower regularly sent birthday greetings and letters to Pershing through the years, and he personally attended the elderly officer during his final days at Walter Reed Army Hospital.[11]

Eisenhower's immediate reward for his services to Pershing was an appointment to the Army War College in Washington, D.C. In theory the school represented the pinnacle of an officer's postgraduate training. But unlike Leavenworth, the War College was less than met the eye. Students spent more time being bored by lectures from civilian and military superiors and attending capital social functions than anything else. The chief benefit of the appointment for Ike was that it gave him additional opportunity to spend time with his family and with Milton and his circle of government friends. Upon graduating in June 1928, he hoped for an assignment with the Army General Staff. But Mamie was eager for a vacation from Washington, and the Battle Monuments Commission again sought his services, this time in France to collect information for an update of the guidebook. By the time he left for France with his family, he was already nearly thirty-eight years old, had completed nearly two decades of intermittent formal education, and was still only a major, despite the assistance from Conner and Pershing. Even their support could not clear away the logjam of officers blocking his rise in the service. He had been given the army's best training to date, but he still waited for the rank and opportunity to use it. By 1928, he had nearly exhausted the possibilities for career assistance that cooperative but controversial heroes of the Great War such as Conner and Pershing could provide.[12]

As long as the country remained at peace and the army remained at its shrunken force levels, Eisenhower would have to seek new avenues of advancement, probably by associating himself with one of the relatively small number of officers now making their mark in the War Department. When he returned to Washington in November of 1929, he obtained an assignment to the office of the assistant secretary of war, with responsibilities for helping prepare contingency plans for a future world war. In the late 1920s this exercise, which eventually resulted in the development of the department's Industrial College, had an otherworldly quality about it. The Great Depression was in its early stages, and both private citizens and public officials were more concerned with the nation's domestic economic health than with preparations for a second world war. And yet, with millions of Americans jobless and in breadlines, with the economy in decline, and with the Hoover administration insisting on spending restraints and budgetary balance, Eisenhower and his colleagues spent late nights preparing plans for wartime plant expansion, rationing of goods and services, manpower allocation, controlled increases in the federal budget and in deficit spending, and cooperative schemes between industrialists and the War Department. Some of these wartime emergency measures, ironically, might have made sense in fighting the depression, especially those involved with federal job creation and allocation, increased government spending, and industrial cooperation. But there is no evidence that it occurred to Eisenhower, his superiors in the War Department, or the industrialists involved to advocate a similar approach in fighting the depression.[13]

Eisenhower's years of service in the War Department in the late 1920s and early 1930s were an important transition period for him. His immediate superior at the department in 1929 was Maj. Gen. George Van Horn Moseley, a former chief of supply under Pershing but a better friend of a rising star in army ranks, and a Pershing opponent, Gen. Douglas MacArthur. One of the items that linked Moseley and MacArthur was their politics, which were decidedly right wing. Moseley eventually was accused of being a fascist, and he later became a political ally of the anti-Semitic demagogue Gerald L. K. Smith. Although he was also conservative in his inclinations, Eisenhower privately questioned some of the more outrageous of Moseley's political views. Nevertheless, he performed without open complaint the staff officer's duty of representing the views of his superior. He even wrote an article for the *Cavalry Journal,* his first since the ill-fated piece on tank tactics, and it combined an outline of the War Department's contingency mobilization plans for American industry with a Moseley-inspired harangue against the dangers of pacifism.[14]

The industrial planning work of Eisenhower and Moseley had received little but scorn in its early months from Army Chief of Staff Charles Summerall. In 1930, however, MacArthur succeeded Summerall and quickly indicated his enthusiasm both for the project and for its junior architect. With MacArthur's encouragement, and under the sponsorship of a new agency created by Congress, the War Policies Commission, Moseley and Eisenhower produced an overall strategy draft for price controls, rationing priorities, foreign trade agreements, commandeering of plants and manpower, selective service, and public relations in the event of war, with all agencies created for these duties to be placed under civilian control. This war mobilization blueprint was primarily Eisenhower's product, and it would have added to the eventual reputation of the commander of Allied forces in Europe to have also played the key role in the creation of the "arsenal of democracy" at home. Unfortunately, both Congress and the Roosevelt administration ignored the major details of the plan in 1940–41 and instead followed their own piecemeal approach to war preparedness.[15]

Despite the inattention of Congress and the president, Eisenhower's efforts had caught the eye of MacArthur, who was seeking just such a diligent and loyal staff officer. Beginning in 1932, Ike spent the next seven years working directly for that most colorful of superiors. It was an unusual partnership, replete with emotional ups and downs that surprised no one aware of their dramatic differences in personality and temperament. Although Eisenhower was certainly not lacking in ambition, his working style was the antithesis of the flamboyant individualist. He also held strictly to the West Point admonition to keep military business and partisan politics separate. Such characteristics certainly did not describe Douglas MacArthur. MacArthur was vain, volatile, flamboyant in dress and manner, but with a capacity for strategic brilliance. When effectively controlled and channeled, his military capabilities were as great as those of any officer the nation possessed. But his belief in his own infallibility of judgment and his proclivity to meddle in Washington politics was not conducive to effective teamwork, and it could and did lead to personal and professional disasters. For MacArthur, accordingly, the ideal staff man was not one with whom to share the public limelight, or even a protégé, but rather a dutiful servant. At least at first, Ike was willing to oblige.[16]

Eisenhower received an early example of the political dangers of working with the impulsive MacArthur in the summer of 1932. Demanding payment in full for their bonus certificates received for service in World War I, a ragged civilian "army" of veterans and their families descended on Washington, D.C., and encamped, awaiting presidential and congressional action. With the economy continuing to fall and unemployment soaring, the capital had grown rife with fears of incipient revolution. To parts of the Hoover administration, the Bonus Army appeared to constitute the front ranks of Bolshevism itself. In Ike's view, the marchers were merely desperate people in need of sympathy and relief, camped out in "miserable little shacks built out of cast-off materials, tin cans, and old lumber." But MacArthur insisted that "Red organizers" had taken over the protests, despite the absence of any evidence to support the allegation. Urged on in part by MacArthur's claims, the Hoover administration sought to remove the protesters forcibly from their sit-in at the Treasury Department. During the eviction, conducted by the D.C. police, violence erupted, and MacArthur, bestrewn with medals and wearing his dress coat and riding breeches, ordered in the cavalry with sabers drawn. Their orders were not merely to assist in the removal of protesters from the Treasury building but to drive the remainder from their shacks on the Anacostia Flats as well. In carrying out the brutal eviction of the bonus marchers, MacArthur ignored two separate attempts by Secretary of War Patrick Hurley to order him to halt his action.[17]

The sight of General MacArthur in full regalia overseeing the brutal expulsion of a group of petitioning American citizens from the capital provided a field day for the press and photographic crews. As the troops moved in on the marchers' shacks, fires of unknown origin broke out, creating the image that the army troops were burning out the veterans. To Eisenhower, who as MacArthur's staffer had been required to follow him around during the escapade, the entire scene was an embarrassment. The Bonus Army marchers were only citizens who were "ragged, ill-fed, and felt themselves badly abused. To suddenly see the whole encampment going up in flames just added to the pity one had to feel for them." Apparently the only thing MacArthur could add to compound the embarrassment was to hold a press conference in sight of the burning shacks that evening of 27 July. And overruling Eisenhower's advice, MacArthur did exactly that, insisting to astonished reporters that "that mob down there was a bad-looking mob. It was animated by the essence of revolution."[18]

The entire Bonus Army episode, for many Americans, labeled both President Hoover and MacArthur as uncaring ogres, and the taint of association with the incident did not help Dwight Eisenhower either. In its own way, however, it too was part of his education as an officer. With the Bonus Army incident as a specific example, Eisenhower's service to MacArthur in the 1930s would prove most valuable as a kind of negative reference in showing him the command excesses to avoid. MacArthur's endless vanity, his unwillingness to accept conflicting counsel (in 1936 he would insist against Ike's advice that Landon would trounce Roosevelt), and his lack of public moderation all provided object lessons on how not to conduct an effective command.[19]

With MacArthur a political hot potato, it might have been expected that the incoming Roosevelt administration would find him immediately expendable in March 1933. Even the general himself probably did not expect to continue as chief of staff beyond the normal expiration of his term in the fall of 1934. But motivated partly by confusion over a possible replacement, Franklin Roosevelt not only kept MacArthur on but extended his tenure as chief of staff an additional year. If MacArthur stayed, that meant that Eisenhower did also. With the change in administrations and in approaches to fighting the depression, Ike now found himself preparing organizational blueprints for FDR's camp-style program for jobless youth, the Civilian Conservation Corps (CCC). It was a supreme irony of Eisenhower's career that he, who spent much of his later political life condemning "paternalistic" government schemes, was forced to play a central role in launching the CCC program. Despite his unease in the task, however, Eisenhower was actually helping lay a basis for future military preparedness. Besides offering participants jobs, the program provided a form of "basic training" to potential future soldiers. In addition, New Deal agencies, such as the Public Works Administration and the Works Progress Administration, eventually employed Americans not only on make-work projects but in munitions plants, aircraft factories, coastal defenses, and shipyards, where World War II vessels like the aircraft carriers USS *Enterprise* and USS *Yorktown* were constructed. [20]

Although Eisenhower at first appreciated the New Deal's emphasis on national cooperation and Roosevelt's ability to inspire a dispirited public, he soon came to detest the administration's broker-state political methods and what he saw as the effects of its programs on individual initiative. With the exception of his experience with the Bonus Army marchers, Eisenhower had been personally insulated in Washington from the full impact of the depression's human hardships. Given his distaste for partisan politics, as well as his detachment from the economic crisis, it is not surprising that he fell back upon his youthful invocations to hard work, the avoidance of debt, self-help, and voluntarism. It remained for others to seek new answers to the economic problems that lay beyond the reach of private individuals alone to solve. Differing views on how to end the depression originating from varying perspectives were evident even within the Eisenhower clan. By 1934 Dwight considered Roosevelt a legislative dictator usurping congressional powers (perhaps because the administration was seeking executive control over the setting of military force levels). On the personal level, too, he disliked Roosevelt, viewing him as "cruel" to aides and a man with an adolescent lack of personal control. He scornfully recalled to others one occasion in which he had been required to carry Roosevelt to bed after the president had imbibed too much liquor. His brother Arthur, a Kansas City banker, also hated FDR for his frequent use of class-based, antibanker rhetoric. In contrast, Milton, an able and rising bureaucratic holdover in the capital, saw at least some good coming from the New Deal's relief and recovery efforts. [21]

With MacArthur unwilling to soften his right-wing political views, Eisenhower did not have long to wait for a new assignment that would free him from Washington bureaucratic battles or from involvement in New Deal "paternalism." The Roosevelt administration sought an opportunity to rid itself of MacArthur and found it in 1935. Congress had voted to grant the Philippines commonwealth status as a preliminary step toward independence, and the Philippines government required a new security force under U.S. Army tutelage. Having the army assume a major role in training and equipping a national military force for a friendly government was nothing new—America had helped create the national guards and armies of several Latin American states. The Philippines assignment, however, took on additional importance because of Washington's growing awareness of the threat posed by the Japanese Empire to U.S. interests in the Far East. MacArthur was the logical man to head the American contingent to Manila, for he had seen prior duty there—his father once had been military governor of the islands—and Philippines President Manuel Quezon specifically had requested him.[22]

Eisenhower hoped that MacArthur's reassignment would free him for troop duty elsewhere than Manila. But MacArthur insisted that Ike remain his chief staff officer at the new post, and when such a high-ranking superior made a request the wise junior officer did not say no. Neither Dwight nor Mamie was thrilled at the move to another tropical posting—Mamie because three years in Panama had been enough, and Ike because he was tired of MacArthur and of staff dealings with politicians, whether American or Filipino. There were compensations, however. Eisenhower got his pick of assistants for the mission, and he chose a West Point classmate already at work on a Philippine defense plan, Maj. James Ord. Having the chance to organize an army from the bottom up was bound to be a challenge and a partial release from desk duty. In addition, the fringe benefits of the job were attractive. While on detachment from the army, both MacArthur and Eisenhower would receive full pay plus an additional salary from the Philippines government (three thousand dollars a month for MacArthur, nearly a thousand dollars a month plus expenses for Eisenhower). While in Manila they also would be able to lodge at the plush Manila Hotel, replete with servants and obliging Filipino civilian officials.[23]

It was not until the two men were on their way to Manila that they discovered how far MacArthur's reputation had fallen in the eyes of the Roosevelt administration. By telegram the general learned that he had been demoted from a four-star to a two-star general, effective immediately. While in Washington, MacArthur had believed that Roosevelt would allow him to retain his title as chief of staff for a month after his arrival in the Philippines as a favor for peacefully accepting the assignment. He also had thought that he would be permitted to retain his four-star rank permanently. FDR's decision not to oblige MacArthur clearly signaled that the general was now persona non grata in the capital. The dishonor of his exile only made him more irritable toward his subordinates, including Eisenhower. Intensifying MacArthur's personal gloom was the death of his mother, who had been a source of love and inspiration just as Ike's own Ida had been. The pressures upon Eisenhower in working for an unhappy boss eased somewhat with the news that the army had promoted him to lieutenant colonel in July 1936. He also enjoyed his accommodations at the Manila Hotel and the presidential palace, where he socialized and played bridge with American businessmen and President Quezon.[24]

Despite MacArthur's previous ties to the islands, Eisenhower assumed the major day-to-day responsibility for preparing the Philippines' defense force. Within weeks he enjoyed more frequent contacts with Filipino officials, including Quezon, than did MacArthur. He also developed a keener understanding of the realities of the Philippine military situation than did his commander. The original defense plan had called for mini-training stations to be set up in ninety scattered locations. These dispersed garrisons of two-hundred conscripts each were intended to eliminate the need for a single massive training installation that would have been too costly. But even with such cost-cutting measures, the dollars provided by Washington were far too few for anything but the most rudimentary training. The Philippines' air force consisted of a few outdated training planes operated by two U.S. Army Air Corps instructors. In January 1938, Eisenhower's friend and aide James Ord lost his life in a plane crash in one of the vehicles. The little money and supplies Washington allocated was further wasted by the Filipino bureaucracy. Eisenhower personally flew back to the capital to beg army superiors for additional equipment, but he met with no success. Despite his personal lobbying, original spending estimates for the Philippines actually were cut 50 percent, followed by even greater reductions. Filipino trainees settled for obsolete equipment on loan and received only six months' instruction before being pressed into active service.[25]

Eisenhower's experiences in Manila drove home to him the lack of military preparedness in the islands and in America itself. At the same time, they also magnified his sense of social isolation from the plight of the Filipino civilians around him. He was much better educated and realistic about the shoddy state of the Philippines' defense than MacArthur, who issued orders for a showy and expensive troop march to display the army of the Philippines to its people. When Quezon wisely vetoed the idea as too expensive, MacArthur blamed Eisenhower for the misunderstanding rather than himself, a slight his staffer never forgave. But Eisenhower did not develop the same perceptiveness about the flaws of Filipino society as he did about its military capability. His social isolation among the officers, politicians, and businessmen of Manila, as with his previous confinement behind a desk in Washington, limited his understanding of the plight of the islands' needy and the inadequacies of Quezon's government in addressing it. Despite the Japanese threat, in the short run what Quezon needed an army for, more than anything else, was to put down the intermittent threats of revolt from those for whom any real promise of independence also meant food, shelter, and land opportunities. Unfortunately, like those around him, Eisenhower continued to view international relations through the blinders of an American global military strategy that stressed unwavering commitments to allies, in spite of their sometimes repressive consequences.[26]

By the end of 1938, despite a happy reunion with Mamie and his son, John, Eisenhower was more than ready to leave the Philippines. Nazi Germany threatened the peace in Europe, and especially after the appeasement at Munich, he itched for reassignment to active duty with troops. In the islands, the picture was deceptively calm. MacArthur had accelerated the training program, but he also had predicted to his hosts that the Japanese army would never attack the Philippines as long as Americans were stationed there. Despite Ike's desire to leave, MacArthur clearly wanted him to stay, but events forced him to allow a transfer. In September of 1939, Hitler's tanks rolled into Poland. Honoring their defense commitments to that country, Great Britain and France declared war on Germany. Although Eisenhower recognized the tragedy of war, especially one on a global scale, he also recognized its arrival as perhaps a final opportunity to escape the shadows of superiors, to command troops in the field, and to answer his country's call to greatness. Perhaps in the expectation of changing his professional fortunes, he had shortly earlier turned down an offer to head an organization seeking refuges in Asia for Jewish refugees—a job which would have paid the attractive sum of sixty thousand dollars a year plus expenses. He also had rejected repeated offers in Washington and Manila to resign his commission for a military correspondent's job, at pay considerably higher than army wages.[27]

He was under no illusions about the sacrifices he and thousands of others would be asked to make. After hearing Neville Chamberlain's war message to the English people on 3 September, he wrote to his brother Milton, "After months and months of feverish effort to appease and placate the madman that is governing Germany, the British and French seem to be driven into a corner out of which they can work their way only by fighting." He added, "It's a sad day for Europe and for the whole civilized world." Eisenhower predicted that a protracted and bloody conflict would create anarchy and poverty, thereby sowing the seeds of communism and the loss of individual freedom. In order to prevent that eventuality, or the recurrence of world war, the Allies would have to defeat Hitler completely, and he added, "Germany will have to be dismembered."[28] Though not a pleasant prospect, a new world war was a call to duty. Given the especially odious nature of the Nazis, it even assumed the character of a latter-day crusade against a new breed of barbarians in Europe. He quickly fixed a departure date of 13 December 1939 for his return to the Untied States, and he refused all pleadings from MacArthur and Quezon to remain in the Philippines. After a formal send-off from Manila, he arrived in Hawaii on Christmas Day, 1939. By New Year's Day, 1940, he was back in San Francisco.

4

WAR AND OPPORTUNITY

The outbreak of World War II in Europe abruptly ended America's official complacency toward the aggressive designs of the dictators abroad. During the three years from 1939 to 1942, the United States Army faced a mobilization task of awesome and unprecedented proportions. Because of the military advances of other industrialized societies and the changes in war tactics they spawned, the army now had to produce new kinds of weaponry, discard old fighting doctrines for new ones, and recruit, equip, and train a new generation of soldiers. In that three-year span, the army would be called upon to mushroom from a level of 190,000 troops to over 5 million. A preparedness miracle was being asked of the military, and a major burden of responsibility now fell upon the group of officers who had persevered during the service hard times of the 1920s and 1930s.

Dwight Eisenhower was one of those officers for whom the growing specter of war, a conflict predicted by mentor Fox Conner, offered both a tragic sequel to the "war to end wars" and a personal opportunity. Because of his shortage of field experience with troops and his advancing age, it was an even greater chance for him than others of his rank. For the army to consider anyone a "capable and well-rounded officer," field troop duty was essential. But from the time he had left Conner in Panama until his return to America in late 1939, Ike had spent only six months with troops. The bulk of his experience was as a staff man, a "paper pusher." The label grated upon him, even though his superiors had appreciated his services to them. Now, it was not only likely that he would receive a field command (especially given the scarcity of officers to handle the recruit influx), but if America entered the war, a combat assignment probably would follow.

The army had another temporary dose of humility to administer, however. Eisenhower's original orders had directed him to go to Fort Lewis, Washington, for troop duty. But instead, a change in army plans forced him to stay in San Francisco and assist with Selective Service and National Guard activations. A frustrated Eisenhower went over his immediate superior's head directly to the War Department and soon secured his release to Fort Lewis. As it turned out, Ike's superior in San Francisco probably could not have detained him much longer, for the army chief of staff had ordered an immediate mobilization of personnel for concentrated training exercises on the West Coast. The United States Third Army was assembling its various units, numbering about a quarter of a million men, and the exercises required as many trained and experienced officers as could be obtained on short notice.[1]

At Fort Lewis, Eisenhower assumed his new duties as a regimental executive in the Fifteenth Infantry of the Third Division, but he quickly moved up to command of the First Battalion. He reveled in the opportunity to escape a desk. He even seemed to enjoy the long hours, the poor food, and the ever-present mud. He drove his charges hard, but he never asked them to do what he was unwilling to do himself, and his attitude and approach enabled him to build a cooperative spirit among his men. Building such an esprit de corps was more difficult than it seemed. The inadequacy of rail facilities for shipping troops expeditiously to camp meant reduced training time, equipment was in short supply, and the trainees themselves were a diverse lot, hailing from all sections of the country. But Ike succeeded in building good morale and discipline, and his public modesty and down-home manner lessened barriers between him and his men. Eisenhower's joy at commanding troops once again swelled even more when he learned that son John had earned admission to West Point in a competitive examination. The decision of a son he had feared would become a "mama's boy" to follow in his own footsteps made him very proud, especially since, because of the MacArthur taint, he had been unable to pull strings for John's automatic admission.[2]

He still wanted as large as possible a role for himself in the big show unfolding in Europe. Nazi panzer armies had rolled over Allied resistance in the Low Countries and even France itself by the early summer of 1940. England awaited a German invasion, and American officers expected their country to enter the war against the Axis before much longer. With great excitement Eisenhower received a request in September from Col. George Patton, now commander of the Second Armored Brigade, to join him as a regimental commander. Ike relished the prospect of serving with his old friend, but the transfer would be difficult because it required shifting from the infantry to a sister corps. Given the infantry's growing need for training officers, he doubted whether his superiors would approve. Nevertheless, he wanted the assignment so much that he contacted a colleague from earlier days, now serving as an aide to the chief of infantry—Mark Clark. If the transfer could not be arranged, Eisenhower stressed, his desire remained at least to receive troop duty once his reassignment orders arrived. During this period of intense lobbying, Ike also was solicited by his old Leavenworth roommate, Leonard Gerow, for a staff position in the War Plans Division of the War Department, but he referred Gerow to Clark in an effort to derail the staff request.[3]

When Ike's new orders finally arrived on the last day of November 1940, he felt as though Thanksgiving had arrived again. Although his transfer request to the Armored Corps had been rejected, he had received a troop assignment, and an important one at that. Having escaped another round of staff duty in the capital, he found himself assigned as chief of staff to the Third Division at Fort Lewis. With good staff officers in constant demand from higher-ups, Ike's continued good performances quickly led to even better appointments. In March 1941 the army appointed Eisenhower chief of staff to the Ninth Army Corps and promoted him to temporary full colonel. For years he had told friends and family that he did not expect ever to exceed the rank of colonel, and for that reason his attainment of the rank at age fifty was cause for great celebration. But his rapid and sudden rise was not yet over. On 11 June 1941, Lt. Gen. Walter Krueger, in search of a staff officer for the Third Army with "broad vision, progressive ideas, a thorough grasp of the magnitude of the problems involved in handling an army, and lots of initiative and resourcefulness," named him his deputy chief of staff. Barely two months later, Krueger named Eisenhower chief of staff for the Third Army—the chief operations officer for 240,000 men scattered from New Mexico to Florida.[4]

The principal reason for the Third Army's assemblage in the South in the summer of 1941 was because Army Chief of Staff George Marshall had ordered a massive war-game training exercise called the "Louisiana maneuvers." The mock war, held in late August and September, pitted Krueger's force against the Second Army of Gen. Ben Lear, comprising 180,000 troops. In the war-game scenario, Lear's force was defending Louisiana against Krueger's invasion force, which possessed more troops but less armor. Because he was Krueger's chief staff officer, Eisenhower carried the main responsibility for designing and carrying out a successful attack plan. It was his greatest opportunity to date to demonstrate his mettle for battlefield command. Because of his Leavenworth training and his twenty-five years of experience in the army, he had definite advantages over younger adversaries in handling the emotional stresses of the situation and in coolly assessing strategy. The exercises were at best only a rough approximation of the battlefield, because such variables as gasoline supplies were controlled by the rule makers, and both sides had to substitute papier-mâché tanks and civilian trucks for still-scarce military hardware. The situation Eisenhower faced, therefore, was a kind of middle ground between the battles on maps and paper at Leavenworth and the actual death, destruction, and unpredictability of a real battlefield.[5]

The maneuvers provided a forum for Eisenhower's impressive physical stamina and drive at age fifty, his ability to convert textbook principles to the field, and his ability to keep his head and his spirits up in time of stress. Unanticipated or underestimated complications, including mud, mosquitoes, malaria, and a near miss by a hurricane, taxed even the most resourceful and energetic of officers, and they added both to logistical tangles and to morale problems among the men. Such problems affected both sides in the exercise, but Eisenhower had to cope with them while planning and implementing a massive flank attack on the Second Army. He passed the test with flying colors. During the first phase of the maneuvers, judges scored Ike's attack a clear-cut victory. Reporters covering the event for the national press asserted that if the battle had been real, the Second Army might have been totally annihilated.[6]

The success of Eisenhower's invasion plan augured well by itself for his professional prospects, but it was the maneuvers' reporting by the press that first introduced his name to the American public. Drew Middleton of the *New York Times* lauded his tactics, and Drew Pearson and Robert S. Allen in their "Washington Merry-Go-Round" column colorfully related "Colonel Eisenhower . . . who conceived and directed the strategy that routed the 2nd Army [has] a steel trap mind plus unusual vigor." They added, "To him the military profession is a science and he began watching and studying the German Army five years ago." Certainly the praise was deserved. But it was unusual that so much praise was directed at the Third Army's chief of staff and not at its commander, General Krueger. Besides Krueger's own willingness to acknowledge Eisenhower's role, another contributor to the flood of acclaim was Ike's own role during the maneuvers as public relations spokesman for the Third Army. During the first phase of the exercise his tent served as a home away from home for the correspondents, and they appreciated his honesty in describing the operation and the deficiencies in army equipment and training. Along with Ike's natural charm and good looks, the reporters found that their host was "good copy." While reporters made Eisenhower's name and face familiar to the country over the news wires, Milton and his friends in Washington did their part in the same direction. In other words, without appearing to try very hard, Eisenhower was able to use the maneuvers to boost dramatically his reputation as a rising star in the army's ranks.[7]

Although it was less publicized, the exercises' second phase also proved important to Eisenhower, but for other reasons. The headline grabber this time was George Patton, and the nature of his theatrics underscored the differences in style of the two men and also the limitations of the exercises in duplicating battlefield conditions. As a tank commander in the Second Army, Patton launched his forces in a daring cross-country flanking dash that succeeded in threatening the Third Army's hard-won position. Convinced by his calculations that Patton's "tanks" could not have traveled the distances claimed on the fuel stocks allocated under the rules, Eisenhower suspected, and charged, foul play. He was right. Patton had commandeered gasoline from Louisiana filling stations while on the march in order to supply his vehicles, and his foray was disallowed by the exercise's judges. Patton, however, had made a useful point. War would not be fought by artificial rules, and even the best-laid plans required battle-tough, cagy, and flexible troops to carry them off. Eisenhower might have mastered war by the United States Army's textbook, but wars were not fought in books but on shifting battlefields.[8]

In the aftermath of his Louisiana maneuvers triumph, Eisenhower was promoted to brigadier general (temporary) in late September 1941. Dramatic and shocking events, however, dictated his next assignment. Five days after the Japanese attack on Pearl Harbor of 7 December, which brought America formally into World War II, the War Department summoned him to Washington for emergency duty. Leonard Gerow and his chief, General Marshall, required his services as a staff officer in the department's War Plans Section, later renamed the Operations Division. Although Eisenhower was unaware of it at the time, the reassignment marked the beginning of a long and fruitful partnership between himself and Marshall. Wherever the war took Eisenhower, from War Plans in Washington to supreme commander of Allied forces in the European theater, and however great his own fame, he remained throughout the war Marshall's subordinate in rank and in prestige with their civilian commanders in chief, Franklin D. Roosevelt and Harry S Truman.[9]

Eisenhower had served under various mentors during the lean years of the 1920s and 1930s, but Marshall proved a unique tutor and, in many ways, the best of all. A native Virginian, Marshall possessed an austere, remote personality reminiscent of his own army mentor, John J. Pershing. Intolerant of sloppiness, laziness, or indecisiveness, Marshall wanted staffers around him who could be counted on to take his general strategic directives and run with them rather than require his constant, time-consuming guidance. Like other senior officers Marshall played favorites with assignments, but the overall quality of his protégés, when tested under difficult conditions, testified to the soundness of his personnel judgments. He counted among his trainees from the Infantry School at Fort Benning such later luminaries of World War II and Korea as Joseph "Vinegar Joe" Stilwell, Omar Bradley, Lawton Collins, Matthew Ridgway, and Walter Bedell Smith.

Given Marshall's independence of judgment on personnel matters, even Eisenhower's performance in Louisiana probably did not account for his summons to Washington. The job at War Plans was again staff work, not field command, and Marshall based his estimations of subordinates on personal observation rather than on the recommendations of others. Instead, Eisenhower's appointment was a logical choice dictated both by the disasters in the Pacific theater in the opening days of the war and by his prior service in the Philippines. Following the debacle at Pearl Harbor, the Japanese offensive was pressing forward into southern China and Southeast Asia, and invasion forces had landed in the Philippines. Who better, then, to try to formulate a response to the deteriorating American position in the Philippines than Eisenhower, who had helped organize the islands' defense forces and had served as MacArthur's principal aide?[10]

Marshall already knew what he wanted to do about the Philippine situation. Despite his personal dislike for MacArthur, which was frequently reciprocated, and despite the hopelessness of resupplying or rescuing MacArthur's forces because of a Japanese naval blockade of the islands, he did not want to appear to abandon MacArthur. To do so would send the wrong signals to American allies at a precarious time and would also enflame domestic public opinion. As a test of his new subordinate, then, Marshall handed the Philippines problem to Eisenhower and immediately asked for a summary of necessary policy steps. Within a few hours, after examining the cables and other information from the Pacific, Eisenhower typed out a memorandum that corresponded almost precisely with Marshall's own assessment. The War Department should spare what it could to aid MacArthur, and it should test ways of running the Japanese blockade, but it should recognize the likely doom of the American garrison. Australia would have to be beefed up as the long-term base for future operations in the Southwest Pacific. In addition, the Soviet Union would be urged to assist in the Asian theater as much as possible.[11]

In January and February 1942, the Philippines remained Eisenhower's main theater of responsibility within War Plans. Although the islands still were important for image and morale purposes, they had otherwise already become a backwater region. They could not be saved, and War Department priorities lay with the Europe-centered grand strategy being directed by Marshall. Eisenhower's attempts to fund and organize efforts to assist MacArthur collided with the European supply priority and the arguments of the United States Navy. The navy, which saw itself as the chief proprietor of the American

war in the Pacific, did not itself want to waste already shrunken resources on MacArthur. Not surprisingly, MacArthur insisted that he
was being made a sacrificial lamb by the War Department, and he
bombarded his former aide with messages complaining about the lack
of help for his men. A desperate Filipino president Quezon proposed
to the War Department that, in order to salvage Allied forces and his
own rule, it accept immediate independence of the islands followed
by a neutrality decree. A neutral Philippines ran directly contrary
to the official definition of American strategic interests in the region, and MacArthur's willingness to second Quezon's scheme only
cemented War Department coolness towards the grandstanding
commander.[12]

Eisenhower's own efforts to channel limited aid to MacArthur, including trying to commission private boats to smuggle supplies, failed
to lessen the frequency of his former commander's diatribes. However,
by mid-February, Ike's duties expanded beyond the Philippine problem, as Marshall named him head of War Plans. Now occupying a
position with planning responsibilities around the globe, including
Europe, Eisenhower became fully allied with the Europe-first strategy
and increasingly displayed his impatience with MacArthur. Although
his estimation not only of MacArthur's temperament but also of his
tactical sense was plummeting, he still recognized that the commander's escape from the Philippines had to be arranged. He feared, however, that MacArthur might choose the theatrical but useless example
of staying with his besieged men at Bataan until their capture. To
prevent any such escapade, the War Department ordered MacArthur
out of the Philippines, and in mid-March he was smuggled out to
Australia in a dramatic rescue mission. Under the brave but doomed
command of Gen. Jonathan Wainwright, the American garrison at
Bataan and later Corregidor Island managed to delay its surrender to
the Japanese until 6 May.[13]

With little in the way of military successes to buoy morale, work at
War Plans was long and discouraging. Eisenhower, in marked contrast
to his later presidential image as a leisurely executive, drove himself
unmercifully. Sixteen-hour days were common, as was the daily con-
sumption of four packs of cigarettes. High blood pressure developed,
and the pressures of the job did not help it. On top of his other professional duties and strains, on 10 March he learned of his father's death.
Nevertheless, he continued at his work that day until 7:30, closing

his office door then for half an hour to contemplate and compose a personal eulogy. Insisting, "I'm proud he was my father," he conceded, "It was always so difficult to let him know the great depth of my affection for him." Under such strains, Eisenhower's temper, usually well bottled up in public, exploded ten days later at, of all people, General Marshall. Marshall insisted on making the point that in this war field officers would receive the promotions, and he informed his subordinate that he had turned down two field command requests for him because Eisenhower's duty, if not his glory, was in Washington. Frustrated and resentful at the remarks, Eisenhower shot back, "General, I'm interested in what you say, but I want you to know that I don't give a damn about your promotion plans as far as I'm concerned. I came into this office from the field and I am trying to do my duty." He finished, "I expect to do so as long as you want me here. If that locks me to a desk for the rest of the war, so be it!" After striding to the door, he looked back at Marshall, managing a slight grin. To his surprise, he thought he detected the traces of a return smile on Marshall's face.[14]

Three days later, Marshall promoted Eisenhower to major general (temporary). Almost as if in response to Eisenhower's outburst, Marshall described his aide's new position as not merely a "staff officer" but a "subordinate commander with troops." What the change signified was that Eisenhower had become Marshall's hand-picked man. His responsibilities grew accordingly. Marshall's own chief objectives were to establish a basis for long-term, bilateral military planning and command with the British, and to arrive at an Allied consensus on broad strategic objectives and timetables. Already Eisenhower had been introduced to the intricacies of such cross-ocean military negotiating through his preparatory work for the Arcadia conference of British and American officials the previous winter. Marshall was determined to create multinational theater commands, starting with the Far East region, and Eisenhower had drafted the proposed organizational chart in late December. The ABDA (Australian-British-Dutch-American) structure that had been proposed and adopted placed British commander Sir Archibald Wavell in charge in the Far East, with headquarters in Java. Ironically, the British, who had been skeptical of the command plan, were able to test it for only forty-six days because of rapid Japanese advances. British defeats in the Asian theater only made them more resentful, for in their view they had been given the command of a doomed theater. The British noted that Burma, a threatened area under British command, had been placed within ABDA's strategic jurisdiction, whereas Australia, the American fall-back base for future Pacific operations, had been excluded.[15]

The early confusion of the theater command structure in the Far East did provide useful lessons on the need for greater inter-Allied cooperation in planning and implementation for other theaters. To facilitate such cooperation, U.S. and British officials already had established the Combined Chiefs of Staff (CCS) as the overarching strategic board for the conduct of the war. The Americans, particularly Army Chief of Staff Marshall, held greater clout on the CCS than the British because of the Allies' overall reliance on America's vital "arsenal of democracy." The British, however, were able to express their points of view effectively, often prevailing by taking command disputes to Roosevelt and Prime Minister Churchill for final decision. The dominant dispute between strategists of the two nations involved the timing of a projected cross-channel invasion of Western Europe. A related issue concerned the selection of a commander for the enterprise. Marshall, epitomizing the American preference for direct, decisive early action against Hitler, urged a cross-channel invasion to be launched as early as the fall of 1942. Although the odds of such an expedition failing were estimated at as much as five to one, Marshall still favored taking the risk in order to relieve the pressure of Hitler's armies on Russia. If Germany knocked Russia out of the war, he feared, all hopes of Allied defeat of Hitler disappeared with it.[16]

Eisenhower stayed out of the debate over a second front in the West until he became head of War Plans. He had been preoccupied with other tedious details, such as the replacement of Gen. Hugh Drum for the projected American command in the Far East with General Stilwell, and with prospective discussions with Vichy France regarding a possible Chinese incursion into Indochina. Once Eisenhower joined the fray over the cross-channel invasion, however, he joined his boss in supporting an early assault. Although Marshall favored it, many other American military officials did not. Both General MacArthur and many of the United States Navy brass believed that the idea was merely another example of the folly of the Europe-first strategy. Given Marshall's close relationship with the president, he could manage that opposition. Any alternative invasion in the Pacific would face the obstacles of a crippled American fleet, a dominant Japanese military position, requirements of four times the shipping than the Americans then possessed, and no clear immediate military objective. Any reason for a preemptive strike in Southeast Asia to cut off raw material supplies from Japan, for example, already had been preempted by Japanese gains in the Malay region. It was the British, not the United States Navy, that presented more formidable obstacles to launching an early second front in Europe. Scarred by memories of the costliness of a direct assault strategy in World War I, the British were less concerned about the Russians' fate, more worried about their possessions in the Mediterranean and the Far East, and frankly skeptical of American strategic wisdom and fighting capabilities.

The British alternative to an immediate cross-channel venture, and a plan that tempted even President Roosevelt, was an amphibious invasion of French North Africa in the fall of 1942. Assuming its success, the British then foresaw subsequent assaults against Sicily and the Italian mainland, with Rome the eventual objective. Such enterprises, they argued, would answer their objections against an invasion of France, might cultivate Vichy collaboration and declining Italian morale to raise the prospect of success, and still would provide Stalin with at least a partial answer to his demand for a second front. In response to the British arguments, the CCS directed the preparation of two separate plans for possible North African landings, called Gymnast and Supergymnast. Gymnast differed from its counterpart in featuring amphibious landings only on the Mediterranean side of the Strait of Gibraltar; Supergymnast called for landings on the Atlantic side in addition.[17]

In the views of Marshall and Eisenhower, the British preference for North African landings instead of an immediate assault on France was both worthless and wasteful of resources. From his position as head of the Operations Division (OPD), where he oversaw such varied activities as planning, psychological warfare, economic warfare and allocations, and diplomatic coordination with the State Department, Eisenhower dispatched a memorandum on 25 March reiterating the American proposal for a cross-channel attack in September. This gambling venture, made contingent on the Russian military situation, Eisenhower designated as Sledgehammer. OPD also prepared two other military options for the consideration of the Combined Chiefs, the president, and the prime minister, and as Sledgehammer's prospects faded theirs gained. The first, code named Bolero, entailed a massive staging operation in 1942 as preparation for a future cross-channel assault. The second set of plans, encompassing the invasion itself and code named Roundup, called for an assault on France in the spring of 1943.[18]

Buttressed by Eisenhower's planning work, Marshall insisted to the British that if they rejected Sledgehammer, Bolero and Roundup remained the most effective ways to strike a blow against Hitler and force him to divert troops from the Russian front. British spokesmen on the Combined Chiefs, however, were as opposed to a 1943 invasion of Western Europe as they were to one in 1942. Besides their predictions of failure and massive casualties, they pointed out the inexperience of the Allies in amphibious operations and the continuing shortages of landing craft. An invasion of North Africa, the British maintained, would provide necessary experience in a less hazardous setting. Bolero also had the drawbacks, according to the British, of requiring them to accept less American material help in their ongoing campaigns in Egypt and China, of limiting the amount of Lend-Lease aid available for the Soviets, and of restricting supplies to the Pacific theater. The Americans acknowledged these difficulties, but they based their strategy on the immediate goals of keeping the Atlantic supply lanes open to Britain, holding (but not necessarily expanding) the India–Middle East buffer zone between Germany and Japan, and massing remaining resources for the direct blow against Fortress Europe. Marshall and Eisenhower's fear, which proved correct, was that any Gymnast-style African campaign would doom prospects not only for the 1942 assault on France but for Roundup as well.[19]

Sensing the diminishing prospects for a 1943 invasion of France, Marshall still directed Eisenhower to organize a Bolero planning group and to draft guidelines for the selection of an American corps commander for its staging operations in Britain. The Eisenhower memorandum of guidelines for the staging commander's selection, sent to Marshall in mid-May of 1942, appeared to suggest that its author was the best qualified candidate. The Bolero commander, Eisenhower wrote, required the trust and confidence of Marshall, had to agree with his strategic goals, and had to have the training and temperament to take over Marshall's job in Washington once Roundup was under way and Marshall himself assumed direct command of the operation. One other, unstated requirement of a Bolero commander was that he be able to maintain reasonably harmonious relations with his British hosts and fellow commanders.[20]

Marshall agreed completely with Eisenhower's conclusions. But before any choice for Bolero commander was made, the British had to be sounded out on their preference for the post and on the organizational arrangements. Marshall dispatched Eisenhower directly to London to meet with various British military leaders and to undertake a scouting operation of the fledgling U.S. presence already on the island. Although his instructions did not indicate so, it seems clear that Marshall's reason for sending his OPD chief was so that the British could look him over as the primary Bolero candidate. When Eisenhower arrived, he found the American command in a shambles. Fortunately, his own personal diplomacy with the British went much better, despite some initial awkwardness. Despite suffering the humiliation of being ordered by Lieutenant General Montgomery to put out his cigarette during a briefing, and despite the open skepticism displayed by Chief of the Imperial General Staff Sir Alan Brooke, Eisenhower kept up a public posture of good humor and cooperation with his hosts that impressed most of them. Especially fond of him was Vice Adm. Lord Louis Mountbatten, who already had organized a joint staff of British army, navy, and air force officers for the planning of amphibious assault tactics.[21]

In contrast to his superior's bulldog defense of the American point of view, it was Eisenhower's very self-effacement and apparent malleability to British concerns that appealed most to his hosts. The British did not want a strong-armer as Bolero commander or as Roundup head; they did not want Marshall in particular because of his stubborn insistence on the priority of the cross-channel assault, and because of his vigor in defending American national prestige in all multinational operations. What they wanted was an American officer receptive to "appeals to reason"—someone who by temperament and, frankly, by a lack of combat command experience would give British field officers maximum flexibility, and would possess the organizational and staff skills to unsnarl the tangled knots of invasion preparation. If that was what the British saw in Eisenhower, Marshall saw a different man. He saw a forceful advocate of his strategic vision—a man who could strongly but diplomatically stand up to British pressure. In part, these differing perceptions of Eisenhower derived from his acquired ability to appear as different things to different people. At times this gift stood him in good stead in mollifying disgruntled subordinates and superiors, as well as soothing nationalistic egos. But it also left him open to the later charge, true in part, that his final judgments on disputed tactical points tended to reflect the opinions of the last commander, American or British, who forced a hearing.[22]

Eisenhower returned to Washington on 3 June 1942 with the plans for Bolero and Roundup still stalled by nationalistic disagreements. He formally recommended for command of the invasion corps his friend Mark Clark, while suggesting Army Air Force Maj. Gen. Joseph McNarney, an early advocate of the cross-channel invasion, as commander for the entire European theater. Despite his written recommendations, the person Marshall had in mind for the assignment was the author of the report. In addition to his suggestions for the command posts, Eisenhower had recommended that whoever was named theater commander should be promoted to the rank of lieutenant general in order to lend that individual the necessary prestige to deal effectively with the British. As might have been expected, Marshall ignored the names submitted by his subordinate and leaked to Eisenhower the news that the theater command was his. Three days later, on 11 June 1942, Dwight D. Eisenhower officially assumed his new duties as commander of the European theater of operations.[23]

5

TIME OF TESTING

Dwight Eisenhower arrived in England with little fanfare on 24 June 1942 to begin his duties as a European theater commander. It was one of the last times he could claim such anonymity. To official Washington he was still "Milton's brother" or "Marshall's assistant." To the American public he was scarcely known at all. But the inattention would not last long. Americans craved a hero, and the decision to concentrate multinational commands under individual theater commanders naturally focused popular attention upon those key men. This was especially true of the European command, given its priority role in the overall war against the Axis. Along with that greater visibility, however, came greater public scrutiny and responsibility. The decisions Eisenhower would make would have the greatest importance to victory, and equally important would be his public conduct as a symbol of the Allied nations.

He brought to his task several important assets. First, he looked the part of the simple, courageous soldier of democracy. Absent was the aristocratic flamboyance of a MacArthur or the militaristic bombast of a Patton. His relaxed public manner, his good looks and reassuring smile, his quiet confidence, and his conservative but well-tailored attire embodied the definition of courage as "grace under pressure." His relative openness to reporters paid off in good copy, and his preference for down-home slang and straight talk appealed to American readers back home. Highly publicized accounts of his search for less elaborate personal accommodations in London only added to the budding description of Eisenhower as the quintessential American—the unpretentious soldier doing his duty to the nation.[1]

Such descriptions of the new commander were not the products of chance alone or of just personal attributes. They were cultivated actively by the general and by his official family. The admiring Pfc. Mickey McKeogh served as Ike's striker, while Lt. Ernest R. "Tex" Lee, a former San Antonio salesman, handled office details and controlled outside access to the general. Harry Butcher, a former CBS vice-president and a longtime friend of Milton Eisenhower, supervised his press relations. The other important member of the entourage, whose name would frequently be gossiped about in later months, was Eisenhower's British driver and secretary, Kay Summersby. Despite the later rumors of a relationship between the two, reporters viewed Eisenhower and Summersby primarily from the outset as personal symbols of Anglo-American wartime partnership. Even Ike's choice of a pet at his headquarters, Telegraph Cottage—a Scottie appropriately named Telek— was interpreted in the same vein. Back in the United States, reporters descended upon Abilene and discovered an Eisenhower background sufficiently close to a Horatio Alger story to make excellent, morale-boosting copy. All these efforts and embellishments only added luster to the general's own natural gifts at public relations. As Butcher admiringly remarked after an early press conference, "Watching Ike deal with the press, I don't think he needs a public relations advisor. He is tops."[2]

In his first year as a theater commander, however, Eisenhower found it necessary to draw upon every personal asset and resource he had. During 1942 and early 1943, his abilities to command battlefield forces decisively were severely tested, and he faced the first serious threats to his reputation since the outbreak of the war. He found his tactical abilities questioned by superiors and subordinates alike. He found his diplomatic judgments sharply criticized and his maturity and experience for major command doubted. Both for Eisenhower personally and for the command structure he led, the period from June 1942 to the end of 1943 entailed a major shakedown process. Eisenhower himself nearly became a serious casualty of that shakedown.

Eisenhower's initial duties in London centered upon creating harmony in the new command and upon directing the staging operations for Roundup. By the summer of 1942, the war still was going badly for the Allies, and public opinion in Britain and America craved good news from the various fronts. In the Soviet Crimea, the Germans had taken the city of Sevastopol. In Egypt, Gen. Erwin Rommel's Afrika Korps had pushed within a few miles of the Nile Delta, while in the Mediterranean the British fortress of Tobruk had fallen. The deteriorating military situation in the Middle East encouraged the British anew to pressure the Americans into abandoning a 1943 invasion of France and substituting an invasion of French North Africa. Eisenhower again opposed the suggestion initially, fearing that his command would be relegated to a backwater operation immediately upon his having arrived. But in Washington, opinion was turning in the British direction. Marshall, as always, still advocated the early cross-channel assault. The United States Navy, however, had intensified its lobbying for additional activity in the Pacific, and, most important, President Roosevelt himself had been won over to the idea of a North African campaign as a prelude to Roundup.[3]

With Roosevelt now siding with Churchill in behalf of a North African invasion, the CCS informed Eisenhower of the formal switch in plans. He did not have time to become overly depressed at the news, for in late July he received word that he would command the new North African enterprise, code named Torch. The good news should have been expected. Eisenhower had been one of a handful of Allied officers who had been in on the ground floor of organizing a multinational command, and the only thing that had really changed was that North Africa rather than Europe now was the theater of operations. Roosevelt, Churchill, and the CCS agreed that Torch's commander should be an American, both to acknowledge the United States' status as "senior partner" in the war and to circumvent the problem of British relations with the French, which were especially bad. Many Frenchmen, Vichyites or not, still harbored resentment of the British "abandonment" at Dunkirk and of British air attacks on the French fleet. The Allies hoped that an American commander would have greater luck in secretly negotiating Vichy nonresistance for the landings. Given the limited state of preparation for an amphibious operation anywhere in 1942, Vichy cooperation was seen as vital to the success of Torch. In other words, Allied planners envisioned a successful Torch less as an invasion than a liberation. Once landings had been secured, Eisenhower's American and British forces would drive eastward rapidly, taking Morocco, Algeria, and Tunisia, while the British Eighth Army would push westward from Egypt towards them.[4]

The larger significance of the decision to take North Africa first was that as a practical matter it doomed any chances for a cross-channel invasion in 1943. Eisenhower regretted the decision, believing as did Marshall that Torch represented cautious, defensive thinking. Given his views, it is worth considering whether the choice made was a correct one or not. Certainly a successful cross-channel thrust in the spring of 1943 would have altered the dividing lines between East and West and would have changed the postwar map of Europe in significant, if unpredictable, ways. Such an outcome obviously would have affected the course of U.S.-Soviet relations for decades. Some subsequent information also suggests that a 1943 assault might have been feasible. German production of tanks, planes, and other armaments did not reach their peak until late 1944. Wehrmacht troop strength in the West was at its greatest in 1944, not 1943. German troop concentrations, beach obstacles, and gun emplacements along the French coast were twice as strong by the spring of 1944 as they had been a year earlier. In addition, with German units still fighting deep within Russia in 1943, the Nazi difficulty of shifting reinforcements and supplies from its Eastern front was greater at that time than it was a year later.[5]

On the negative side, however, an equally impressive list of reasons against attempting a cross-channel invasion of France in 1943 could be compiled. Allied air cover was vital to the success of an amphibious operation, and the German Luftwaffe was far stronger in 1943 than it was a year later. By 1944, fuel shortages finally had begun to limit the range and effectiveness of German air power. More important, numerous Allied deficiencies and shortcomings made any amphibious operation in 1943, especially one against the European mainland, extremely risky. The Allies' new command hierarchy would have gone in untested against the Germans, and with less assistance available from intelligence and code-breaking sources, fewer combat aircraft, fewer American divisions, and a scarcity of landing craft. All these facts would have dictated an invasion on a narrower beachhead, carrying with it a far greater risk of failure. In other words, if a 1943 invasion of France promised greater potential rewards, it also carried with it extreme risks at a time when failure could have been devastating to Allied war morale.[6]

Although Allied planners deemed it a safer operation than Roundup, Torch itself was a risky venture. In addition to the lack of Allied experience in amphibious tactics, the North African invasion plan had the disadvantage of requiring coordination over long distances. It was eight hundred miles from Casablanca, a landing site on the Atlantic side of Gibraltar, to Algiers, and another four hundred miles from it to the third prospective landing site of Tunis. Choosing among the scattered landing sites offered an uncertain mix of benefits and drawbacks. Within the Allied command, those who argued for landings on each side of Gibraltar pointed to the threat posed to supply lines on the Mediterranean side by Franco's fascist Spain. The disadvantage of the western landings was that they placed American forces even farther away from the projected battlefronts with the Germans in Algeria and Tunisia. Those who opposed dual landings argued instead for a concentrated set of landings closer to the bulk of the German forces, making possible a quicker campaign. Ironically, it was the British, given their special stake in the Middle East, who pushed hardest for landings on the Mediterranean side alone.[7]

Eisenhower and the CCS did not resolve the deadlock over landing sites for Torch until early September. The result of the delay was that Eisenhower found himself making hasty logistical decisions for an invasion that was now scheduled for barely two months away. After the United States Navy grudgingly yielded additional support, Eisenhower selected three landing sites—at Casablanca, Algiers, and Oran—encompassing both sides of Gibraltar. At the same time, he decided not to attempt landings at all near the city of Tunis. Because Tunis lay farther to the east, his choice meant that none of the invasion forces was likely to engage the Germans immediately. Eisenhower had chosen the most cautious invasion plan possible, but even it carried great risks. The key to a successful invasion and a rapid advance eastward toward Tunisia, now more than ever, lay in securing cooperation and nonresistance from the French. His method of obtaining it proved controversial, and it nearly cost him his job.[8]

Eisenhower's entire approach to the issue of dealing with the French in North Africa focused on the immediate need to minimize opposition on the beaches. But securing that objective meant engaging in unpredictable secret diplomacy with known fascists and Nazi collaborators who had imprisoned or executed Jews, political opponents, and members of the French Resistance. In trying to bargain with Vichy officials, he ran the parallel risks of Vichy betrayal and of loss of the moral high ground against the Germans if the deals became public. Eisenhower's indifference to moral niceties in the negotiations might have been forgiven if the primary objective of preventing French military resistance to the landings had been achieved. But this approach proved not only cold-blooded and amoral but also less than successful in preventing American casualties and paving the way for a rapid advance from the beaches.

Eisenhower tried to ensure against the possibility of Vichy betrayal by dealing privately and separately with Vichy and its Resistance opponents at the same time. While seeking nonresistance from the French military, he set up contacts with the Resistance for designing a sabotage campaign against government forces on the beaches. Of the two secret negotiations, however, he placed greater emphasis on those with Vichy officers, seeking their cooperation and immediate surrender. Making this game of intrigue more risky was the fact that Eisenhower had to rely upon the overly simplistic analyses of French politics and power in North Africa that were being supplied by State Department operative Robert Murphy. Murphy insisted that the key French officer in securing Vichy nonresistance to the invasion was a retired general in France, Henri Giraud, despite the fact the Giraud held no official position in the French military or civilian administration. In the light of hindsight, there was little reason to suppose that French forces in North Africa would lay down their arms for Giraud, but Murphy predicted just such a response.[9]

As a partial hedge to his bet on Giraud, Murphy advised Eisenhower to open up additional contacts with Adm. Jean Darlan, the commander in chief of Vichy forces. Darlan clearly held more reliable official credentials than Giraud, but he was an even more distasteful figure to deal with because of his well-known record as a fascist and

Nazi collaborator. Still, cooperation with Darlan held out the hope of neutralizing the French fleet, and the obstinate Giraud already was insisting on being named the invasion commander as his price for cooperation. Prime Minister Winston Churchill, for his part, advised Eisenhower to "kiss Darlan's stern if you have to to get the French navy." The secret negotiations with the "Frogs," as the supreme commander disparagingly called the French, continued until the very eve of the landings. Eisenhower offered generous concessions to both Giraud and Darlan, agreeing to make Giraud the "governor-general," or chief political officer, of North Africa and Darlan the commander in chief of North African French forces. He even dispatched Gen. Mark Clark, his deputy ground forces commander, on a daring cloak-and-dagger mission into occupied Algiers. Clark returned with additional information on Vichy troop strength and location, but no additional guarantees of cooperation from Darlan.[10]

Just how shaky the assurances of Giraud and Darlan were became evident once the landings commenced on 8 November 1942. Barely fourteen hours before the first troops hit the beaches, Giraud arrived in Gibraltar, refusing to issue a surrender declaration to French forces unless he was granted supreme command of the entire operation. Eight hours of wrangling followed, and only after Eisenhower threatened to abandon him completely did Giraud agree to release a surrender statement over the radio. But even then, French troops refused to recognize his authority and kept on fighting. American forces met open French resistance at Casablanca and Oran. In Algiers, Darlan also refused to issue a command for his men to cease fighting until he personally saw Eisenhower and wrested control of the civil administration from Giraud. It was not until five days after the landings that Eisenhower secured a reasonably reliable agreement with Darlan to cease Vichy resistance in North Africa, and only then after Darlan had invented the ruse that he was surrendering under "secret orders" from Marshal Petain, therefore not committing treason against Vichy. Darlan proved the short-term winner of the diplomatic maneuvering with the Americans, for his purchase price was the reversal of the previous deals with Giraud. Now Darlan was the "high commissioner" of North Africa, and Giraud his subordinate as French military commander.[11]

The price of the sloppy secret diplomacy was costly, both in lives and in American moral prestige. The invasion forces suffered eighteen hundred casualties, and because the Algiers landing site had been relocated at the last minute to preserve secrecy, Vichy troops had needlessly slaughtered Resistance forces awaiting the Americans at the prior location. To top matters off, North Africa had been handed on a silver platter to a known fascist. Stunned by the immediate surge of criticism from the Western press for his part in the "Darlan deal," Eisenhower privately lashed out—"I can't understand why these longhaired, starry-eyed guys keep gunning for me. I'm no reactionary. Christ on the Mountain! I'm as idealistic as Hell!" But while he sincerely believed his declarations, Eisenhower's conduct in Torch displayed an early example of a consistent willingness to view military or other international crises in the detached, amoral calculus of the military strategist. [12]

The firestorm of protest ignited by Eisenhower's handling of Torch secret diplomacy nearly cost him his first command before he had even engaged the Germans. In defense of his action, he reminded Roosevelt and Churchill through channels that they had approved of his efforts to secure Vichy cooperation. In Washington, General Marshall, anxious to protect the reputations of the army and his protégé, blasted press critics of the deal and credited it with saving sixteen thousand American lives. Marshall conceded that under Darlan, French jails in North Africa remained crammed with Jews, communists, Spanish republicans, and anti-Vichy Frenchmen. But he insisted to reporters that continued criticism would weaken American standing with the Allies and could trigger Eisenhower's replacement with a British commander. In turn Milton Eisenhower, now the number-two man in the Office of War Information, lobbied President Roosevelt into issuing a statement in his brother's behalf. Dismayed at its mild tone, he flew to North Africa to conduct his own housecleaning of the American public relations operation in Algiers, railing against local radio commentators who continued to refer to Ike as a fascist. Fearing that unless drastic action was taken his brother's career could be irreparably damaged, he insisted to Robert Murphy, "Heads must roll." They did, under the direction of OWI representative and later Eisenhower administration psychological warfare expert, C. D. Jackson. [13]

The Allies actually gained little from the Darlan episode, save public relations nightmares. The point of securing the admiral's cooperation had been to absorb the French army in Tunisia for use against the

Germans and to capture the French fleet at Toulon without a shot. But French forces in Tunis melted into the countryside rather than join the Allies, and French ships were scuttled before either the Allies or the Germans could seize them. Mercifully for Eisenhower, the burden of Darlan lasted for only a month and a half. On Christmas Eve 1942, news reached his command that Darlan had been assassinated by a former member of one of Robert Murphy's subsidized Resistance groups. Within forty-eight hours of the suspect's arrest, he was executed by order of General Giraud, and all records of the case were destroyed. Exactly who authorized Darlan's murder remains a mystery, but not for lack of willing volunteers. Any number of individuals and groups, from the Americans themselves to Giraud to the Resistance, had ample motivation. In the words of American general Mark Clark, Darlan's "removal" was nothing less than "an act of Providence. . . . His removal from the scene was like the lancing of a troublesome boil. He had served his purpose."[14]

Darlan's death came too late to be of any use, however, in speeding the American sweep through Tunisia before the arrival of German reinforcements. In the landings' aftermath, the delays in advancing inland and eastward from the beachheads clearly displeased Eisenhower's superiors on the CCS. British general Brooke offered the opinion that the theater commander had allowed himself to become "far too immersed in the political aspects of the situation" at the expense of the military campaign. Attempting to respond to Brooke's criticism, Eisenhower buried himself in tactical detail and drove himself unceasingly to make up for lost time, only to contract influenza and be bedridden. The combined effects of the Darlan fiasco and the slowness of the campaign encouraged the commander's critics to hope that he might be relieved of his command by Churchill and Roosevelt at the Casablanca Conference scheduled for 15 January.[15]

Partly because of the American insistence that a United States Army commander head the theater command chain, Eisenhower kept his job, but at the cost of some reshuffling of subordinates and redefinition of responsibilities. In order to satisfy British concerns, British general Harold Alexander was named to the new position of deputy commander in chief of land operations. In Brooke's rather inflated prose, "We were pushing Eisenhower up into the stratosphere and rarefied atmosphere of a Supreme Commander, where he would be free to devote his time to the political and inter-Allied problem, whilst we inserted under him . . . our own commanders to deal with the military situations and to restore the necessary drive and coordination which had been so seriously lacking." Then and afterward, Eisenhower resisted all attempts to portray the shift as a reduction of his battlefield responsibility, but despite Brooke's anti-American bias, the change did reflect a lingering skepticism of Ike's command abilities that pursued him for most of the war. The rough design of command established at Casablanca, with Eisenhower as overall theater commander, but with British subordinates for ground, air, and naval operations, persisted until September of 1944, well after the Normandy invasion. Partly to soothe any hurt feelings, Marshall recommended Eisenhower for promotion to full, or four-star, general, and the promotion came through on 10 February, placing him on the same lofty plateau as Marshall himself and MacArthur.[16]

Before the command changes could be implemented, however, the American armies in Tunisia suffered additional humiliation from the Germans. Taking advantage of poor American defensive preparation and communication, both symptoms of the belief that the Germans would not attack, Rommel's troops administered a bloody antidote to American lethargy at the Kasserine Pass. Ironically, Rommel's surprise attack had been aided by Allied overreliance on Ultra intercepts (captured German radio messages), which had led American commanders at the front to assume that any prospective German counterattack would occur farther north. After the advance was halted, Eisenhower took advantage of the embarrassment to launch a thorough housecleaning of American corps and divisional commanders in North Africa. On the advice of his eyes and ears at the front (others less kindly referred to him as the hatchet man), Gen. Omar Bradley, he relieved Gen. Lloyd R. Fredendall of the II Corps, replacing him with George Patton and subsequently Bradley himself. His orders to Patton for shaping up the II Corps were blunt and unmistakable—"You must not retain for an instant any man in a responsible position where you have become doubtful of his ability to do the job. . . . I expect you to be perfectly cold-blooded about it."[17]

During the late stages of the Kasserine battle, General Alexander arrived to assume his duties as ground forces commander. Despite the temporary setback at Kasserine, the Allies' overall position in North Africa had improved, largely because of the British Eighth Army's rapid advance from the east. Montgomery's forces continued their drive westward toward the Americans and the Tunisian frontier. Alexander, however, discovered to his dismay that Eisenhower had become so entangled in immediate details that he had not drafted any overall plan for the final conquest of Tunisia. Alexander proceeded to draft a plan, but when it gave American troops only a secondary role, Eisenhower faced him down into granting the Americans a chance to avenge the Kasserine embarrassment. Even before his confrontation with Alexander, Eisenhower had found himself refereeing quarrels between Patton and Montgomery over front priorities and between Patton and Air Marshall Sir Arthur Coningham over the adequacy of British air cover for American troops. By the beginning of the final offensive in Tunisia, the American II Corps, now under Bradley's command, had been granted the responsibility for pushing eastward along the Mediterranean coast to Bizerte, but Eisenhower's nerves had been worn thin by the command infighting. As Harry Butcher described it, "Ike's position just now is something like that of a hen setting on a batch of eggs. He is waiting for the eggs to hatch, and is in the mental state of wondering if they will ever break the shell."[18]

The final Allied offensive in Tunisia began on 30 April, and the results heartened Eisenhower and the entire command. British and American armies drove German forces into a narrowing corridor from both east and west. By 13 May, some six months after the Torch landings, the last Axis forces still in North Africa had surrendered. The victorious Allies captured 275,000 enemy troops in Tunisia, more even than the Russian bag at Stalingrad the previous winter. The campaign had taken longer than its planners had hoped, and it had been more costly—nearly 11,000 dead and 72,000 casualties. But it was a victory—one in which Americans had played a key role—and a victory commanded by an American, Dwight D. Eisenhower. Combined with the earlier triumphs at El Alamein, Midway Island, and Stalingrad, the Tunisian campaign signaled an irreversible turning of the tide of the war. And whatever errors of omission or commission he had made, Eisenhower was America's symbol of that newfound success.[19]

Although he was pleased at the successful conclusion of the North African campaign, Eisenhower's happiness was tempered by the knowledge that its length had ruled out any last chance of an invasion of France in 1943. The path was now clear for the British to advocate a continuation of the Mediterranean offensive from North Africa into

Italy, probably through the stepping-stone of Sicily. In Washington, Marshall and his colleagues still favored shutting down the operation in the Mediterranean in favor of the cross-channel assault, if not after Tunisia, then at least after taking Sicily. Marshall's view—and in hindsight it was probably a correct one—was that even a Mediterranean commitment limited to Sicily would accomplish the primary goal of any Mediterranean campaign—tying down German troops on the Italian mainland away from northern France. Eisenhower, however, having tasted victory once, now found himself in disagreement with his mentor. After all, he reasoned, if the invasion of France could not take place until 1944 anyway, should not some offensive momentum be continued in 1943?[20]

In their May planning sessions, the Combined Chiefs agreed to disagree, concurring on a 1944 invasion of France but leaving the decision on whether to continue the Mediterranean operation after Sicily to Eisenhower. With Eisenhower itching for a new challenge, his decision to push ahead for Italy was no surprise. It triggered, however, a renewed debate within his command over strategy and over the priority of American and British assignments for the upcoming campaign. Although all of Eisenhower's subordinates wanted to attack Italy, their methods differed. General Bradley, reflecting the direct approach taught by his mentor, General Marshall, favored bypassing Sicily altogether and striking immediately on the Italian mainland. Patton and Montgomery, in contrast, favored taking Sicily first, but each man's plan gave his own forces strategic priority over the other's. Faced with renewed wrangling, Eisenhower managed to extract some personal satisfaction by overruling British warnings of high casualties and carrying off a preliminary amphibious assault against the Italian-held island of Pantellaria, which bagged eleven thousand prisoners in the process.[21]

Eisenhower ruled that the next major target would be Sicily. But following his growing tendency to assuage the British, and his renewed respect of the Germans, he gave approval to Montgomery's more cautious invasion plan for the island. The plan called for side-by-side landings of U.S. and British forces on the southeastern coast, followed by a push by Montgomery's troops northward towards the key port of Messina. While the British drove for Messina, the only strategic spot on the island because of its proximity to the Italian mainland, Patton's American forces would be relegated to guarding their western, interior flank. Because of shortages of landing craft, D-day for the Sicily invasion had to be postponed until 10 July 1943. Making matters worse, following the delay in the jump-off of the campaign, the capture of the island proved much slower than Eisenhower had anticipated. The campaign lasted a full month, and the slowness of Montgomery's advance exacerbated the nationalistic rivalries within the command. The Germans conducted a skillful fighting retreat after offering little resistance to the initial landings, and their defense drew out Montgomery's native caution. Patton, furious at his counterpart's sluggishness and frustrated at Eisenhower's rejection of his own plan, abandoned Montgomery's flank and struck out westward on his own, capturing the largely defenseless and strategically worthless city of Palermo. Once in Palermo, Patton again changed the script and drove eastward along the northern coast of Sicily toward Messina, as his own original plan had advocated.[22]

With his commanders improvising their own strategies at variance with the original plan, the theater commander had enough headaches, but Patton proceeded to add yet another. A week before Patton's troops entered Messina ahead of Montgomery's on 17 August, the general slapped a hospitalized GI suffering from battle fatigue and accused him of cowardice. Frustrated both at Patton's glory-seeking and at his lack of personal control, yet aware of his battlefield value, Eisenhower chose not to reprimand him officially but privately chastised him by letter. When reporters obtained the story weeks later, Eisenhower temporarily succeeded in convincing them not to report it because of his colleague's military value. The slapping incident, added to Patton's other misdeeds, did convince Ike that his longtime friend should not be given the command of American ground forces for the next spring's invasion of France. The appointment needed a commander with the capacity to submerge his ego for the sake of multinational cooperation, something Patton could not do. Instead, he judged, the choice would have to be Bradley. Bradley, in Eisenhower's words, had proven himself "master of every military maneuver, lacking only in the capacity—possibly the willingness—to dramatize himself."[23]

The immediate concern, however, remained Italy. Having been given the power of decision by the Combined Chiefs, he had decided to back an invasion of the Italian mainland. Despite Marshall's objections it made more sense to Eisenhower to employ the existing concentrations of Allied troops in the Mediterranean in an effort to knock Italy out of the war than to leave them idle. He again hoped, as he had with the French in North Africa, that a confused and war-weary Italian command could be persuaded to surrender before the Germans could fully occupy the peninsula. Again, he was disappointed. Partly because of the embarrassment from the Darlan deal, the CCS gave him less room for diplomatic maneuver with the Italians. The unconditional surrender decree of Roosevelt and Churchill at Casablanca also left him with few enticements to coax a quick Italian capitulation. While he squirmed and fretted, the Germans hastily funneled more troops into Italy to shore up Axis defenses. By the time Eisenhower sent a full report to the CCS outlining a plan for cooperation with Italian marshal Bagdolio, who had replaced the toppled Mussolini, the Nazis already occupied the country. Ike was forced to cancel planned parachute operations near Rome because of the changed military situation. And once again, this time only twelve hours before the initial American landings at Salerno, Italian officials backed out of their deal to announce a surrender proclamation to their population.[24]

Italian noncooperation threatened the success of the entire campaign, and despite the landing of Montgomery's Eighth Army in the Italian "toe" (designed partly to increase leverage on Bagdolio), the official foot-dragging continued. Forcing the marshal's hand, Eisenhower unilaterally (and falsely) announced over Radio Algiers that the Italians had formally surrendered, and he ordered the reading of Bagdolio's surrender statement without authorization. An hour later, the marshal yielded and added his own call for surrender over Radio Rome. American forces under General Clark landed at Salerno on 9 September, but German counterattacks the next day nearly drove his troops back into the sea. Besides Clark himself, whose fighting spirit Eisenhower had begun to doubt, he blamed the Italian army, which had disintegrated rather than assisted, for the unexpected troubles. He also blamed the CCS for not relinquishing enough bombers and landing craft from the cross-channel preparations in England, an ironic complaint given his own role earlier in establishing the supply priority for the invasion of northern France.[25]

Following two weeks of intense fighting, the Americans and British pushed inland from their beaches in southern Italy and linked up along a continuous front across the peninsula. In the process, the

American Fifth Army suffered fourteen thousand casualties, compared to only six hundred for the sparsely opposed British Eighth Army. Despite the slowness of the early campaign, or perhaps because of the effectiveness of the German resistance, caution again prevailed in Eisenhower's assessment of the campaign ahead to Rome. Marshall urged a bold leapfrogging amphibious assault behind German defenses closer to Rome, but his theater commander committed himself to the longer, but less risky, overland route up the rugged Italian peninsula. Although the Italian front had been stabilized, the Allies would not reach Rome until June 1944. With the landings accomplished and the Allied presence secured in Italy, the campaign began to revert to a secondary theater, as preparations continued for the projected assault on Hitler's Fortress Europe the following spring.[26]

Eisenhower observed the official preparations for the cross-channel assault on France with more than academic interest. With the invasion, now code named Overlord, firmly fixed for the spring, both he and his personal staff believed that he had earned the right to a major, even *the* major, role in its direction. He had led an Allied multinational command to victories in North Africa and Sicily despite the assorted political, military, and personal aggravations. He had gained valuable, if sometimes painful, experience in directing a complex command against a battle-hardened adversary. And he alone in the European theater had the practical experience of overseeing and carrying out a major amphibious invasion. But ever since the topic of the invasion first had been broached, all had assumed that its chief champion and Roosevelt's trusted officer, General Marshall, would direct the enterprise. Knowing that likelihood, Eisenhower did not broach his sentiments about the Overlord command publicly, but he did let it be known to colleagues that he wanted, at the least, a field command somewhere rather than a recall to Washington and a desk job, even if it was Marshall's.[27]

In the late fall of 1943, the odds seemed to be against Eisenhower receiving either command of Overlord or a field assignment. If Marshall assumed command of the cross-channel invasion, nationalistic considerations dictated that Alexander receive the Italian command and another British officer be named as Marshall's chief deputy commander. Since Washington wanted to avoid anything that appeared to be a demotion of Eisenhower, a field command for him under Alexander would not be possible. Therefore, despite his protestations to

Butcher that he was not "temperamentally fitted for the job." Eisenhower appeared destined for the chief of staff's chair in Washington. On 1 October, the same day the Italian city of Naples fell to the Allies, Secretary of the Navy Frank Knox leaked to reporters the likely selection of Marshall as Overlord head and Eisenhower's probable nomination as his replacement. While Eisenhower, in Butcher's words, was "sweating out" the deliberations "in big drops," Lord Mountbatten also indicated Roosevelt's insistence on Marshall for the invasion command. Chief of Naval Operations Ernest King and Gen. Henry "Hap" Arnold of the Army Air Corps agreed that Marshall deserved the assignment, although they expressed concern about his departure from the Combined Chiefs.[28]

While keeping his discomfort within private channels, Eisenhower did relay his preference for field duty to Marshall through theater chief of staff Walter Bedell Smith, a Marshall protégé. His efforts were helped indirectly by the growing sentiment on the Combined Chiefs and from the professional service journals that Marshall remain at Roosevelt's side in the capital. Eisenhower's own feelings about the command shifts were not without some bureaucratic clout of their own, for he was already a popular hero at home. Walter Winchell, for example, speculated that Roosevelt might make him his running mate in 1944 in order to head off a MacArthur presidential boomlet by the Republicans. Eisenhower himself squelched any rumors of political ambitions, and once again, on 15 November, the president informed the service chiefs of his intention to reward Marshall with the Overlord assignment.[29]

Roosevelt arrived in the Mediterranean prior to the Cairo Conference with the Combined Chiefs partly to share his thoughts on the Overlord command with Eisenhower. During a tour of the Tunisian battlefields he repeated his determination to ensure Marshall's reputation in history by giving him the invasion command. Eisenhower, in turn, demonstrated his own mettle for the job by delivering a impressive presentation on the progress of the Mediterranean campaign to date to the CCS. Following a huge dinner party, however, Marshall ordered Eisenhower to take a well-earned vacation from the war. He toured the sights of Luxor, Jerusalem, and Bethlehem, but his thoughts were on his immediate future and the Overlord choice, neither of which he seemed to have much control over.[30]

Following the Cairo meetings, Roosevelt and Churchill continued on to Teheran for conferences with the Soviets. Marshal Stalin viewed the public appointment of a commander for Overlord as necessary evidence of the Western commitment to a 1944 second front. Consequently, a decision from Roosevelt was expected by the end of the conference. Roosevelt was wavering in his choice in the face of the argument that he needed Marshall in Washington, but he was still willing to give Overlord to the chief of staff if he asked for it. However, Marshall, ever the dutiful soldier, only indicated to the president his willingness to serve wherever assigned. Roosevelt did not relish the procedural tangles of Marshall's serving as a theater commander under lower ranking officers in Washington, nor the solution of asking him to accept a demotion in rank. But probably the biggest single consideration was the British preference for Eisenhower as Overlord head. The British saw Ike as the superior diplomat in smoothing over command frictions, and if he had shortcomings as a field commander, he was a known quantity with whom British commanders had operated successfully. Eisenhower was not the bold strategist Marshall was, but the British often viewed Marshall's boldness as rashness. Given the tinkering in the command structure that had produced victories in the Mediterranean, Eisenhower now appeared well suited by experience and temperament to serve as the link between the CCS and field commanders as Overlord's chief.

Franklin Roosevelt made his decision. With some reluctance, he summoned General Marshall for a final meeting before his departure from Teheran. While he dictated, Marshall transcribed a fateful, and personally heartbreaking, message to the Soviet head of state. The telegram read: "From the President to Marshal Stalin: The immediate appointment of General Eisenhower to command of Overload operation has been decided upon."[31]

6

CRUSADE IN EUROPE

After a brief vacation and a series of meetings in Washington, Eisenhower arrived in London in mid-January 1944 to assume command of Overlord. Once again, as in the Mediterranean, he was planning and coordinating an amphibious operation against the Germans on very short notice. This time, however, the stakes were even higher. Failure meant no new assault against Hitler's Fortress Europe until 1945 at the earliest, and little hope of an early end to the war. Only slightly more than 140 days remained for him to make the necessary preparations for a 1944 invasion. On the positive side, his experiences in North Africa and Italy had seasoned him well, both personally and professionally, for the difficult assignment. He was now fifty-three years old, but still looked far younger, and despite the stresses of command he exuded a sunny warmth and confidence to officers and enlisted men alike. Although not a dominating physical presence, he projected a personal strength that turned heads when he entered the room. Having gained a reputation for success and a personal understanding of the tools of command, he was in turn resilient, adroit in press dealings, publicly self-controlled, and apparently even lucky when necessary.

A multitude of issues and problems awaited him in London. Despite the fact that weather and tide conditions dictated an invasion no later than June, key decisions had awaited the appointment of a supreme commander. Where would the landings take place? How many landing sites would there be? How large should the invading force be? What air support strategy should be adopted to soften up German defenses in France and facilitate the landings? Could coordination with the French underground be secured for sabotage operations? Would there be sufficient landing craft for the enterprise? How would the forces on the beaches be supplied? And how could the enemy's response be hindered through deception about the timing and location of the assault? These questions merely addressed the controllable variables. The uncertain weather conditions in the English Channel could undermine even the best laid plans, especially given the relatively narrow window of time provided by suitable tide and moonlight conditions. Any invasion would have to occur in either early May or the first or third weeks of June.[1]

Even before these sticky issues could be resolved, the new commander had to assemble a working staff and a command hierarchy to administer the huge, sixteen-thousand-member apparatus known as SHAEF (Supreme Headquarters, Allied Expeditionary Force). Serving again as Eisenhower's official gatekeeper and chief of staff was Gen. Walter Bedell Smith. Despite Marshall's requests that Smith return to Washington, Ike managed to retain the "dour Prussian with ulcers." As in North Africa, the Combined Chiefs had decided to select British deputies to serve under Eisenhower. Although he preferred to have Alexander as his assault phase commander, British official and public opinion dictated General Montgomery's selection. Air Marshal Sir Trafford Leigh-Mallory assumed the duties as chief for air operations, and Adm. Sir Bertram Ramsay took control of naval forces for the expedition. Rounding out SHAEF's upper echelon was an Eisenhower favorite, Air Marshal Sir Arthur Tedder, serving as a deputy supreme commander without portfolio.[2]

As he had done in the Mediterranean campaign, Eisenhower agreed that within the general guidelines of the invasion plan subordinates should be allowed considerable independence. But the crucial final decisions on planning and logistics were his, and in making them he had to wear many hats at the same time. The supreme commander of SHAEF was the ultimate guardian of communications channels and authority to the Combined Chiefs, coordinator of public relations for a multinational enterprise, an overseer of censorship and civil affairs, the final arbiter of supply priorities and shipping decisions, a planning coordinator, and a morale booster for the thousands of individuals, high ranking and low, who made up the invasion team. His command was at one and the same time the most visible individual responsibility of the European war to the West, and one that required the personal self-effacement to persuade a complex bureaucracy to work as one rather than at cross-purposes. Observers then and later compared his activities to the duties of a chairman of the board of a huge corporation. Given the overall strategic authority of the president of the United States, the British prime minister, and the Combined Chiefs, a "regional manager" might have been a more appropriate comparison. Although Eisenhower chafed at such descriptions of his duties, seeing them as another form of denigration of his field command abilities, on occasion he described them similarly himself.[3]

Once he had settled the organizational details, Eisenhower could turn to the substantive problems of the assault plan. Already British lieutenant general Frederick Morgan, working from an early proposal drawn up by Ike himself for Roundup, had designed a plan calling for landings of three divisions of troops on the Normandy coast of northwestern France. Both the smaller numbers of troops projected for the landings and the choice of the Normandy site reflected the British preference for indirect engagements and wars of maneuver, rather than the blunt, direct approach favored by the Americans. American strategists generally favored employing far greater resources and manpower along a wider beachhead at the section of the French coast nearest to England—the Pas de Calais region of northeastern France. Eisenhower's own choice, again reflecting his tendency toward caution and his search for a middle ground between nationalistic approaches, accepted Morgan's Normandy location, but it called for five landing sites instead of three and required a landing force of at least five divisions. The element that made Eisenhower's choice hard to carry out was the acute shortage of landing craft available for Overlord in the spring of 1944. A second amphibious invasion along the Mediterranean coast of France, code named Anvil, had been scheduled to coincide with

Overlord, and in addition, the British command in Italy now was pushing for their own amphibious landings to accelerate the advance up the Italian boot. Eventually, because of the Allied landings at Anzio and the supply needs of Overlord, the Anvil operation had to be postponed.[4]

The Normandy site chosen for Overlord created additional complications for Eisenhower and his command. Invasion at Normandy meant accepting greater distances from the assault's jump-off points in England to the beaches, and the lack of immediate access to major port facilities carried the risk of slowing the advance inland even after the beachheads were secured. For those reasons, deception of the German armies in northern France to delay Nazi reinforcement and counterattack became even more vital. SHAEF had one great ally in measuring the success of deceiving the Nazis on the landings' timing and location—its access to intercepted coded German radio messages known as Ultra. Ironically, Eisenhower's earlier decision not to give General Patton command of the American First Army, which had been earmarked for a key assault role at Normandy, also aided the Allies' deception of the Germans. In an elaborate enterprise called Operation Fortitude, Patton assumed command of a dummy army in Dover directly across the Pas de Calais. Patton's presence, combined with Hitler's unshakable conviction that the main assault would occur at Calais, helped freeze Nazi reinforcement units inland in the belief that any Normandy operation was merely a deception. Ultra, in turn, allowed the Allies to confirm through the Germans' own words that their trickery had worked.[5]

Despite the assistance deception offered, it could not be counted on alone to meet the task of preventing German reinforcement and resupply to Normandy, particularly once the initial surprise had worn off. As a consequence, any assistance the French underground could provide in stalling the Nazi response through sabotage operations was an added asset. Given Eisenhower's less than pristine record in dealing with the French Resistance in North Africa, concern existed that Free French leader Charles de Gaulle might hesitate in assisting with the necessary coordination of a sabotage campaign with the Overlord operation. But Eisenhower proved willing to express his regret at the diplomatic snafus in North Africa and to submerge his own ego for the sake of cordial relations with the imperious de Gaulle. Eisenhower gained as the payoff for his diplomacy toward the Free French leader the full assistance of the French underground, both before and after the landings.[6]

Of even greater value than the Resistance in sowing confusion and disorder among the Germans, however, would be a successful air campaign. Deciding on an appropriate air strategy proved difficult, and it became one of the most significant decisions Eisenhower made in the weeks before D day. His air advisers themselves were divided between two approaches to the campaign. One, dubbed the Oil Plan, was advocated chiefly by Army Air Force General Carl Spaatz. It called for the Allied air forces to concentrate their attacks inside Germany and its Balkan possessions in an attempt to cut off Nazi oil production. The Oil Plan, its advocates reluctantly admitted, offered but limited help in the short-term task of securing the beachheads. It held forth the prospect of longer term benefits, however, once the Allies began their drive into the French heartland. At that point, Spaatz and his supporters argued, a fuel-depleted Wehrmacht would be ripe for a sweeping campaign that could end the war in Europe by the end of 1944.[7]

The other approach to the air campaign, advocated chiefly by Air Marshal Tedder, became known as the Transportation Plan. It promised more immediate help for the invasion, but less value for the subsequent campaign. By using Allied air power to disrupt the transportation and communication network inside France for weeks leading up to the invasion, the Transportation Plan could limit the enemy's ability to reinforce coastal defenses or to launch a counterattack against the beachheads. Given the high casualty estimates being projected for Overlord, any plan that offered to reduce the invasion's initial toll was welcomed by Eisenhower. The plan's chief drawbacks were that an air campaign directed at French transportation routes would endanger the country's civilian population to a greater degree, and if the Allied breakout from the beaches proved faster than anticipated, the very effectiveness of the air campaign in destroying the French transportation network would slow the Allied advance toward Germany. Because of the immediate risk of failure of Overlord itself and the need to ensure its success, Eisenhower opted for the Transportation Plan and faced down its skeptics, which included both Prime Minister Churchill and British Bomber Command.[8]

In retrospect, Eisenhower's choice proved a wise one. Relatively few military historians have since questioned his decision to employ the Transportation Plan. Another major issue tied directly to the choice of the Normandy landing sites was less easily resolved, however—the problem of supply. In the short run, until the Allied invading forces could expand their beachheads and could seize the northwestern French ports of Cherbourg and Brest, or even more distant facilities, SHAEF would be required to improvise an untested system of resupplying the beachheads. Engineers constructed fuel pipelines, intended to extend across the English Channel to the Normandy beaches, and erected huge, floating artificial harbors, called "mulberries." Operation Mulberry eventually provided a short-term stopgap in the days after the landings, but in the subsequent French campaign the Allies' inability to secure port facilities nearer the fronts in eastern France continually slowed the push towards the Rhine.[9]

The already brief preparation time for the invasion, and the delay in obtaining landing craft because of the Anzio operation, quickly dashed any thoughts of a May cross-channel assault. Ruling out May, of course, only narrowed further the tide and moonlight window of time periods acceptable for the amphibious landings. Eisenhower rescheduled Overlord for 5 June 1944, and from 15 April a censorship on diplomatic contacts and a ban on visitors went into effect in southern England. By then the supreme commander and his staff had made most of the basic decisions, and the waiting began. In that pressure cooker of silence and tension, some of Eisenhower's greatest gifts as a supreme commander came to the forefront. The Overlord contingent, from the deputy commanders to the first-wave GIs, was his team, and like a good coach he did his utmost both to protect the game plan and to shore up confidence and morale. The waiting gnawed at him, as it did at everyone, but it was up to him to convince even the most skeptical that success was in the cards. Among those needing the most shoring up was Winston Churchill, who had never liked the cross-channel invasion but had come to respect Eisenhower's soundness of judgment. After an upbeat briefing on 15 May, even Churchill confessed to him, "I am hardening toward this enterprise." Eisenhower himself professed elation that the long-awaited day was drawing near, remarking, "The smell of victory is in the air." He conveyed that attitude to his troops, engaging in small talk with American, British, and Canadian units, and making clear his personal regard for their welfare.[10]

Over 23,000 airborne paratroopers, 130,000 soldiers, 11,000

planes, and an armada of ships and landing craft were poised for the attempt to breach Hitler's vaunted Fortress Europe. SHAEF had prepared for every possible contingency—save one. Although tide and moonlight conditions could be predicted, the weather could not, and in the haste of other preparations, no contingency planning had been done to prepare for the eventuality of a weather delay. Throughout 3 June and into the morning of 4 June, Eisenhower and his colleagues received a battery of depressing weather reports at SHAEF headquarters at Southwick House. A decision had to be made on whether to go for landings on the fifth or to postpone for twenty-four hours. All the reports indicated storms in the channel, with high winds buffeting the landing craft and dense clouds preventing effective Allied air cover of the beaches. With General Bradley's First Army landing forces already aboard ships and in the channel, Eisenhower ordered a postponement, and the ships navigated difficult seas back to base.[11]

The stage had been set for one of the most dramatic, and dramatized, command decisions of the Second World War. It proved not exactly an individual decision, but instead, befitting the supreme commander's style, a choice made after a consensus first had been solicited. On the evening of 4 June, with severe winds and rain lashing Southwick House, SHAEF's weather experts reassembled with the commanders to deliver surprisingly optimistic news. Despite the storm raging outside the windows, they predicted that the bad weather would abate by morning and that up to thirty-six hours of relatively good conditions would ensue. For an invasion of the magnitude of Overlord, it was a small and uncertain weather window being predicted, but the alternatives to going ahead on 6 June were even less appealing. A tentative decision had to be made at once for the initial invasion vessels to break port. If, as on the night before, they had to be recalled, they could not be readied again until 19 June. The latter date represented the absolute last chance to launch an invasion for months. Soliciting opinions from around the room, Eisenhower received urgings to give the go order from Smith and even from the usually cautious Montgomery. Tedder, however, counseled postponement. After stating the meeting's consensus, Eisenhower declared, "I am quite positive that the order [to go] must be given." Following this first, tentative decision, Eisenhower reassembled the command several hours later, at 3:30 A.M. of 5 June, for a final weather report which corroborated the earlier predictions. The second gathering abruptly terminated with one simple sentence from the supreme commander—"OK, let's go."[12]

Within thirty seconds Eisenhower found himself alone in the room, as subordinates rushed to their invasion posts. For him, this was the hardest time—the time when, like a coach, all he could do was sit on the sidelines and await the outcome of the difficult preparations, but with the stakes far higher than any athletic contest. He tried to kill time by playing checkers with Butcher and then drafted a note to his superiors assigning himself ultimate responsibility for the enterprise in the event of its failure. As a form of absolution for the deaths that he feared would be many, he personally saw off a group of paratroopers from the 101st Airborne Division. After his session of small talk with the camouflaged soldiers, he returned to headquarters, offering only the taciturn comment, "Well, it's on." Propped up in bed reading a western novel, he worriedly smoked cigarettes through the early morning hours of the sixth and waited anxiously for news by telephone from Admiral Ramsay.[13]

The news proved gratifying. Before 7 A.M. on 6 June, Eisenhower received word that the paratroop drops had taken place with lighter than expected casualties. While he paced and fretted in England during the day, his mood swayed between optimism and concern, but the general indications of the updates were good. The British and Canadians had established their beachheads, Gold, Juno, and Sword, with only token resistance. The American landings at Utah Beach, although slightly off target, had also gone forward with little difficulty. Less pleasant was the news from Omaha Beach, where American troops had encountered fierce German resistance. After hours of heavy fighting and with the vital assistance of U.S. naval batteries, the Omaha beachhead finally was secured by day's end. At the same time that these events preoccupied the thoughts of the supreme commander, another cause for personal joy had unfolded half a world away. For on the same day that Allied troops struggled ashore on the Normandy coast of France, Eisenhower's son John had graduated from West Point.[14]

The gamble to proceed with the invasion on 6 June had paid off handsomely. Only six days later, Eisenhower enjoyed the opportunity to tour the scene of the triumph with Marshall, King, and Arnold. Not only had the Allies returned to the shores of France, but to the surprise and pleasure of the command, they had done so with less than ten-thousand ground casualties. The air campaign that had helped make it possible had cost slightly more, for in the two months leading up to D day, the Allies had lost twelve-thousand airmen. The "Eisenhower luck" had worked again, aided in no small measure by a well-drawn attack plan and a successful deception of the enemy. The ultimate wisdom of the decision to go on 6 June was underscored two weeks after D day, when on 19 June, the only fallback date for Overlord, the most severe channel storm in twenty years wracked the French coast and destroyed a series of temporary harbors. In a brief note to his chief weather forecaster at SHAEF, Eisenhower scribbled, "Thank the gods of war we went when we did!"[15]

Weeks of growing frustration, however, followed the immediate success of the landings. Montgomery, who had promised a quick capture of the vital transportation hub of Caen, failed to pursue the attack vigorously. Eisenhower was partly to blame for the Briton's sluggishness, for although he had recognized the importance of Caen, he had failed to give him decisive orders. With Goodwood, Montgomery's assault on Caen, stalled, the British commander now insisted to associates that his plan all along had been intended solely to tie down enough German troops to facilitate the Americans' advance farther west. General Bradley, unfortunately, faced his own difficulties in breaking out from his beachheads, not least of which were hedgerows that paralyzed American armor. Montgomery, seeing himself the strategic superior of any American and especially Eisenhower, did not take kindly to the supreme commander's renewed proddings to take Caen. To Eisenhower, however, the consequences of delay were extremely serious. The memory of stalemated trench warfare in World War I haunted the entire Allied command, and the terrorist attacks of V-1 rockets launched from the Nazi-held northeastern coast threatened English civilians.[16]

Whether by intent, as Montgomery claimed, or by accident, the breakout from Normandy began on 25 July with an attack plan of General Bradley's, called Cobra. Bradley's forces, which soon included a Third Army commanded by George Patton, broke through German defenses at St. Lo and raced southward and westward in early August toward the Brittany ports and the French interior. Even before the Americans could reach the ports of Brest, l'Orient, and St. Nazaire, Hitler offered them an opportunity to destroy the Wehrmacht in northern France. In a move known to the Allies through information gathered from captured POWs and Ultra fragments, Hitler had ordered German forces to counterattack westward at Avranches in order to split off Patton's tanks, south of the salient, from the remainder of Bradley's army group. But while Bradley's forces kept the Germans at bay, Patton wheeled his armor eastward and then northward in a drive to encircle the German divisions. With Montgomery's forces finally driving southward from Caen toward Patton's, a linkup of the Americans and British near the towns of Falaise and Argentan threatened to bag an entire German army group. The remaining gap between Allied forces was only ten miles wide by mid-August.[17]

Fortunately for the Germans, the Allies never completely cut off the corridor of escape between Falaise and Argentan. American and British commanders blamed each other for the failure to capture the entire German force. Despite the escape of forty-thousand enemy troops, however, and despite the recriminations, which Eisenhower desperately sought to keep private, the Allied armies did capture fifty-thousand of the Wehrmacht and killed ten-thousand others. Those who managed to escape the Falaise killing ground did so at the cost of abandoning their equipment and armor. Although the battle plan that had produced the breakout at St. Lo and the subsequent Falaise encirclement had not been his, but rather an improvisation of Bradley's, Eisenhower had seen his command break the stalemate and win the battle for France by the end of August. As he toured the battlefield, he remarked that the scene was one that "could only be described by Dante. It was literally possible to walk for hundreds of yards at a time, stepping on nothing but dead and decaying flesh." Allied troops liberated Paris on 25 August, and instead of finding themselves weeks behind schedule, as they had been after the initial landings, Eisenhower's armies were now eight months ahead of the timetable for the reoccupation of France.[18]

Eisenhower was not immediately aware of it in the heady aftermath of Falaise, but his internal command headaches were entering a new and more serious phase. According to Eisenhower, Marshall, and most of SHAEF, the original plan for the French campaign had called upon Montgomery to be the deputy in charge of ground forces from the time of the invasion until 1 September. At that time Eisenhower would assume direct command of the land battle. But emboldened by the recent success of the campaign, Montgomery, backed by Brooke, fought against the change. Why limit his successful leadership, he

argued, even though by most accounts, including those of Bradley and
Patton, Montgomery had been more an obstacle to progress than an
a catalyst of it. With the benefit of hindsight, it is fair to say that
Eisenhower's very looseness of command structure, designed to minimize nationalistic frictions, had emboldened subordinates such as
Montgomery to see themselves as the essential ingredients of victory
and to view their supreme commander as inessential window dressing.
As long as the previous structure had been maintained and victories
had produced enough glory for all, Eisenhower had been able to minimize disputes over battlefield authorities. But unfortunately for him,
at the same time he reasserted direct control over land operations in
September 1944, the Allied advance toward Germany began to slow.
His critics inevitably linked the two developments as cause and
effect.[19]

Eisenhower's method of soothing Montgomery's hurt feelings, as he
had done before, was to massage his colleague's massive ego and to
show willingness to yield in part to the field marshal's strategic views.
Bowing even partly to Montgomery's wishes presented other problems, however, for both the British commander and his American
counterpart, Bradley, wanted their sectors given top priority over diminishing fuel supplies and troop reinforcements. Each man in particular wanted his troops to receive the prized assignment of heading a
single thrust across the Seine River toward the German border. Eisenhower's compromise approach called for a broad-front rather than a
single-thrust strategy and a flexible policy on fuel priorities to the
commanders, depending on the speed of their advance at any given
time. Much of the wrangling over supplies and offensive priorities had
been created by the very speed of the Allied push in August, which
had stretched supply lines taut before even the Brittany ports could be
wrested from their isolated German garrisons. Anvil, the delayed invasion of southern France, had taken place on 15 August, and it had
resulted in the capture of Marseilles. But the lack of a major port
closer to the fronts in northeastern and eastern France was depriving
forward units of the gasoline necessary to take advantage of German
disorganization after Falaise.[20]

The need for advanced port facilities made Eisenhower's decision
to approve Montgomery's paratrooper offensive in the lower Rhine
basin of Holland particularly ill advised. Although the Allies needed
to secure a bridgehead across the Rhine (in Montgomery's words, a

"swinging door") in order to breach Hitler's West Wall defenses into Germany, the plan, called Market-Garden, was risky and underestimated the Germans' continuing capacity to resist. As Market-Garden's failure tragically demonstrated, German defenses along the Rhine were not going to collapse as a result of a single, poorly coordinated incursion on their northern flank. Making matters worse, Montgomery's desire for a breakthrough in his sector led him to ignore the priority of taking Antwerp. SHAEF knew that no final campaign in Germany could be conducted without the use of Antwerp's port facilities, but despite the fact that German control of the surrounding Scheldt estuary still prevented their use by the Allies, Eisenhower allowed Montgomery to give his paratroop enterprise at Arnhem higher priority.[21]

The failure of Market-Garden in late September ensured that with winter soon to come, no Allied victory in Europe would be achieved in 1944. The realization of that frustrating fact led to yet more squabbling within SHAEF over land strategy for the spring campaign and over ground forces command. Renewed attacks against the retreating Germans did enable American forces to reach the Roer and Saar rivers by the end of the fall, but the Rhine remained unbreached. Making matters worse, only on 28 November did the first Allied convoy reach the docks of Antwerp. Ironically, despite their minimal success on other sectors of the front, the only place where the Allies were not pressing attacks by November was in the Ardennes forests. The Ardennes roughly marked the dividing line between Montgomery's forces in the northern half of the front and Bradley's command to the south. In the Allied center bordering on the Ardennes, troop concentrations remained noticeably thinner. On 7 December, Eisenhower made the observation to Bradley that American troops in the Ardennes were spread dangerously thin. But Bradley feared that strengthening the Allied middle would weaken his offensive operations farther south. Anticipating no sudden German actions in the area, he judged that any surprise attack could be repulsed from both flanks before it reached the Meuse River.[22]

The entire SHAEF command had underestimated Adolf Hitler's willingness to take rash offensive risks. Intelligence failures also added to the German prospect of surprise. Because the Allies had driven the Germans so far back toward their own borders, the Wehrmacht no longer needed to send most of its military messages by wireless, which had the effect of limiting Ultra's ability to warn of an impending Nazi assault. Illustrating the Allies' lack of anticipation, Field Marshal Montgomery asked for leave on 15 December in order to visit his son in England. On the very next day, the Germans launched the attack known as the Battle of the Bulge, throwing two panzer armies of twenty-four divisions against an American army corps of only three divisions. Because of the apparent German chaos during the Allied sweep through France, accompanied by the diminishing usefulness of Ultra, no one in SHAEF had expected an offensive through the Ardennes, especially one in greater strength than the Germans had amassed in 1940.[23]

Although the Nazi attack presented a serious threat to the Allies, it also offered a fresh opportunity to destroy the Wehrmacht once and for all in open battle. And it was Eisenhower, in perhaps his finest hour as a field commander, who most quickly grasped the possibilities of counterattack presented by the German gamble in the Ardennes. Facing down a reluctant Bradley, he ordered the isolated American units north of the German bulge into Montgomery's command. He ordered Patton's tanks to the south to abandon their offensive against the Saar and to push northward toward the besieged town of Bastogne. With British forces under Montgomery pushing southward upon the salient and Americans driving northward, Eisenhower hoped to repeat the successful strategy employed at Argentan-Falaise once more. As early as 19 December, even while the German advance continued toward the Meuse River, Eisenhower had laid the groundwork for a counterattack aimed at nothing less than the annihilation of the German army in the West.[24]

The jump-off of Eisenhower's counteroffensive was delayed by bad weather, which hampered air support, and by Montgomery's slowness once more to press his advantage. But this time, when Montgomery took advantage of the American confusion in the Ardennes to again demand overall command of the land battle, Eisenhower called his bluff by threatening to take the issue directly to the Combined Chiefs. Montgomery's slowness, the Americans later estimated, prevented an even larger prisoner bag from the Battle of the Bulge. And his willingness, even eagerness, to claim public credit for the entire operation infuriated an American contingent in SHAEF already embarrassed at its initial failure to anticipate the German attack. But as at Falaise, the victory was nonetheless impressive. By 9 February 1945, Allied forces had closed again to the banks of the Rhine River all along the front. Facing the pressure of a Russian offensive in the East, which had begun a month earlier, Hitler also was being forced to withdraw some of his troops from the West Wall. Once the Allies actually bridged the Rhine, victory would be within grasp.[25]

Once again, however, Eisenhower first had to put down a challenge to his authority in the theater. General Alexander, having completed the successful Italian campaign, had been summoned by the Combined Chiefs from the Mediterranean to replace Tedder as Ike's deputy. Seeing the move as a new scheme to limit his battlefield responsibilities, Eisenhower forced a newly chastened Montgomery to "volunteer" the judgment to their superiors that the existing command arrangement needed no such alterations. Under Eisenhower's pressure, the Combined Chiefs opted to retain Alexander in Italy rather than place him at Ike's side. Soon afterward, renewed debates over strategy, this time concerning the final campaign into Germany itself, replaced the command disputes as Eisenhower's chief headaches. Showing renewed resolve, the supreme commander again flexed his official muscles. Despite British desires for a new single-thrust strategy that would feature Montgomery's northern forces, Bradley's successful breach of the West Wall at Remagen bolstered Eisenhower's insistence on a broader, two-front approach, which gave the Americans an equal if not greater role in the campaign for Germany.[26]

The debate over single thrust versus broad front would not go away, however, because it bore directly upon the larger geopolitical issue of the capture and occupation of Berlin. Should the Western Allies abandon the broad-front approach for a single massive push designed to beat the Russians to the German capital? With Prime Minister Churchill increasingly skeptical of Russian intentions in the Mediterranean, Eastern Europe, and Germany, he urged Eisenhower to abandon the broad-front strategy. The supreme commander could not object to Churchill's pleas on the basis that no plans for such a campaign had been drafted, for the previous fall, when the pattern of the Rhine campaign had still been conjectural, SHAEF had drawn up an offensive plan with Berlin the chief focus of a drive from Montgomery's northern sector. So the issue remained—why not enter the race for Berlin?[27]

In Eisenhower's view, overriding reasons existed for not abandoning the broad-front strategy for an all-out Berlin push. By March 1945, the Red Army lay only thirty-five miles from the German capital, whereas Western forces stood over two hundred miles away. In addition, Eisenhower feared that die-hard Nazis would attempt to establish a mountain retreat in the Alps, from which continued guerrilla warfare against Allied troops would be directed if southern Germany was not secured quickly. Even if the Americans and British chose, against the odds, to try to beat the Russians to Berlin, the effort required traversing fifty miles of lowlands, crisscrossed with lakes and canals. The cost of the enterprise was estimated by General Bradley at as many as 100,000 casualties. As Bradley put it, "A pretty stiff price to pay for a prestige objective, especially when we've got to fall back and let the other fellow take over." The Yalta Conference with the Russians had already taken place, and Berlin lay within the agreed-upon Soviet zone of occupation. Eisenhower's political superiors in the Roosevelt administration still hoped that continued gestures of good will, including not trying to race the Russians to Berlin, would promote Soviet cooperation on other issues of dispute. A broader front strategy, employing thrusts north and south of Berlin, also might help in neutralizing German V-2 sites and in gathering German atomic and rocketry information located at Stuttgart. Finally, personalities and nationalistic considerations dictated against a single-minded emphasis on Berlin in Eisenhower's thinking. With Eisenhower and Montgomery now barely on speaking terms, the supreme commander preferred not to add to the field marshal's glory through a drive for Berlin, but chose to give greater priority to Bradley's southern thrust toward Dresden.[28]

Having made the decision not to press for Berlin, Eisenhower even wired Stalin about the final SHAEF attack plan as a sign of American good faith. But following surprisingly rapid Western advances by early April, he was presented with a final opportunity to change his mind. The last Russian push for Berlin still had not yet commenced, and Allied forces now stood only fifty miles from the German capital. The forces involved even belonged to an American, General Bradley. Nevertheless, Eisenhower stuck with his original decision and vetoed the new request, this time from Bradley, to go for Berlin. In his view, even though the mileage gap with the Russians had dramatically narrowed, the Americans still had only a small bridgehead of less than fifty thousand men across the Elbe River. In contrast, the bulk of the Red Army remained poised on the eastern approach to the capital.

The American advance had gone so rapidly that it also had outdistanced its fighter support. Most important, Eisenhower feared that if his forces went for Berlin rather than Lubeck, located farther north, the Russians might take advantage of the situation and occupy Denmark. Upon presenting Prime Minister Churchill with these arguments against an assault on Berlin, Churchill concurred.[29]

The Russians' own massive assault on Berlin commenced on 16 April 1945. The victorious end of the war in Europe was now unquestionably at hand. But during an inspection trip through the occupied German heartland with his fellow American commander, one final incident drove home to Eisenhower the ultimate meaning of Allied victory and conclusively demonstrated to all who witnessed it that the supreme commander was anything but a glad-handing lightweight. Following the Allied liberation of one of the smaller German concentration camps, the Ohrdruf Nord facility near Gotha, Eisenhower, Bradley, and Patton arrived at the site on 12 April. Ironically, on the same date half a world away, another tragic scenario was playing itself out, as President Franklin D. Roosevelt collapsed and died at Warm Springs, Georgia. Inside Ohrdruf Nord the sight and stench of corpses were everywhere; so revolting was the scene that battle-hardened soldiers turned ashen. Patton, "Old Blood and Guts" himself, finally abandoned the group to vomit in a corner of the camp. But Eisenhower, aware as perhaps never before of the full extent of the Nazi horror, refused to yield to his nausea and willed himself into viewing every inch of the camp before finally agreeing to leave.[30]

It was his recognition of the cost and the necessity of total victory that steeled his determination not to give the Nazis any hope of exploiting fears of the Russians for leniency. German resistance in the West crumbled, and following Hitler's suicide on 30 April, a group of German officers headed by Adm. Karl Doenitz sought a separate deal with the British and Americans. Despite renewed wrangling among his political superiors, Eisenhower refused to accept any limited surrender in the West while Germans still fought Russians. He insisted on the presence of a Russian representative at the surrender negotiations, and he eventually permitted only a forty-eight-hour postponement of surrender implementation for outlying German units. He even refused to be present in the same room as German chief of staff Alfred Jodl for the formal surrender ceremony, held at 2:00 A.M. on 7 May. Instead, he merely summoned Jodl to attend him alone afterward in order to insist upon his full compliance with unconditional surren-der. After a brief photo opportunity for reporters and the recording of a short newsreel and radio message, Eisenhower ordered his aides to draft a formal telegram of victory to the Combined Chiefs. Rejecting their flowery efforts, he thanked them for their services and dictated the final message himself. It was, as befitted its author, a simple state-ment of fact: "The mission of this Allied force was fulfilled at 0241 local time, May 7, 1945."[31]

7

RETURN OF
THE HERO

By the summer of 1945 Dwight D. Eisenhower had become America's most famous citizen. With Roosevelt dead, Churchill soon to be replaced by Clement Attlee as head of the British government, and Harry S. Truman still largely an unknown quantity, he was unrivaled as a personal symbol of the victorious Western democracies. His image was that of the gentle Christian warrior, the noble crusader returned from the war against the Nazi infidels, and he inspired immense public confidence and pride. In a society that in spite of (or perhaps because of) its sweeping organizational changes and growing complexity still worshiped at the altar of individual initiative and accomplishment, Eisenhower was a great national treasure. In the midst of this overwhelming tide of adulation, he became the postwar symbol both of his country's global commitments and of its dedication to individual freedom. Countrymen from all walks of life did not hesitate to consider him for virtually any national job or challenge, from secretary-general of the United Nations to governor of postwar Germany or president of the United States.

The public Eisenhower offered his countrymen a simple stereotype of courage, cooperation, and congeniality. The private Ike, of course, was far more complex and rather less pristine. But with his rise to fame and his immense symbolic value to the free world, both he and his official superiors in Washington found it useful to protect his public reputation from the slings and arrows of criticism and controversy. A symbol of national dedication, Allied unity, and democratic values like Eisenhower was hard to find, and accordingly national leaders had a stake of sorts in preserving the patriotic good feelings about him and about the American role in World War II. What complicated the task was the fact that the image was expected to remain static, but Eisenhower's life could not stand still. As a top-echelon military officer in his mid-fifties, he was still young enough to be seeking new challenges rather than the comforts of retirement. In pursuing those new personal and professional challenges, he would have to guard at the same time the heroic reputation he had earned. The glories of Normandy and Rheims, however, were difficult feats to duplicate, especially in peacetime.

At first, the task of protecting his fame and image as the archetypal "soldier of freedom" was easy, given the celebratory mood in America and Western Europe in the summer of 1945. Victory ceremonies were held in all the major cities of the West. For Eisenhower, the crowning centerpiece took place in London, at the Guildhall, on 12 June. Driven into the city in a horse-drawn carriage, Eisenhower received the sword of the Duke of Wellington and gave the principal speech for the occasion. Recognizing the importance of the event, he had worked on the speech for three weeks beforehand and had memorized it both to avoid wearing glasses and to give it a "spontaneous" feeling. The speech appropriately reinforced his image as a humble, dutiful servant of democracy and a member of a noble multinational team. "Had I possessed the military skill of a Marlborough," he proclaimed, "the wisdom of Solomon, the understanding of Lincoln, I still would have been helpless without the loyalty, vision, and generosity of thousands upon thousands of British and Americans."[1]

Despite the public disclaimers of greatness, such a lofty impression of Eisenhower was exactly what Western public opinion held, and the rounds of ceremonies only cemented the public adulation and affection for him. Celebrations in Prague, Paris, and other European capitals were followed by ticker-tape parades in New York and Washington, D.C., and another "extemporaneous" speech before a joint session of Congress. The general selected the occasions and settings for his public addresses carefully, and from Washington to Abilene the themes of his "impromptu" speeches remained the same—patriotism, teamwork, duty. If the real Eisenhower contained more contradictions than the public symbol displayed, few Americans knew it, and both he and his superiors intended to keep it that way. Neither he, for reasons of privacy and dignity, nor official Washington wanted his private life minutely scrutinized or the wartime arguments at SHAEF aired in public.[2]

During the war the most important people in protecting the public Eisenhower had been his personal staff, the wartime family whose loyalty and discretion had known few bounds. But with peacetime that family scattered, and the public clamor for information about the new national hero and about the inside story of the war enticed several into contracting for wartime memoirs. The first to do so, Mickey McKeogh, began work on a book of his experiences almost immediately, entitled *Sergeant Mickey and General Ike*. Although Eisenhower could not block its publication, he refused to lend it his sanction by contributing a foreword. Also at work on a memoir was Harry Butcher, and the general demanded that he destroy any personal notes of their private wartime observations on people and events. Butcher secretly kept the notes rather than comply with Eisenhower's request, but he did not feature them in his book and concealed them from public view for three decades. Ironically, despite Eisenhower's qualms, both the McKeogh book and Butcher's *My Three Years with Eisenhower,* released in 1946, only added to the general's lofty reputation. Nevertheless, he was angered by the modest revelations of his wartime disharmony with other SHAEF commanders, notably Montgomery. In Eisenhower's view, such revelations not only damaged his own image and that of SHAEF but also publicly compromised still active international actors such as Churchill and Marshall. To Churchill he lamented, "I am perfectly helpless in the matter. As long as an ex-aide turned into a Boswell type of reporter there is nothing I can do about it except to shudder." To Tedder he added the advice, "If ever I have to go to war again I am not going to take along with me someone that wants to write about the matter when it is all over."[3]

Potentially more damaging were the continuing rumors concerning Eisenhower's wartime relationship with British driver and personal aide Kay Summersby. With hindsight it is apparent that Kay's feelings toward Ike, particularly after the death of her American fiancé in North Africa, were visibly more intense than his toward her. As the general viewed their experiences, Kay had provided pleasant and relaxing personal companionship during the most stressful days of the war. But he had never consummated a sexual relationship with her, and he had no intentions of abandoning Mamie for her, despite the strains placed on their marriage by war and separation. During the war military aides and colleagues, including General Bradley, had been aware of the Eisenhower-Summersby gossip—rumors fanned by the supreme commander's own attendance of social functions in London and elsewhere with her. Then, however, the motto had been, "Leave Ike and Kay alone. She's helping him win the war." Correspondents covering the general had cooperated. But with the new demands of peacetime, Eisenhower knew that the Summersby connection had to be severed gracefully and quietly. At first he tried gentle methods, attempting to secure a job for Kay in Germany with his successor, Gen. Lucius Clay. But she resisted the separation, and after she secured American citizenship, Eisenhower firmly put down all overtures for any kind of continuing friendship. After a chance encounter in New York in 1948, he never spoke to her again.[4]

For the most part, the various minor threats to Eisenhower's image were contained successfully or were deflected from public attention. The net effect of all the staff reminiscences, including Summersby's own sanitized first memoir, *Eisenhower Was My Boss*, was to enhance rather than mar his reputation as an honest, fair, and courageous wartime leader. Despite their limited revelations of disharmony in the high command, their respect for the man they had served had not waned. Adding to the ever-more heavily documented portrait of the war hero was a semiofficial biography of the general, entitled *Soldier of Democracy*, written by a young Kansas State University journalist, Kenneth S. Davis. Davis obtained the cooperation of Eisenhower, his staff, and his family, and the book combined a generally admiring tone with an unmatched wealth of detail about his boyhood years in Abilene. Again, however, Eisenhower was not totally satisfied with the final product, complaining once more that too much emphasis had been placed on wartime disputes between himself and other commanders.[5]

Eisenhower soon had his own chance to set the record straight. A multitude of publishers and agents had swamped him ever since the end of the war for rights to his memoirs. At first he was not certain that enough time had passed for him to write dispassionately about his dealings with Montgomery and others. The time pressures he suffered under as commander of the American occupation zone in Germany also precluded much writing in 1945. Nevertheless, as early as the late summer of that year he notified his brother Milton that he had begun work on "an outline of my personal story covering the war years." In 1946 he arranged for Richard Simon of Simon and Schuster to review two sample chapters for style and content. Intent on capturing the simple eloquence of his public talks, he reread the memoirs of Ulysses S. Grant for stylistic guidance. By late 1947, with his duties in Washington as chief of staff winding down, he finally began in earnest the task of preparing a complete manuscript for Doubleday and Company. As befitted his working style, the drafting was a staff enterprise. The general gathered the necessary documentation and read it; then he dictated the written text to any of three secretaries at a sixteen-hour-a-day pace. Doubleday released the wartime memoir, *Crusade in Europe*, in late 1948, and it became an immediate best-seller. For Eisenhower it was a financial boon as well, for he received $500,000 after taxes from the publisher for the book's rights and paid only capital gains tax on the entire transaction. More important, though, reviewers across the country hailed it as the best military memoir since Grant's, and "the work of the best soldier-historian since, perhaps, Caesar and his commentaries."[6]

As the public response to *Crusade in Europe* demonstrated, nothing Eisenhower did in peacetime realistically could be expected to match or surpass the drama and excitement of the war and Eisenhower's role in it. Anything he chose to do after V-E Day was bound to appear an anticlimax. But he was far from the day when he expected to settle into a cozy retirement, and as postwar international fears and concerns rose, he was called upon repeatedly to render necessary, if often unglamorous, service to the nation. His first such assignment represented a carryover from his duties of SHAEF. After completing his round of public appearances in Europe and the United States, he assumed the task of head of the American zone of occupation in western Germany, staying in that post until the end of November. From December of 1945 to February 1948, he served in Washington as Marshall's successor as chief of staff. Both jobs provided more headaches than glories, but he loyally served his professional calling and his country.

During his term as overseer of the American sector of Germany, two related sets of problems confronted him. The first involved the ongoing debate over how harsh the Allied treatment of the defeated country should be. Should Germany's economy be permanently "pastoralized," or should a pro-Western industrial infrastructure be rebuilt? How extensively should the de-Nazification of the country be pursued? This first set of issues, in turn, weighed heavily upon a second major preoccupation—the increasingly turbulent relations between the Western Allies and the Soviet Union. Actions to restore German industrial health or to rehabilitate former Nazis, for example, only would add to growing Soviet suspicion and noncooperation on a host of East-West issues. Providing visible illustration of the dilemmas posed for Eisenhower by the American occupation role was his own headquarters in Frankfurt, located in the offices of I. G. Farben, the manufacturer of poison gas for Hitler's concentration camps.[7]

Eisenhower's approach to occupation issues walked a middle ground between the views of committed antifascists and those of cold war hard-liners within the Truman administration. On the one hand, his position toward former Nazis was relatively stern, for he condemned American fraternization and administrative cooperation with former officials of the Hitler regime. At the same time, however, his views on German economic reconstruction gradually moved away from pastoralization and toward assisting industrial revival. His wartime references toward Germany, reflecting the passions of the moment and ignoring his own ethnic ancestry, had been brutal, full of such statements as "the German is a beast." As with other Americans, however, as the war's memory faded and cold war tensions heated up, his views on postwar German reconstruction softened. But he maintained his firm stance against extensive Nazi influence, and this forced a final showdown with longtime friend George Patton. Patton's obvious willingness to collaborate politically with former Nazis against the Russians forced Eisenhower to fire him, something he would never have done in wartime. To Patton's replacement, Lucian Truscott, he issued

renewed instructions to be "stern" toward the Nazis and to give reset-
tlement priority to displaced Jewish refugees.[8]

Although he maintained a policy of limiting contacts with former
Nazi officials, Eisenhower advised President Truman, in a reversal of
his wartime endorsement of pastoralization, to rehabilitate the industrial Ruhr. Probably the most influential individual in changing his
views on economic restoration in Germany was his chief deputy in
Frankfurt, former West Point classmate and Philippine associate Lucius Clay. Clay's counsel, along with Eisenhower's own evolving mistrust of the Russians, encouraged the shift in thinking, and once
American overall policy in the occupation zone had been developed,
Eisenhower left more and more of the day-to-day operation of his office to Clay. He openly welcomed the opportunity to escape his desk
responsibilities for economic, political, and financial supervision in
the zone, and he trusted Clay's judgment implicitly. Under Clay's daily supervision, the previous plans of the Roosevelt administration and
the military services for the dismantling of German industry slowly
were relegated to bureaucratic mothballs.[9]

Despite his own growing mistrust of the Russians, Eisenhower was
not as quick to abandon avenues of cooperation and coexistence in
the summer and fall of 1945 as were Truman and many of his advisers.
Displaying a certain amount of geopolitical naïveté, Eisenhower clung
to the hope that a foundation of U.S.-Soviet cooperation could be
built alongside a revived, reindustrialized, pro-Western Germany. One
consequence of this continuing hope on his part was his lack of enthusiasm for employing the atomic bomb to end the Pacific war, for
he feared its effect on Soviet perceptions of American global intentions. When Secretary of War Stimson asked him for his views on the
use of the A-bomb against Japan, Eisenhower, almost alone among
the advisers, opposed its use on the grounds that Japan was already
defeated and that it would shock world opinion. His desire to maintain communication with the Soviets also extended to German and
Eastern European issues. Despite urgings by Churchill and others to
maintain American troops in the Russian occupation zone both to
provide leverage against possible Russian moves against Austria and
to ensure Western access rights to Berlin, he negotiated a plan for
American withdrawal from most of the zone and Soviet acceptance of
Western forces in Berlin with Marshal Grigori Zhukov.[10]

The mutual respect and friendship between Eisenhower and Zhukov briefly delayed a total freeze in U.S.-Soviet relations over Germany. In recognition, the Russians even invited Eisenhower to Moscow to meet Joseph Stalin. But he soon discovered that, as he had feared, the employment of the atomic bomb had added a new and chilling element into the big-power dialogue. As he had commented to a journalist, "Before the atom bomb was used, I would have said yes, I was sure we could keep the peace with Russia. Now, I don't know. . . . People are frightened and disturbed all over. Everyone feels insecure again." He continued to try keeping the doors of contact open, arranging the controversial dismantling and relocation of selected German plants to Soviet-held territory in exchange for recognized Western air corridors and land access rights to Berlin. Soon, however, new orders summoned him back to the United States. President Truman had accepted General Marshall's resignation as chief of staff as a preliminary move to reassignment to new diplomatic duties, and Truman wanted Eisenhower to take Marshall's place.[11]

Eisenhower assumed his new post on 20 November 1945. Although it represented the zenith of the army establishment, to Eisenhower it was "nothing but straight duty." He hated the return to Washington desk work. The new assignment did afford him the chance to put together a new personal staff, many of whom remained with him through the presidential years. For his assistant in charge of running the office, he tabbed Maj. Craig Cannon to replace the departed Tex Lee. Maj. Robert Schulz handled his travel arrangements, and Maj. Kevin McCann assumed Harry Butcher's old role as press adviser and speechwriter. Being in a high position in the military in Washington meant, as it had in Europe, that Eisenhower relied heavily on the loyalty and efficient service of his staff personnel. It was said at times, and apparently accurately, that from his rise to high rank in the army until his retirement from public life some twenty years later, Eisenhower never had reason to drive himself in an automobile or even to dial his own telephone calls.[12]

Such perquisites of office did little, however, to ease the drudgery of being chief of staff of a demobilizing army. His chief value to the Truman administration was not as a manager of demobilization but as a popular hero, employed to ease the growing public impatience with the slowness and confusion of the return to peace. He left the day-to-day administration of his office to staffers and traveled around the country, giving morale-boosting speeches in support of controversial War Department proposals such as universal military training, armed services unification under civilian control, and the continuation of selective service. He did not object to his role as a public spokesman for the military, for it freed him from his desk, kept him in the public view, and gave him the chance to speak in behalf of positions formulated by his predecessor with which he agreed.[13]

What Eisenhower increasingly did dislike about his job, however, was the fact that President Truman viewed him merely as window dressing and placed little stock in his advice on international military and political issues. For Truman even more than for Roosevelt, when strategic advice was needed it was Marshall who was consulted, not Ike. Despite his visibility as the symbol of the military establishment, Eisenhower had little input into such major decisions as the military budget, the Truman Doctrine, military aid to Greece and Turkey, and the international control of atomic energy. Part of the reason may have been that in addition to his unintellectual demeanor and the formidable presence of Marshall, Eisenhower still was less openly militant in his anti-Communism than Truman's chief advisers in the State Department and Moscow. Because of his firsthand knowledge of the weakened state of Soviet military power at the end of World War II, he did not accept the exaggerated cries of danger posited by such alarmists as former ambassador William C. Bullitt. By the end of his tenure as chief of staff, Eisenhower was as dedicated an anticommunist as anyone, but he continued to be more critical of what was, in his view, an overreliance on conventional military force and a tendency to overstate the dangers of localized trouble spots such as Greece and Turkey.[14]

One other factor cemented the growing distaste of Eisenhower for his commander in chief. Given his long-standing contempt of partisanship and broker politics, it was scarcely surprising that Ike found little to admire in Harry S Truman, the personification of the career partisan politician in the White House. Always playing the role of the dutiful soldier, however, Eisenhower did not make his split with Truman public until after the 1948 elections. But if his advice was ignored by the president and the White House inner circle, he was discovering anew that life in Washington did have its compensations. He enjoyed a comfortable, if not gaudy, style of living, and he was accumulating a growing circle of wealthy and powerful admirers on the banquet circuit through his speech-making trips as chief of staff. It is all too easy to spot a conspiracy in the way more and more corporate titans flocked to his side, but it is fairer to state that they sought his company often out of the same curiosity and hero worship that motivated so many of their countrymen. The difference, of course, was that the average American seldom enjoyed similar access to Washington's famous and powerful.[15]

Many of this group of influential businessmen had just recently begun enjoying the revived prosperity and public esteem that had been so lacking during the hard times of the depression. Wartime partnership with the federal government in the production effort had helped restore their prestige in official circles. Eisenhower, having been stationed for most of the war out of the country, had not been acquainted with most of them during his own rise to fame. But within a period of two to three years after the end of World War II, he included them among his closest personal friends. Where once he had been accompanied only by an official family of staffers and reporters, he now spent his leisure time playing bridge or golf in the company of such corporate luminaries as Thomas J. Watson of IBM, Robert Woodruff of Coca-Cola, Cason Callaway of U.S. Steel, New York investment banker Clifford Roberts, W. Alton "Pete" Jones of the Cities Service Company, and publisher William Robinson of the *New York Herald-Tribune*, the chief voice of northeastern internationalist Republicanism. With an official income still of only fifteen thousand dollars a year, he now enjoyed the good life at such plush locales as the Chevy Chase Club in Washington, D.C., the Blind Brook Country Club in Westchester County, New York, and the Augusta National Golf Club in Georgia.[16]

Eisenhower's widening circle of corporate friends remained his close personal companions for the rest of his life, and their influence upon him extended beyond their ability to provide him with collegiality and a comfortable private life. Being men who moved in powerful company, they naturally held strong political opinions and liked to express them, and Ike proved a ready and sympathetic listener. Almost without exception Eisenhower's business companions were internationalists, advocating an expanded global political, economic, and military role for the United States, and conservatives, desiring to reign in the governmental activism of the broker state. Eisenhower found that not only did he enjoy their company and their flattering attentions but that his own version of patriotic nationalism and his distaste for divisive class and partisan warfare blended well with their convictions. Increasingly he called upon them for support and counsel in personal matters and in political ones as well.[17]

It was, in fact, the ardent solicitation by one of Eisenhower's corporate friends that led to his next career move in 1948. After two frustrating years as chief of staff, he was ready to leave active service, and offers had never ceased flooding in from a variety of directions. One that he nearly accepted came from Amory Houghton, chairman of the board of Corning Glass and president of the Boy Scouts of America, urging him to become the scouting organization's new executive director. But ever since 1946, Thomas Watson, who in addition to being IBM's chief executive was a trustee of Columbia University, had been pursuing Eisenhower with the idea of making him Columbia's presidential successor to the aged Nicholas Murray Butler. Initially Eisenhower had rebuffed Watson, citing his academic inexperience, and he had offered the name of his brother Milton instead. But Watson wanted Ike, and he resumed his solicitation in the summer of 1947. Again the general expressed reluctance, citing Mamie's fragile health and the social demands the post of Columbia's first lady would place upon her. Watson gave assurances, however, that the social obligations of both husband and wife largely would be assumed by the trustees. Watson argued that Columbia would offer him a nationally respected forum for the presentation of his political, social, and international views, and he maintained that it was the general's duty to serve the nation from the Columbia chair. Accepting the post, Watson pointed out, also would help remove his name from speculation regarding the 1948 presidential race. Eisenhower was not yet personally willing to test the presidential waters, and most of Columbia's trustees themselves were solidly lined up behind New York Republican Thomas E. Dewey.[18]

As a result of his lengthy negotiations with Watson, by the time Eisenhower accepted the Columbia presidency in June 1948, his duties had been carefully restricted. It was difficult under the circumstances to consider him a university president in any comprehensive sense. The job had been fundamentally altered so as to offer him a visible public forum for selective appearances and national policy debate, without burdening him with the usual administrative duties of academic decision making. He declined involvement in purely academic matters affecting the school, acknowledged no extensive role in fund solicitation (although his name alone attached to a Columbia letterhead loosened its share of alumni purse strings), foreswore most entertaining and social chores, and left the day-to-day details of administration to subordinates. He was able to pick and choose his public appearances and their contexts, while his academic affiliation protected his privacy and his public reputation. His ability to play a major role in national affairs was unrestricted, and he could speak his political mind without having to defend himself in the rough-and-tumble world of partisan politics itself.[19]

It was said by critics of Eisenhower's brief tenure as president of Columbia that he was not a bad president, for he was not one at all. The criticism only slightly exaggerated mattters. Eisenhower's relations with Columbia's generally liberal faculty were nonexistent. Teachers and administrators alike complained about his inaccessibility and about the efficiency of his "palace guard" of protectors. Ignoring the complaints, Eisenhower collected his twenty-five-thousand-dollar-a-year salary, worked on *Crusade in Europe,* took up oil painting in his house on Morningside Heights, and broke his reclusiveness occasionally to host policy forums on national issues. His own personal discomfort with life in the hustle and bustle of New York City only increased his desire for solitude. As he was driven to his various functions, he exercised the "soldier's right to grouse" and went into a brown study as he surveyed the congested metropolis. According to his later recollections, he asked himself on those occasions, "How could these men and women be moved in unison to channel some portion of their energies and talents to assure their children and grandchildren an even richer heritage?"[20]

Part of his answer to that question lay in his self-appointed mission to "help Columbia help America" find answers to national problems, as he defined them. But many in Columbia's faculty thought little of Eisenhower's intellectual depth. To them, his distaste for lengthy discussion and his demand for boiled-down summaries of academic policy recommendations indicated a shallowness of thought. The military way of decision making was not the university's, but Eisenhower was determined to treat it as if it were. After six months of frustration and boredom, he simply quit attending faculty meetings, turning over his duties to the graduate dean. His attempts to make Columbia "a more effective member of the American national team" also grated on faculty sensibilities. They preferred to see slightly more skepticism of the altruistic claims of patriotic nationalism expressed by many politicians and business executives. His chief contribution to the national policy dialogue, the American Assembly, demonstrated the ideological chasm that separated him from his intellectual critics. The organization, a floating collection of business, financial, educational, and other leaders, was designed to formulate policy ideas that, in Eisenhower's words, would prevent "the paralysis of bureaucratic controls, deficit spending, subsidies, and just plain handouts" of the modern state. Little wonder, then, that he found his organization criticized as a latter-day Liberty League and his personal views scorned as those of a "Boy Scout master" in public affairs.[21]

If some of Columbia's professors cared little for Eisenhower's stewardship, most of the trustees were not displeased at all. His personal magnetism helped the university retain the services of football coach Lou Little and Nobel laureate physicist Isidor Rabi. Although the subjects of his speeches around the country seldom emanated from Columbia issues or even general academic topics, they still attracted public attention to the school. And despite the grumblings about the complacent conservatism of the American Assembly forums, their existence did bring Columbia prestige as a place where prominent leaders wrestled with contemporary problems and issues, and they did bring additional financial contributions to the university. It was an irony of Eisenhower's tenure at Columbia that despite his distaste for fund-raising, the economic boost his very presence gave the school's solicitations for its building program was probably his greatest single academic accomplishment.[22]

Eisenhower was not a happy man at Columbia, however, and after a short time he again yearned for a more active role in national decision making. Columbia offered, for all its advantages, no real opportunity for heroic service to the country, and such forums as the American Assembly provided only limited substitutes. Only six months into his Columbia presidency, in early 1949, he returned to Washington as a consultant to Defense Secretary James Forrestal. His main task was to aid in overcoming navy resistance to unification of the armed forces. While in the capital, he suffered a severe intestinal ailment, diagnosed years later as chronic ileitis. He took the opportunity, at his doctors' advice, to quit smoking completely after having indulged a four-pack-a-day habit for many years. Upon his recovery, the Truman administration asked him to serve as informal chairman of the Joint Chiefs of Staff until an official replacement, General Bradley, could be installed. But even in that brief time, disagreements surfaced again with Truman over the size of the military budget, with Eisenhower advocating a larger allocation. [23]

In retrospect the dispute between Eisenhower and the Truman administration over the military budget had all the earmarks of a tempest in a teapot. The sum of money in dispute amounted to barely more than $1 billion, with the president publicly committed to holding defense expenditures to less than $15 billion and Eisenhower insisting on $16 billion. A year later, the administration would scrap its own limitation and adopt a far more massive program than even Eisenhower had called for. Eisenhower's readiness for a fight over military spending and his adoption of a new health regimen both hinted at a newfound willingness to become heavily involved in national partisan politics. He professed to all who would listen that such a perception was false, claiming that the capital would "never see me again except as an occasional visitor."[24] In truth, he was being less than candid with both himself and the public. The bug of national politics had bitten him, and Harry Truman's shocking defeat of Thomas Dewey in November 1948 had once again thrust his name into the forefront of presidential speculation for 1952. The pressures on Eisenhower to heed the political call—to provide a new brand of unifying national leadership—could only build in the months ahead.

ight Eisenhower with fifth grade class, Lincoln School. Dwight second
m left, front row.

Milton, David, Dwight,
Ida, and Earl outside
Eisenhower home in 1907.

Ike as a West Point football star, 1912.

Eisenhower as instructor at Camp Meade, Maryland, for the Tank Corps, 1919.

Mamie, Doud Dwight ("Icky"), and Dwight Eisenhower, ca. 1919.

General Fox Conner.

Eisenhower at family reunion, Abilene, 1926. Front row, left to right: David, Milton, Ida.
Back row: Dwight, Edgar, Earl, Arthur, Roy.

Eisenhower (partly concealed) with General
MacArthur, Bonus Army incident, 1932.

Capt. T. J. Davis, MacArthur, and
Eisenhower, Manila, 1935.

Brigadier General Eisenhower
in photograph sent to his
parents,
14 November 1941.

Eisenhower and Marshall. *Source: United States Army.*

TOP: Eisenhower with President Roosevelt, Carthage, North Africa, 7 December 1943. *Source: United States Army.*

BOTTOM: Eisenhower and aide Kay Summersby, North Africa, ca. early 1943.

TOP: Eisenhower and Montgomery, North Africa, ca. spring 1943. *Source: United States Army.*

BOTTOM: Eisenhower chatting with paratroopers of 101st Airborne Division, D day eve, 1944. *Source: United States Army.*

Eisenhower interviewing prisoner at Ohrdruf Nord concentration camp, 13 April 1945.
(Eisenhower commented with suspicion at the time that the man looked too well fed to be
a prisoner. Within days the individual was killed as a collaborator by his fellow inmates.)
Source: United States Army.

Columbia University president
Eisenhower, ca. 1948. *Source:
Columbia University.*

Army Chief of Staff Eisenhower, Hawaii, 1946. *Source: United States Army.*

Eisenhower and Taft, 1952. Eisenhower desperately sought, and secured at the "Surrender at Morningside Heights," the Ohio senator's active support in the general election campaign. *Source: Republican National Committee.*

Eisenhower shaking hands with Sen. Joseph McCarthy, Milwaukee, Wisconsin, October 1952.

Eisenhower and Secretary of State John Foster Dulles, 25 October 1954.
Source: National Park Service.

Eisenhower and Soviet leader
Khrushchev, Camp David,
Maryland, September 1959.
Source: United States Navy.

The expressive Eisenhower face on display at a news conference, 8 June 1955. *Source: National Park Service.*

Eisenhower and Vice President Nixon renominated, Republican National Convention, San Francisco, California, 1956. *Source: Republican Senatorial Campaign Committee.*

Eisenhower advises President Kennedy after Bay of Pigs disaster, Camp David, Maryland, 22 April 1961. *Source: United States Navy. Courtesy of the John F. Kennedy Library.*

Ike and Mamie in retirement, Gettysburg, Pennsylvania, 1966.

8

CINCINNATUS
IN POLITICS

Thomas E. Dewey's surprising loss to Harry Truman in November 1948 carried with it enormous ramifications for Dwight D. Eisenhower. Besides Truman, Eisenhower without question was the big winner in the election, and with the publication that same fall of *Crusade in Europe* his own political fortunes received a huge boost. In the aftermath of the election he continued to express no interest in campaigning for the nation's highest office. But he had said such things before and been disbelieved. Whether he chose to admit it to himself or not, ever since the end of World War II he had let slip occasionally an interest in the idea of becoming president. Although the pressures to become a presidential contender in 1952 accelerated in the aftermath of the 1948 election, it was not the first time he had given the matter serious thought.

Given Eisenhower's enormous popularity, it was not surprising that members of both major parties had solicited his candidacy for president since the summer of 1945. As early as July of that year, Harry

Truman himself had told the general, "There is nothing that you may want that I won't try to help you get. That definitely and specifically includes the presidency in 1948." Truman's infatuation soon faded, but in early 1946, before that year's congressional victories led to Republican overconfidence about the prospects for 1948, GOP politicians had also courted Eisenhower. Although his standard response was that the military was his career and partisan speculation only hampered his service, he had not refused categorically to accept a presidential nomination.[1]

Eisenhower's refusal to issue a Shermanlike denial of presidential ambitions at that early time suggested at the very least that the prospect of assuming presidential leadership intrigued him. At the same time, his personal and professional code of honor required him to foreswear the expression of such ambition, particularly within the forums of partisan politics. So what were the conditions under which Eisenhower might consider making a presidential race? First and foremost, he had to be able to reconcile such a decision with his code of honor, to convince himself that in accepting a party's nomination, he was not seeking it but simply answering the call of the nation. Whether or not the actual sequence of events reflected that scenario, Eisenhower had to be able to convince himself that it did. The nomination could not appear to be the result of a routine partisan selection process; rather, it had to be consistent with his self-image as a leader who transcended divisive partisanship, or at least seem so to Eisenhower. His sense of history had to convince him that the times demanded a new, unifying national leadership, and that in his nation's hour of need only he could provide it. He had to be nominated and elected "by acclamation," or at least perceive that he had been chosen by a public groundswell of opinion.

What Eisenhower required, in short, was a political setting that would enable him to appear at the proper moment as the new American Cincinnatus, the indispensable soldier-statesman reluctantly but dutifully answering his country's call. He wanted to be seen as, and sought as, a twentieth-century George Washington. What he learned only slowly, however, was that American politics of the modern variety were not those of 1788, and especially not in the presidential selection processes. America in 1788 had lacked formal political parties, had been a struggling infant nation, and had held to a political philosophy that still required a national strongman—if not a king, a president—to embody the national virtue and serve as a force to cement a shaky national unity. Modern America lived by a different, more complex code of competing class, racial, and social interests, channeled and organized within the political parties. Any prospective twentieth-century president sought nomination and election not by some mystical anointment by a handful of state leaders or by a consensus of political elites but by the rough-and-tumble processes of partisanship. Any modern presidential hopeful required a campaign war chest provided by wealthy benefactors and grass-roots supporters, and a savvy vote-counting and delegate-collecting operation run by skilled professionals.

Eisenhower's recognition of his inability quickly to accumulate such a war chest and a campaign organization had influenced his decision not to run in 1948. Other factors, however, had been even more important. By early 1947, with the Truman administration taking a terrible beating in public opinion polls, Republican desperation at a decade and a half of presidential exile had given way to overweening confidence. Governor Dewey, who had run a respectable race against Franklin Roosevelt in 1944, had appeared to be a candidate destined to secure victory. If any party had needed a savior in 1947, it had been the Democrats, and as a sign of their desperation Truman again had offered privately to forge a presidential ticket with Eisenhower at the top and himself as the vice-presidential candidate. The offer had contained its flaws from Eisenhower's standpoint, for it was likely that Truman expected in any such arrangement that he would continue to run the executive branch from the vice-presidency, making the general little more than a figurehead. In any event, Eisenhower's growing dislike of Truman and the Democratic party—in his estimation a more divisive, class-riven group than the Republicans—had precluded any desire to be its nominee. His answer to Truman, accordingly, was a flat rejection.[2]

Despite his early repudiation of Truman's offer, he still had waited for months before finally issuing a definitive statement of noncandidacy in 1948. Friends, after all, had told him for months and even years that history called and that he must be prepared to answer. In November 1946, historian Douglas Southall Freeman, the biographer of Robert E. Lee and editor of the *Richmond News Leader*, had urged him to change his "wholly negative attitude toward entering politics." As Eisenhower recalled, "He saw it as my simple duty to the nation."

The country had appeared to be crying out for leadership, factionalized as it was over rising prices, controversial strikes, and the growing fear of communism and internal subversion. But after a quick education in the organizational requirements of a presidential campaign, he had confessed to Cornelius Vanderbilt, Jr., that "no man since Washington has been elected to political office unless he definitely desired it." After soliciting further advice from his brother Milton, he had concluded that "we are not children and we know that under the political party system of this country it would certainly be nothing less than a miracle" for an outsider to be drafted at a major party convention.[3]

Henry Wallace's break with the Democrats and his formation of a Progressive party candidacy had erased Eisenhower's remaining contemplation of a 1948 candidacy on the only party ticket he would have accepted—the Republican. At the time he had written in his diary, "Wallace's third party move has completely taken me off the spot. He has increased the confidence of the Republicans that anyone can win for them." His own circle of business friends had lined up behind Dewey, and the only important dissenter among them from the conventional belief in Dewey's invincibility had been publisher William Robinson, who had predicted either an attempt by conservatives to block the New Yorker's nomination or a Truman comeback in November. In January 1948, after a New Hampshire supporter had entered an Eisenhower delegate slate for the 9 March primary, the general had finally made his noncandidacy public, answering *Manchester Union-Leader* publisher Leonard Finder's open letter urging his candidacy with a disavowal on 22 January. Basing his decision not to run on the principle that civilian and military power should never be merged, he had declared, "My decision to remove myself completely from the political scene is definitive and positive." Similarly, at the Democratic convention in mid-July, he had squelched an attempt by Sen. Claude Pepper of Florida to place his name before the delegates.[4]

The decision had made good political sense at the time. But given the expectation of Dewey's victory in the fall, Eisenhower had made it knowing that his hopes of ever becoming president might have vanished with a Republican landslide. If Dewey had won, as expected, he likely would have sought reelection on the Republican ticket in 1952. Eisenhower's scenario for rising to the presidency could never have encompassed challenging an incumbent Republican for renomination.

But by the end of a second Dewey term in 1956, Eisenhower would have been sixty-six years old, presumably too old to run. Political pundits therefore had assumed, as had the general himself, that his decision not to seek the presidency in 1948 had sealed his future as a prospective candidate for the office.

Harry S Truman's "give 'em hell" campaign in the summer and fall of 1948, however, had changed all that. Although Eisenhower had preserved his public neutrality and had given no speeches in Dewey's behalf, he had expected the New Yorker to win and had told friends he planned to vote for him. Nonetheless, by maintaining his public silence he had carefully preserved his room for maneuver within the Republican party and in national politics if by some miracle the unexpected took place. It had. In one of the most shocking upsets in presidential election history, Harry Truman had defied the odds and won a new lease on the White House on 2 November. Avoiding public comment on the election returns, Eisenhower immediately transmitted a congratulatory letter to the president, praising his "stark courage and fighting heart." More important, within hours after the election he resumed his rounds of public appearances on the banquet circuit before audiences of businessmen and other interested groups.[5]

For a man of Eisenhower's faith in destiny and divine providence, it came as a kind of sign that Truman had won, since the upset thrust his own name immediately back into presidential speculation for 1952. With Dewey defeated a second time, the Republican party was unlikely to seek his services again, and the other likely GOP possibilities for four years hence might drag the party in the direction of narrowly based domestic reaction and foreign policy isolationism. Eisenhower continued to profess no special interest in the presidency, but now his actions conveyed a different message. For while he denied that he was pursuing the White House, he and his followers charted and carried out a carefully orchestrated series of steps designed to place him in the position of being the "inevitable man" for 1952.

Eisenhower needed to perform a variety of tasks to prepare himself for 1952. To preserve his image as a national leader above the political fray, he had to maintain a public stance as a reluctant candidate who shunned party labels. His speeches had to be rallying points for a middle-of-the-road consensus on public concerns, without being specific enough to invite detailed criticism. He had to put clear distance between himself and the Democrats, especially Harry Truman, without appearing to do so for any other reason than that of sincere apprehension for the nation's welfare. He had to retain and expand his backing within the Republican party from those who could provide him with the financial support, the press coverage, and the organizational skills to carry the day, all without appearing to exert undue partisan effort. He needed to reassure important elements in the business community, concerned about the drift toward "paternalism" and "statism" in the Fair Deal, that his own views on taxes, government spending, labor relations, and the economy were "sound." Above all, he had to maintain his unique position of respect and admiration in the eyes of the American public—to preserve the image of the gentle modest hero who could get things done.[6]

Eisenhower's earliest political pronouncements were little more than a collection of general themes and homilies, sounding to cynical reporters like pure midwestern hokum but to many of the American people as inspired truth. In Eisenhower's description, American democracy was "a system that recognizes and protects the right of the individual and that ascribes to the individual a dignity accruing to him because of his creation in the image of a supreme being, and which rests upon the conviction that only through a system of free enterprise can this type of democracy be preserved." What the country needed, he insisted, was a new spirit of cooperation and patriotism instead of special interest selfishness, which would "produce a healthy economy, raise living standards for all, and preserve individual liberty." When he suggested to a group of eastern industrialists that they specifically foreswear price increases for a year as an example, however, he received a stony silence. As time went on, he learned to avoid directing such examples of sacrifice at the business community, choosing instead to highlight the need for labor restraint and reduced government spending as examples of national cooperative endeavor and the avoidance of "paternalism."[7]

Beginning the very day after the Truman victory, Eisenhower plunged into a series of dinner engagements with leading businessmen and publishers from different sections of the country. At the request of Alabama native and investment banker Ed Bermingham, he addressed an audience of Chicago-area executives, including the presidents of the Santa Fe Railroad and the Pullman Company, the city's three major newspaper publishers, and the chief executives of Sears, Montgomery Ward, Swift, Armour, and International Harvester. His script teemed with references to the evils of big government, labor power, and high taxes. In New York, Winthrop Aldrich of the Chase Manhattan Bank hosted a reception in his honor at the Racquet & Tennis Club of Manhattan. For the next two years, while ostensibly president of Columbia and still a consultant to the Defense Department, his schedule overflowed with similar appearances around the country, selling both himself and his political creed.[8]

He spent his time during his travels not merely talking but also listening to corporate leaders eager to advise him in the ways of the modern American economy. One of them, advocating the use of a different term than *capitalism* to define the American economic system, described it to him as "an overall system of individual endeavor profitable to management, labor, and ownership, with vast numbers of labor among the stockholders and thus having ownership in their business." Eisenhower liked that description, for it softened the hard exploitive image capitalism sometimes conveyed and stressed the common stake of all in profit and business prosperity. Besides economic theory, he also received advice in political tactics during his trips. While in Denver in the late summer of 1949, William Robinson relayed valuable words from former Republican party officer and *Saturday Evening Post* contributor Clarence B. Kelland. Kelland urged the general to speak at regular intervals on the broad theme of preserving freedom, while avoiding any identification with "radicals" of either the Right or the Left. Suggesting that Ike "win the friendship of party leaders in a private way," he added that in a year or two, "it would be easy to bring about spontaneous movements . . . to demand a draft. These things do not happen of themselves but require organization and skillful handling." He concluded, "Let there seem to be . . . a voluntary public demand dissociated from obvious party leaders. . . . These things do not happen. They must be contrived. And they cannot be contrived by amateurs."[9]

Consciously or not, Eisenhower followed Kelland's advice down to the last detail. Already Republican party professionals were approaching him in the gloom of the Dewey defeat as the sole hope for the party's presidential salvation. Among the solicitors was Dewey himself, who in July 1949 urged him to run in order to "save this country from going to hades in the handbasket of paternalism, socialism, dictatorship." As Kelland had advised and as his own instincts guided him, Eisenhower called in his public addresses for a restoration of the "middle way." He warned of the dangers of growing governmental power and labor strife, and he advocated a greater unity of purpose among labor, management, and government in a "far tighter voluntary cooperative unit than we now have." When he lapsed into specifics, however, he still got into political trouble. In Texas in December 1949, he appeared to assail Social Security, declaring that "if all Americans want is security they can go to prison," and adding that those who had died in the last war had "believed in something more than trying to be sure they would not be hungry when they were sixty-seven." After the remarks hit the newspapers, Kelland fired off a hasty message to William Robinson, now acting as Eisenhower's chief adviser: "For God's sake get your boy to close his trap and crawl into a hole for a while. A few more speeches and he'll be up the creek without a bucket."[10]

The speaking trips, listed under the auspices of the American Assembly, continued well into 1950. They enabled Eisenhower to expand his list of contacts with America's wealthy and powerful to include oilman H. L. Hunt of Texas, Robert Cutler of Boston's Old Colony Trust Company, and Harry Bullis of General Mills. His message remained the same—gently but not conclusively rebuffing overtures to seek the presidency, while warning of the dangerous growth of government paternalism. In order to touch base with all major segments of the Republican party, he sought more cordial relations with the right wing by sojourning to the Bohemian Grove resort in California. There conservative millionaires held court in the presence of the reigning symbol of political conservatism, Herbert Hoover. Eisenhower made the trip on a special train provided for him by the president of the Santa Fe, and he delighted his audience, which included a young congressman named Richard M. Nixon, with his infectious grin and his willingness to assail the New Deal.[11]

Despite the success of his travels, it did bother Eisenhower privately that he was giving in to his ambition, or at the least allowing cracks to appear in the foundation of his code of selfless honor. He still needed to believe that the times were so critical they justified his taking what were for him extraordinary personal steps. Events soon cooperated. On 25 June 1950, North Korean communist forces invaded their neighbors to the south. In Eisenhower's view, the Truman administration's response to the assault on South Korea demonstrated indecision, particularly its slowness to launch a rapid overall rearmament program. By 1950 his views on the communist menace had become those of a hard-liner, supportive of American internationalism and of economic, political, and military intervention around the globe. An early backer of the Marshall Plan, he also had come to favor a closer political and economic partnership of the United States and Western Europe. As early as 1947, he had advocated a defensive alliance system for the region, a controversial idea for the time because of the traditional American aversion to peacetime military alliances. In 1949, his idea had been formalized by the Truman administration in the defensive umbrella known as the North Atlantic Treaty Organization (NATO).[12]

With an unhealthy boost from the Korean invasion, American nerves had become strained to the breaking point in 1950. Continuing concern over Soviet-inspired aggression in Europe and Joseph McCarthy's well-publicized hunt for subversives within the U.S. Government only added to the tension. In response to the calls of militant anticommunists, Truman had committed the nation to a massive rearmament program planned to triple the defense budget, and Western Europe began its own tentative buildup. But NATO remained an untested alliance in need of someone to convert it into a fully functional European command. A joint command structure had to be devised in such a way as to preserve the firm American commitment to Europe's defense and yet not trample upon European national sensibilities. With such critics at home as Sen. Robert A. Taft of Ohio challenging Truman's authority even to dispatch American troops to Europe in peacetime, NATO also needed a spokesman to sell the expanded American presence abroad to its own citizens. Europe and America both required as NATO's first commander a man in whom the people of the West would place their trust and confidence. Dwight D. Eisenhower was the obvious choice.[13]

The call from Truman came in October 1950. Eisenhower insisted that the president "order" rather than "request" him to the post, ensuring that his service would not be construed as an endorsement of the current administration's overall defense and foreign policies. The job itself proved well suited to his talents, without unduly hampering his presidential prospects. In Paris he found himself under less pressure to comment on domestic political issues or on the still open question of his own presidential candidacy. At the same time, the importance of his mission ensured worldwide press coverage of his actions and enhanced his image as a troubleshooting soldier-statesman whose services transcended party labels. The growing sense of crisis in the West also fed his belief in himself as a man chosen to fill a role by destiny. As he wrote boyhood friend Swede Hazlett, "I rather look upon this effort as about the last remaining chance for the survival of Western civilization."[14]

During his service as NATO supreme commander, his role as public salesman of the alliance to American politicians and the public added extra urgency to his own political considerations. To be willing to take the plunge into the waters of presidential politics, he had always needed to believe not only that the nation was in grave danger but that only he could provide it with the necessary direction. He had already soured on Truman and the Democratic party, and his encounters with his most likely Republican rivals in 1952 now convinced him as well that they were not suited for the tasks of national leadership. At the top of any list of prospective Republican challengers, of course, was Taft, the darling of the party's conservative, neoisolationist wing and the presumed front-runner for the nomination. To convince himself of Taft's unsuitability, Eisenhower arranged a private meeting with the Ohio senator in December 1950, in which he sought Taft's public support for NATO. If he received the assurances, Eisenhower told himself, he would consider ending any further speculation about his own presidential ambitions. But as expected, Taft remained noncommittal even on issuing a vague endorsement of the alliance, and he specifically criticized sending any additional American divisions to Europe. After Taft left, Eisenhower tore up a previously prepared statement of noncandidacy and decided to maintain "an aura of mystery" about his presidential plans.[15]

By the beginning of 1951 Eisenhower had committed himself to a path leading to the Republican presidential nomination. All his preconditions for candidacy were being met. Public opinion polls indicated that he was the country's first choice, and the groundswell of support cut across party lines. The Republicans' other prominent possibilities were growing ever more isolationist and negative. Taft, McCarthy, and others, in his estimation, presented a "sorry picture" of hate. The Democrats, in turn, were directed by a crowd of "unworthy men," headed by Harry Truman. The present administration appeared incapable of inspiring public confidence or of charting a firm but steady international course. Deficit spending, in his view, threatened the nation's economic future. "How we need some brains and some selflessness," he observed. Deep down he felt he knew where those attributes could be found. And his own occasional aches and pains reminded him that at age sixty-one, his moment of destiny might be short-lived.[16]

His circle of eastern financial advisers and internationalist Republicans began putting the wheels of a presidential organization in motion in the summer of 1951. With Eisenhower's knowledge, a volunteer organization, called Citizens for Eisenhower, was formed with the financial sponsorship of close friends who included Clifford Roberts, Pete Jones, Ellis "Slats" Slater of Frankfort Distilleries, and financiers George Whitney, John Hay Whitney, and L. B. Maytag. With the guidance of Citizens for Eisenhower, local booster organizations called "Ike Clubs" began springing up all over the country. Ike's private boosters advised the professional politicians in his circle to keep their distance from these initial efforts so that they would assume the appearance of a spontaneous public demand for the general. In August, Eisenhower's former public relations officer and speech writer, Kevin McCann, started work on a campaign biography entitled *Man from Abilene.* Eisenhower remained in close touch with his backers from his office in Paris, requesting and receiving briefing books on major public policy issues. From George Whitney and Paul Hoffman of the Ford Foundation he got "lectures on economics," including a feasibility study on a possible return to the gold standard. Through Hoffman he solicited additional studies from the Ford Foundation on the "farm problem" and on schemes to reallocate regulatory authority from Washington to the states.[17]

While Eisenhower made his plans in Paris, President Truman, still uncertain whether to seek another term in 1952, tried to sidetrack him with another political offer. Two years earlier, Truman had relayed through a close friend of the general and a Democrat, George Allen, an offer of the U.S. Senate nomination in New York. Eisenhower had quickly turned the offer down. In November 1951, Truman repeated to Eisenhower his 1947 offer to run as a vice-presidential candidate alongside the general's Democratic presidential candidacy. Eisenhower would have none of it. He protested vigorously to Truman, "You can't join a party just to run for office. What reason have you to think I have ever been a Democrat? You know I have been a Republican all my life and that my family have always been Republicans." By making the offer, in fact, Truman had lowered himself even more in Eisenhower's estimation. Truman had tried to pull off the typical partisan's deal by openly appealing to another man's narrow personal interest. The action symbolized Eisenhower's main complaint with the Democratic party's philosophy as a whole. The fact that Truman was willing to make the offer also told him, however, that many Democrats as well as Republicans would support him if he made the final decision to run for president [18]

Unfortunately, he was learning the hard way that orchestrating a grass-roots movement for his nomination was not sufficient to obtain it. While Ike Clubs hosted rallies, Robert Taft collected Republican delegates. It had been growing clearer for months that if Eisenhower was serious about winning the nomination, he would have to unleash the political professionals within Citizens for Eisenhower and construct a staff operation to oversee the grubby business of delegate hunting. In early September, Sen. Henry Cabot Lodge, Jr., of Massachusetts had delivered that message to Paris, and trusted friend Lucius Clay soon began the process of incorporating professional political expertise into the organization. On 25 October William Robinson issued the clarion call for an open Eisenhower declaration of candidacy on the front page of the *New York Herald-Tribune*, attributing the general with "the vision of the statesman, the skill of the diplomat, the supreme organizing talents of the administrator, and the human sympathies of the representative of the people."[19]

A campaign staff meeting on 10 November followed Robinson's public call to arms. The gathering included such political notables as Clay, Lodge, Dewey, Sen. James Duff of Pennsylvania, and a number of Dewey staffers from the 1948 campaign, including campaign manager and lawyer Herbert Brownell and economic adviser Gabriel Hauge. The group agreed on Lodge as campaign manager for the nomination race, owing both to his obvious energy and political savvy and his lack of ties to the Dewey failure of 1948. Dewey himself offered a final word of advice as the conferees dispersed—"And don't forget, let's get a hell of a lot of money." With the help of Dewey and financial backers such as Harold Talbot of Chrysler and John Hay Whitney, they did. Sigrid Larmon, an executive in the Young & Rubicam advertising agency and an Eisenhower golfing partner, was hired by the campaign to handle publicity. Gabe Hauge received the task of coordinating issues research and creating an economic advisory panel for the general.[20]

But one thing was still missing—an open declaration of candidacy by Eisenhower himself. Without it the necessary public enthusiasm could not be generated and delegate support could not be collected in sufficient numbers. His friends and advisers, including by now his brother Milton, bombarded him with pleas to announce his candidacy, underscoring his duty to answer his country's call. But he hesitated to enter the delegate fight, which ran against his cherished vision of selection by public acclamation. Time was running out, but despite that fact, Lodge's decision to announce that Eisenhower's name would be placed on the New Hampshire primary ballot brought a rebuke rather than an acceptance from Ike. Shunning the preconvention politicking, he still insisted to Robinson that "the seeker is never so popular as the sought. People want what they think that they can't get."[21]

It finally required the pressure of events and the supplying of "proof" of public demand to get Eisenhower formally into the race. On 21 January 1952, President Truman submitted his budget, which contained a projected deficit of $14 billion. Two weeks later, Herbert Hoover, Robert Taft, and sixteen other prominent Republicans publicly called for the removal of American troops from NATO. Now, Eisenhower believed, only he could arrest the slide to the twin disasters of bankruptcy and isolationism. On 11 February, exactly one month before the New Hampshire primary, aviator and personal friend Jacqueline Cochran carried with her to Paris for Eisenhower's private viewing a two-hour film of a fifteen-thousand-member Eisenhower for President rally at Madison Square Garden. The actual sight of thousands of Americans shouting "We want Ike!" apparently shattered the general's last remaining doubts. In an emotional scene witnesses described as full of tears, Eisenhower's recollections of his mother, and reassurances from Cochran that his candidacy was necessary for the country, he finally let slip the long-awaited words, "You can tell Bill Robinson that I'm going to run." The next morning he dictated letters announcing the decision to his closest friends. The message was the same each time—that he now realized that he had a "mandate" from the people to run and that he was deeply moved by their confidence and trust in him.[22]

Having finally made the commitment to run for president, Eisenhower prepared himself for the battle ahead. At a strategy session in London with Clay, Texas oilman Sid Richardson, and George Allen, he learned that Taft already had amassed 450 pledged delegates, and another 70 or so were leaning to the senator. Eisenhower could count on about 450 delegate votes himself, with about 300 remaining delegates still uncommitted. With that 300 likely to stay unpledged until the national convention, which would prevent Taft from going over the top early, Eisenhower found that he could follow his wishes and remain at his NATO post until 1 June. While he stayed in Paris, his backers staged impressive performances in the New Hampshire and Minnesota primaries of 11 March and 18 March. In New Hampshire, Eisenhower defeated Taft and Harold Stassen with 50 percent of the vote to their respective 38 percent and 7 percent. In Minnesota, Stassen's home state, Eisenhower nonetheless received only twenty-thousand fewer votes as a write-in candidate than did his rival, with Taft not entered at all. Privately the delegate results were even better, since Stassen had assured Eisenhower of his support after the first ballot of the Chicago convention. When Eisenhower returned to the United States in June, he immediately plunged into meetings with groups of state delegates, first in Abilene, then at Gettysburg, and finally in Denver. Many of the unpledged delegates were conservatives, so he denounced the Yalta Accords, blamed the Democrats for the "loss" of China, and downplayed his own wartime attempts to cooperate with the Russians. In these small group meetings with delegates he was superb, flashing his famous grin and displaying the down-home touch they loved. By the time the Republican convention opened in Chicago in early June, he was in position to wrest the nomination from Taft.[23]

Besides winning over as many uncommitted delegates as possible, in order to get the necessary 604 votes for nomination Eisenhower needed to strike deals with several powerful state delegations. In addition, he had to win his credentials challenge of Taft delegates, known as the "Fair Play Amendment." The Fair Play issue had arisen out of the actions of the Texas Republican party, which had disqualified the precinct convention votes of thousands who, upon signing a pledge to participate in the party, had voted overwhelmingly for Eisenhower delegates to the state convention. Because the pro-Taft organization had disfranchised these "one-day Republicans," two delegations each claimed to represent the state at the national convention. By the opening of the convention, the delegate contest between Taft and Eisenhower remained so close that the nomination rode upon the outcome of Fair Play on the convention floor. While Eisenhower took the high road of moral outrage, campaign manager Lodge made deals with state delegation leaders. Because of Lodge's efforts, the amendment barring contested Taft delegates from voting on their own seating carried by 110 votes. The convention then rejected a Taft delegation from Georgia and proceeded to seat the Eisenhower delegates from Texas.[24]

The effort extended to key state delegations on the convention floor: Richard M. Nixon secured California's votes for the Eisenhower cause, and the Pennsylvania and Michigan groups cooperated as well. Stassen also threw his Minnesota delegation behind Fair Play, and the successful credentials fight maneuvers signaled an impending Eisenhower victory in the presidential nomination contest the next night. By the end of the first ballot, Eisenhower stood only 9 votes away from nomination. At that point, as Stassen had promised, Minnesota switched its 19 tallies from its favorite-son cause to the general, putting him over the top. As evidence of the bruising nomination fight, however, die-hard Taft delegates refused to end the balloting with a show of unity and shouted down a motion to make Eisenhower's selection unanimous.[25]

The successful but divisive outcome at the Chicago convention defined Eisenhower's main political task in the interval between his nomination and election day. With the Democrats in disfavor because of the Korean War stalemate, corruption in the Truman administration, and the fear of internal subversion, about the only way he might lose in the fall was if the Taft wing of the Republican party decided out of spite to sit out the contest. Eisenhower accordingly spent much of his postnomination time repairing the wounds of the primary fight. In the process, he yielded vast amounts of rhetoric and platform planks to the conservatives. The healing process began with a unity meeting between the two combatants in Senator Taft's hotel suite. Eisenhower followed the session with his selection of Nixon, a senator of impeccable anticommunist credentials, as his running mate, and his acceptance of a platform that accused the Democrats of "shielding traitors," damned containment, and called for the "liberation" of Eastern Europe. Eisenhower's own acceptance speech, a call for a "crusade" against "wastefulness" and "arrogance and corruption in high places," also sought the restoration of party harmony for the campaign ahead.[26]

The Republican Old Guard, however, insisted not just upon a temporary rhetorical concession to their aims but a continuing commitment by the nominee. Eisenhower's conduct of the campaign against his Democratic rival, Gov. Adlai Stevenson of Illinois, tried too hard to provide such reassurance. In opposition to the views of his primary campaign staff, who were mostly Deweyites the conservatives detested, Eisenhower decided to open his whistle-stop campaign with a September foray into the South. On his southern swing, he pleased party conservatives by promising the states of Louisiana and Texas freedom from federal government control of their offshore oil reserves. To further conciliate the Republican Right, he borrowed its call for "liberation of the satellite countries" of Eastern Europe, while being deliberately vague on how he would accomplish the goal. Despite his private disgust at such scenes, he even allowed himself to be photographed embracing such party reactionaries as Sen. William Jenner of Indiana, who had heralded the crusades of McCarthy and had opposed the United Nations, the Marshall Plan, NATO, foreign aid, and virtually every piece of New Deal or Fair Deal domestic legislation. Eisenhower's appeasement of the Republican Right culminated in a second meeting with Taft in New York on 12 September, producing a joint statement that defined the campaign as one of "liberty against creeping socialism," called for drastic cuts in federal taxes and spending, and dismissed their own foreign policy differences as merely matters of "degree." Democrats gleefully referred to the statement as the "surrender at Morningside Heights," but Eisenhower had gained his assurance that Taft would work hard for the ticket.[27]

While Eisenhower compromised with the Republican conservatives, his running mate eagerly catered to their passions, poking fun at opponent Stevenson's "egghead" image and referring to the Illinois Democrat as a graduate of Secretary of State Dean Acheson's "Cowardly College of Communist Containment." On 18 September, however, news broke of a secret personal fund maintained for Nixon by wealthy California supporters. On the surface, the story was not big news, for many congressmen in the days before stringent ethics codes routinely accepted such personal favors. It was Nixon's own self-righteousness on the stump that, as much as anything, turned the secret fund into a major issue. Concern spread among the Eisenhower entourage, for the choice of Nixon as a running mate had been a marriage of convenience, and revelations of the Nixon fund threatened to deny the general the use of the corruption issue against the Democrats. The Old Guard, as expected, insisted that Eisenhower stand by his vice-presidential candidate and denounce the charges.[28]

Eisenhower declined to make a hasty decision either to drop Nixon or to defend him. Instead, he refused comment on his running mate's fate one way or the other, but offered him the opportunity to win over the public and save his place on the ticket through a televised defense of his record. In a famous address in which he employed the example of a cocker spaniel puppy, named Checkers, as representative of the gifts he had accepted, Nixon saved himself with an impassioned presentation. In the process he also managed to box Eisenhower not only into keeping him on the ticket but into disclosing his own personal finances. Within days, the financial statements of the Democratic ticket had also been forced into public view. Eisenhower, who always hated to reveal any portion of his private life, seethed at Nixon's tactic, but the overwhelming response to the Checkers speech forced him to retain his running mate, albeit at a distance.[29]

The political infighting and maneuvering with members of his own party, and the requirement of opening up his private life to greater scrutiny, had not been what Eisenhower had envisioned his procession to the presidency to entail. Further disillusionments were in store, both for himself and those who looked to him for moral leadership. The issue of McCarthyism, and specifically of Eisenhower's silence toward the Wisconsin senator's charges of malfeasance and even treason against General Marshall, had grown as the campaign had worn on. Eisenhower's broad statements on the subject of internal security, designed to appease party hard-liners, implied that the Democrats' sloppy practices had made McCarthyism possible. At the same time, however, he insisted that he did not condone "unfairness." Aware of McCarthy's popularity (he had just won renomination in Wisconsin by 100,000 votes), Eisenhower excused his silence toward McCarthy's reckless methods by lamenting that if "I should oppose him on the ground that he is morally unfit for office, I would be indirectly accusing the Republican electorate of stupidity, at the least, and of immorality, at the most."[30]

The entire question of whether Eisenhower would specifically condemn McCarthy's reckless charges, or whether he would implicitly discredit them through a public defense of Marshall, became a litmus test of his capacity for leadership to the national press and to liberal observers. With the candidate scheduled to cross Wisconsin on a campaign train ride in early October, speech writer Emmet Hughes urged Eisenhower to issue a defense of his former mentor while in McCarthy's home state. Aides inserted a paragraph into his standard stump speech praising Marshall "as a man and as a soldier," and stating that disloyalty charges against him constituted "a sobering lesson in the way freedom must not defend itself." But at the urging of staff director Sherman Adams and Wisconsin Republican politicians, Eisenhower dropped the Marshall references. News of the statement's existence already had filtered to the campaign press, and the candidate's failure to use it became instant national news. Five days after Eisenhower had left the state, Adlai Stevenson highlighted the crucial issue raised by the incident by quipping, "My opponent has been worrying about my funnybone. I'm worrying about his backbone."[31]

The incident revealed more to Eisenhower about the strength of his own personal ambitions than he had ever been forced to admit before. For years afterwards memories of the event were painful, and he even tried to avoid addressing it entirely when drafting his presidential memoirs ten years later. But although the incident left its scars upon the candidate, it did not cause his campaign any major damage amidst the bitterness and mudslinging of the 1952 race. The minor gains Stevenson made soon were erased by Eisenhower's late-hour pledge of 24 October that if elected he would travel personally to Korea to seek a quick end to the war. The idea of an Eisenhower postelection trip to Korea was little more than a public relations gesture, since he could learn little more there than he would from official briefings in Washington. But the offer, coming barely two weeks before the election, cemented the verdict of the voters. Those who believed that the inspection trip would serve as a prelude to an attempt to win the war militarily were appeased, and those who wanted merely a quick end to the fighting were encouraged to believe that he could find a way through the diplomatic impasse.[32]

Election day, 4 November 1952, dawned with pollsters burned by their experience four years earlier carefully hedging their predictions of a comfortable Eisenhower margin. This time, the expected did occur. For the Republicans and their standard-bearer, it was an impressive triumph. Eisenhower received over 55 percent of the popular vote and 442 electoral votes, in contrast to the game but outgunned Stevenson's 89. His coattails, along with popular disaffection with the Democrats, were even sufficient to usher in a Republican Congress—an eight-seat majority in the House of Representatives and a tie in the Senate that Vice-President Nixon's vote could break. His decision to campaign early in the traditionally Democratic South had paid rich dividends, for he carried five southern states, including Texas, and missed only narrowly in two others. Most gratifying of all to the candidate who had sought a personal summons to duty from the American people, virtually every analyst attributed the election results to his personal presence rather than to a deeper long-term voter realignment. His personal rise had reached its logical culmination. As he sat in his chair in the Oval Office on his first day as president of the United States, he wrote, "Plenty of worries and difficult problems. . . . Today just seems like a continuation of all I've been doing since July '41—even before that."[33]

9

OLD ASSUMPTIONS
AND A NEW LOOK

When Dwight Eisenhower entered the White House in January of 1953, he believed his primary responsibility was to promote and maintain American national security. By outlook, training, and personal preference, he intended first and foremost to be a foreign policy president. To that task he brought various assumptions about the postwar world and the American role in it. With the depression and World War II as his frame of reference, he saw the promotion of American prosperity and power around the world and the halt of the spread of totalitarianism as essential and complementary goals. To him the communist threat was real and was centrally directed from Moscow. Third World countries were dominoes in a gigantic big-power game, and Western economic and military security depended on preventing the Soviets from triggering the fall of these national dominoes through either overt aggression or internal revolutionary subversion. Third World nationalism was genuine, but it inevitably had to swing to one big-power pole or another. Like Truman, he posited a stable, supportive Western Europe as the chief anchor of American global security, and despite his earlier campaign rhetoric, he did not share the Asia-first orientation of the Republican Old Guard.

In his view, the nature of the communist enemy was such that, although American policy had to be based upon moral ends, America had to play by the same amoral rules as the opponent. Wars, whether hot or cold, required a cold-blooded calculus of strategy and tactics. As befitted the bridge-playing Eisenhower, the cold war was an analytical, almost mathematical, sequence of global responses and counterresponses. And like a good cardplayer, he kept his decision-making processes and his geopolitical tactics secret except when public diplomacy itself proved useful for public relations purposes or as bluff. As Vice-President Nixon described it, "He always applied two, three, or four lines of reasoning to a single problem and he usually preferred the indirect approach where it would serve him better than the direct attack on the problem."[1]

Despite the attention paid to the public fulminations of Secretary of State John Foster Dulles, Eisenhower was in firm control of foreign policy in his administration. His preferred agency for crucial decisions was not the cabinet, but the National Security Council (NSC) and its smaller informal subgroups. Although the NSC had been created in 1947, President Truman had seldom used it. Eisenhower, seeking a more orderly, secretive body for foreign policy advice which would be comparable to a military staff, quickly revitalized it. The NSC's chief note taker and organizer was Robert Cutler, who as special assistant for national security affairs expanded its membership to include the secretary of the treasury and the budget director as well as others on an occasional basis. The major players at the table, however, were Eisenhower himself, the secretaries of state and defense, the chairman of the Joint Chiefs of Staff, and the director of the Central Intelligence Agency. Eisenhower held NSC meetings weekly, prefaced by briefings from CIA Director Allen Dulles, the secretary of state's brother. Despite his numerous serious illnesses during his presidency, Eisenhower missed only twenty-nine meetings of the NSC in eight years. "Its sessions are long, bitter, and tough," he noted. "Out of that sort of discussion we're trying to hammer policy."[2]

What the public saw for the majority of the Eisenhower years was the deceptive sight of Secretary of State Dulles issuing moral lectures on the evils of communism and delivering calls for the "liberation" of

Eastern Europe. Dulles, the long-time Republican party spokesman on foreign policy, had been selected by Eisenhower partly to satisfy the Old Guard. Although Eisenhower respected Dulles's intelligence and the secretary's advice often intrigued him, he by no means always followed it. Dulles proved most useful as a lightning rod for criticism— an official whose visible position enabled him to provide rhetorical bluster at communist rivals when necessary. Dulles also helped Eisenhower convince Americans that he was sincere in seeking to free the "captive nations" of Eastern Europe, although no practical ways to achieve that aim existed.[3]

With hindsight it is easier to see that Eisenhower's approach to foreign policy was dictated in large measure by the contradictory partisan pressures operating upon him. Ever since the debacle of 1948, Republicans had hammered away at the Democrats for adopting a containment policy that they claimed was too "passive," instead of attempting to "roll back" communist gains. At the same time, the Republicans had condemned their partisan opponents for preempting congressional authority while spending too much money and bankrupting the country. Defense spending, however, made up a large share of the increase in the federal budget. How, then, could Eisenhower bolster American alliances in Europe, offer at least lip service to the strident calls for liberation, and reduce American defense expenditures at the same time?

Immediately upon taking office Eisenhower found himself embroiled in the same controversy over liberation in Eastern Europe as his predecessor had been. After only one month in office he faced five different congressional resolutions repudiating the Yalta Accords of 1945 with the Russians. Despite his own campaign criticism of Yalta and of Soviet control of the "captive nations," Eisenhower feared that an open repudiation of the wartime accords would provide the Russians an excuse to deny Western access rights to West Berlin. The administration's own captive-peoples resolution was limited to a call for national self-determination in Eastern Europe, and it chose to blame not the Yalta agreements but their "perversion" by the Soviets as the source of subjugation. To the Republican Old Guard's dismay, after Joseph Stalin's death on 4 March 1953 opened up new prospects for a thaw in the cold war, a more toughly worded resolution died in the Senate Foreign Relations Committee. Following two more years of intermittent furor over Yalta, publication of the official conference proceedings by the State Department in 1955 quieted much of the rhetorical bluster in Congress.[4]

Debates between the White House and the Congress over a captive-peoples resolution soon were joined by the revival of a suggested amendment to the U.S. Constitution proposed by Sen. John Bricker of Ohio. It was designed to give Congress the power to approve or reject not only formal treaties with other nations but executive agreements as well. Although the amendment first had been offered in 1951 as a vehicle for congressional Republican opposition to Truman foreign policy, Eisenhower now found himself its new target. After experiencing nothing but frustration in his attempts to seek an accommodation with Bricker and his supporters that would not tie his hands in foreign policy, Eisenhower succeeded by the narrowest of margins (one vote less than the two-thirds required for Senate passage) in bringing about the defeat of a modified version of the amendment in February 1954. Most aggravating to the president, thirty-two of the sixty Senate votes for the amendment came from members of his own party.[5]

Eisenhower's defense-policy answer to the strident calls from the Republican Right for both fiscal restraint and militant anticommunism came packaged in two phrases—the "New Look" and "massive retaliation." The New Look, formulated in NSC sessions in the fall and winter of 1953, promised a cutback in conventional forces from twenty divisions to fourteen by 1957, and the navy would absorb lesser cuts. But the air force, acquiring thirty thousand more men, would be increased from 115 to 137 wings. Ground forces stationed overseas would be reduced, but in order to preserve sufficient deterrent power against the Soviets and their allies the threat of massive retaliation would become official American defense doctrine. Smaller tactical nuclear weapons would be used in local wars, but the main American retaliatory response around the globe now would be the unpredictable application of massive nuclear force directly against the Soviet Union or China. The intended result would be, in the parlance of the day, "more bang for the buck." By relying to an unprecedented extent upon the air force, the defense budget then could be reduced from $35 billion to $31 billion a year.[6]

Such, at least, was the official strategy, designed as much to pacify conservative Republicans as to humble the Russians and their allies. Unfortunately, the New Look's reliance on massive retaliation did not work except as a strategy of bluff. If the enemy was willing to believe in the American threat of nuclear reprisal, bluff could force diplomatic gains. But the more often massive retaliation was used as threat and not as reality, it would tend to lose its power to intimidate the adversary into concessions. The New Look approach did not mesh with the parallel objective of improved defense cooperation with Western Europe. When crises arose and the United States sought alliance sanction for its use of massive retaliatory response, the European allies resisted joining in, fearing a Soviet counterresponse and the condemnation of world opinion. Eisenhower himself proved consistently unwilling to provoke international opinion by ordering retaliatory action without the protective umbrella of Allied joint participation. Western Europe also opposed any American schemes to increase European levels of military spending and troop strength so that the United States could reduce its own. As a consequence, the New Look's chief accomplishments proved not to be its military and diplomatic results but its contributions to defusing the Republican Right and to temporarily holding down American military spending. [7]

During the Eisenhower years, the massive retaliation doctrine did nothing to halt the Soviets' consolidation of their hold on Eastern Europe. The hollowness of the American threats of massive response and liberation were demonstrated as early as June 1953, when riots broke out in Soviet-occupied East Berlin and spread to other cities. Within twenty-four hours Soviet tanks had brutally crushed the resistance. The only official American response was to open food kitchens in West Berlin for the influx of refugees. Similarly in 1956, bold American words were not followed by bold actions. Following a modest loosening of Soviet policy in Poland that had permitted the installation of moderate Wladyslaw Gomulka as head of the Polish Communist party on 21 October 1956, rioting broke out in Hungary. Rebels demanded a similar relaxation of Russian control and specifically the return of Imre Nagy as Hungarian premier. At first the Russians showed restraint, allowing Nagy's return and pulling Soviet tanks out of Budapest. But while the CIA-funded Radio Free Europe broadcast militant calls to arms into Hungary, all Eisenhower could offer was the comment to a journalist after a campaign stop, "Poor fellows, poor fellows, I think about them all the time. I wish there were some way of helping them." After Nagy announced his intention to pull Hungary out of the Warsaw Pact, the Russians retook the country by force. Thirty thousand Hungarians were killed, 200,000 fled the country as refugees, and Nagy was executed by a Soviet firing squad in 1958.[8]

Administration officials later claimed that employing the threat of massive retaliation had not been a complete failure in moderating Soviet behavior. But interestingly, its advocates' claims of successes could not include Eastern Europe, where the sharpest calls for a rollback of communist control had been directed. The Soviets' possession of nuclear weapons apparently made them less vulnerable to the direct threat of American nuclear attack. Where the use of massive retaliation rhetoric may have made some difference in communist activity was in Asia; the threats there, however, were not directed against the Soviets themselves but against the Chinese. Communist China lacked its own nuclear deterrent, and while they retained a clear memory of the American willingness to use the A-bomb against Japan, Chinese leaders apparently were skeptical of the Soviets' willingness to use their nuclear arsenal in China's defense.

On the occasions when American hints of nuclear retaliation failed to bring sufficient Soviet assurances of aid to the Chinese, the massive retaliation bluff apparently did make Chinese policy more amenable to U.S. diplomatic pressure. Following months of stalemated negotiations in Korea over the issue of prisoner repatriation, Secretary Dulles in the spring of 1953 issued threats through diplomatic channels of possible American air strikes against China, including the use of nuclear bombs. Dulles's warnings, followed by the actual transfer of atomic warheads to forward bases in Okinawa, led to rapid Chinese acceptance of the American prisoner exchange proposal. The death of Soviet leader Stalin in March apparently had contributed to the Chinese conclusion that Russian weaponry to counter the American threat could not be relied upon. Following attempts by South Korean president Syngman Rhee to sabotage the agreement by unilaterally releasing North Korean and Chinese prisoners held in the South, Eisenhower alternated between threatening an American pullout and promising massive U.S. military aid to Rhee if he complied. Through this use of a carrot-and-stick ploy, Eisenhower achieved his objective of a Korean armistice on 26 July 1953.[9]

At other times, however, the American employment of nuclear brinksmanship in Asia either failed to produce major concessions or triggered militant counterthreats that increased the dangers of tragic superpower miscalculation over relatively minor issues. In the spring of 1954, only a year after the apparent success of the American strategy of bluff in Korea, Eisenhower found himself faced with another Asian crisis, this time in Indochina. America's ally France was in danger of losing its control of the region to Vietnamese nationalist communist guerrillas, led by Ho Chi Minh, despite millions of dollars in American aid. Fearing the fall of Asian dominoes all the way to Thailand and Burma, the president sought a way to relieve pressure on the besieged French military garrison at Dien Bien Phu. Operation Vulture, drawn up by Joint Chiefs of Staff chairman Adm. Arthur Radford, called for the use of 60 B-29 bombers and 150 carrier-based fighters, equipped to carry tactical nuclear weapons against the Viet Minh.[10]

Eisenhower refused to authorize the air strikes, however, without the cooperation of the Western Allies and the consent of Congress. The United States would not go it alone, for he wished to avoid the international perception of American actions as a "brutal example of imperialism." Not even the French themselves, however, were willing to give the go-ahead. Instead, they and the British favored pursuing a negotiated settlement at an international conference in Geneva. In late May 1954 Eisenhower upped the military stakes further by authorizing the preparation of nuclear strikes against China itself if it intervened directly in the Indochina war. Shortly afterward, the Russians and Chinese secretly pressured Ho into accepting a temporary division of Vietnam along the seventeenth parallel. With the promise of national elections by 1956 to determine the future of the country, and with his side likely to win such elections, Ho reluctantly accepted the deal at Geneva. Fighting temporarily ceased in mid-July 1954.[11]

Eisenhower's larger objective of a noncommunist Vietnam had not been achieved by the threat of massive response, and its use had caused new fractures within the Western alliance. After Geneva, the U.S. government found itself rather than France the chief Western power in the region. The administration ignored the Geneva-approved ban on new forces and equipment and funneled aid to a new anticommunist nationalist politician in the South, Ngo Dinh Diem. Also ignoring the requirement of nationwide elections within two years, the United States proceeded to build up a separate South Vietnam as its ally and refused to cooperate in national reunification talks. In order to provide the sanction of multilateral support for American objectives, the Eisenhower administration created a new alliance system, the Southeast Asia Treaty Organization (SEATO), which included the United States, Great Britian, France, Australia, New Zealand, Thailand, the Philippines, and Pakistan. But the real burden of maintaining an anticommunist Indochina had been assumed by America, with disastrous consequences in the years ahead.[12]

The Vietnam disaster of 1954, as even Eisenhower's own NSC report described it, clearly revealed that the president's concept of alliance partnership was one that ratified, sanctioned, and even implemented American strategic objectives. In contrast, when the tables were turned, and Western European nations sought U.S. cooperation in pursuing their individual agendas two years later in the Middle East, Eisenhower refused to oblige. After Egypt seized the Suez Canal, owned previously by British stockholders, in late July 1956, Britain and France made joint plans to retake the canal by force and overthrow Egyptian strongman Gamal Abdul Nasser. The French were as eager as the British to topple Nasser, for they blamed his version of Arab nationalism for the rising unrest in their North Africa possessions. Eisenhower, however, not only did not participate in the Allied scheme to retake Suez but condemned the British, French, and Israeli assault in the Sinai on 29 October. Dashing the hopes of the Allies that the United States would accept the occupation as a fait accompli, the president turned to the United Nations as his forum for demanding a complete Western and Israeli withdrawal.[13]

Eisenhower took his action in the Suez crisis on the ground that the imperialistic actions of the British and French had alienated world opinion and served as a pretext for Russian penetration of the region and for new threats to American oil interests. His unilateral policy on Suez won immediate and overwhelming approval in the Third World, and it thrust the United States into the new position of Middle Eastern power broker. At the same time, however, his moves increased the likelihood that if in the future America decided to intervene in the region to protect its own interests, it would have to do so alone. In an attempt to fill "the existing vacuum in the Middle East . . . before it is filled by Russia," the president issued the Eisenhower Doctrine, a unilateral commitment of economic aid, military assistance, and even direct American troop intervention on behalf of friendly Arab states, in the spring of 1957. The doctrine received a lukewarm response from the Arabs themselves, and it did not prevent an attempt by pro-Nasser army officers to overthrow Jordan's King Hussein in April 1957, a successful coup by radical officers in Syria later in the year, and the assassination of Iraq's King Faisal on 14 July 1958. It did provide the justification, at the request of Lebanese Christian president Camille Chamoun, for a Marine incursion onto the shores of Beirut the day after the Iraqi coup to counter an anticipated revolution by Moslem opponents and an attempt at a communist takeover that did not materialize. In the end, the Lebanon expedition displayed the flexing of American military might in the region, but very little else.[14]

The continuing danger that America's use of brinksmanship could lead to an irreversible big-power showdown and a nuclear exchange was dramatically underscored during yet another series of crises in the Far East. This time the confrontation pitted Chaing Kai-Shek's Nationalist Chinese, exiled on the island of Formosa, against the mainland Communists. The focus of the dispute was each side's claim to a series of offshore islands, particularly Quemoy and Matsu. Chiang's forces held the islands, as potential stepping-stones to the mainland, with seventy-five thousand Nationalist troops, while Mao Tse-tung's government claimed them as its rightful property. The first Quemoy crisis had erupted in September 1954, when Communist shelling of the island had killed two American soldiers. Eisenhower had rejected a JCS recommendation to bomb the Chinese mainland, but he had given Chiang an agreement promising U.S. protection of Formosa and "such other territories as may be determined by mutual agreement" in exchange for his agreement to a cease-fire. After a brief cooling-off period, however, Communist shelling had resumed against the Nationalist-held Tachen Islands two hundred miles north of Formosa. In response, Eisenhower strengthened his guarantee with Chiang to include defense of Quemoy and Matsu if he agreed to evacuate the Tachens. In early March 1955, Secretary Dulles coupled Eisenhower's communications to Chiang with vague threats of atomic reprisal against the mainland if the Communists persisted in their aggression in the Taiwan Straits.[15]

The result of Eisenhower's parallel guarantees and threats in the region was a war scare in Washington and Peking, and the initiation of direct discussions between the United States and Communist China in Geneva in August. The shelling of the Nationalist-held islands again stopped temporarily, but the basic issue of the islands' ownership remained unresolved. Not surprisingly, in August 1958, the crisis exploded again, following additional troop buildups on Quemoy by Chiang. In response the Communists attempted, this time through both shelling and a naval blockade, to cut off Nationalist supplies to the island. Again the Eisenhower administration employed the tacit threat of massive response and positioned the Seventh Fleet for a possible attack on the Communist blockade. In the background briefing to reporters, Dulles let it be known that the United States now considered an attack on Quemoy or Matsu as an attack on Formosa itself, which would require a full American military response.[16]

This time, however, official administration statements did not bring forward a Communist withdrawal but instead counterthreats from the Soviet Union. On 7 September 1958, Nikita Khrushchev bluntly warned Eisenhower that "an attack on the Chinese People's Republic is an attack on the Soviet Union." Both sides, staring down the precipice of nuclear war, proceeded to back away from a showdown. Negotiations resumed between the Communist Chinese and the Americans, and although the administration stood by its defense commitment to Chiang, it noticeably cooled its rhetoric. The Communists, in turn, effectively ended their blockade's utility by announcing to the world their intention to scale back shelling of Quemoy to a token, every-other-day schedule. Bemused at this unusual approach to defusing a crisis, Eisenhower remarked, "I wondered if we were in a Gilbert and Sullivan war." Observers were left to speculate on the consequences, however, had both sides stood fast rather than compromised. Privately Eisenhower sought to reassure nervous Allies that he had not intended to use "even tactical atomic weapons in a limited operation." But was even such a use of nuclear bluff wise or necessary in resolving the fate of several offshore islands in the Taiwan Straits?[17]

In the long run, what controversies like that over Quemoy and Matsu demonstrated was that in a world on which two opposing superpowers possessed nuclear arsenals, talking out differences and seeking a basis of accommodation made more sense than games of nuclear blackmail. Despite his skill at the nuclear chess game, Eisenhower himself regularly acknowledged the need for improved relations with the Soviets, as long as such conciliation did not compromise American objectives. But an atmosphere colored by brinksmanship and cold war rhetoric made superpower agreement on nuclear arms control and other outstanding issues virtually impossible.

Eisenhower's initial attempt to establish a dialogue with the Russians had come only two months into his presidency and was triggered by the death of Joseph Stalin. The new Soviet leadership, headed by Georgi Malenkov, had indicated possible receptivity to peaceful overtures from the United States. On 16 April 1953, Eisenhower delivered a speech, over his secretary of state's objections, on U.S.-Soviet relations to the American Society of Newspaper Editors. Written by Emmet John Hughes, the speech conveyed a conciliatory tone and underscored the human cost of the cold war to both sides. However, it asked the Russians to give up many of their postwar gains in exchange for American good will. Although he declared that "every gun that is made, every warship launched, every rocket fired signifies, in the final scene, a theft from those who hunger and are not fed, those who are cold and are not clothed," Eisenhower still insisted on an Austrian peace treaty, a Korean armistice, free elections for German unification, and self-determination for Eastern Europe as preconditions for better relations. The Soviets accordingly received the speech coolly. Eisenhower moreover did not follow up on calls from Winston Churchill for a 1953 summit conference with the Russians.[18]

Pressure for summitry with the Russians had continued to build, however, as both sides perfected steadily more destructive thermonuclear weapons. Wanting to reassure world opinion of America's peaceful intentions, Eisenhower ordered C. D. Jackson, his White House expert on psychological warfare, to prepare a speech outlining plans for the peaceful sharing of atomic energy. Before the UN General Assembly on 8 December, he delivered the "atoms for peace" address. In it he proposed that nations possessing fissionable material make joint contributions to an international atomic energy agency, which would use them for medical, agricultural, and electric power needs around the globe. Cynics dubbed the speech a public relations gimmick, but in 1957 the UN did create the International Atomic Energy Agency to oversee the peaceful global use of nuclear power. Unfortunately, inadequate safeguards resulted in the proliferation of nuclear materials for weapons as well as for peaceful causes.[19]

Fears of superpower nuclear confrontation refused to fade as a result of the atoms for peace initiative. The Soviets already had detonated a hydrogen warhead in August 1953, and the following March in the United States followed with the testing of its first deliverable H-bomb on Bikini atoll in the Pacific Ocean. The danger of radioactive fallout from such testing was highlighted when a group of Japanese fishermen near the blast site contracted radiation sickness. Combined with the continued massing of NATO and Warsaw Pact forces in Europe, these fears made both nations willing by the spring of 1955 to consider anew the idea of a summit conference. Russian signals of receptivity to an Austrian peace treaty were followed by a Soviet speech in the UN proposing the abolition of nuclear weapons, reduction in conventional forces, and even permission for some inspection provisions, long a stumbling block to Russian acceptance of arms control. The two countries arranged a summit in Geneva for mid-July, and although Dulles was unenthusiastic, Eisenhower told the nation that it was his intention to "change the spirit that has characterized the intergovernmental relationships of the world during the past ten years."[20]

Eisenhower presented a bold gambit to break the ice at Geneva—a proposal for mutual aerial inspection called Open Skies. The United States was willing, he indicated, to exchange military blueprints of its armed forces and to permit frequent aerial inspections of its territory if the Soviets would do likewise. In reality, Open Skies was a brilliant propaganda stratagem, devised mainly by C. D. Jackson's successor, Nelson Rockefeller, and Mutual Security Administrator Harold Stassen. Since the Russians already knew the location of most American strategic defense facilities, mutual overflights would yield the United States far more information than their adversaries. Evidence that the Ameican negotiation team at Geneva was less than totally sincere in proposing Open Skies was later provided by Eisenhower himself. "We knew the Soviets wouldn't accept it," he confessed to an interviewer in 1965. "We were sure of that." The long-standing Russian skepticism of Western proposals, especially surprise ones, prevailed, and the expected rejection of Open Skies soon followed.[21]

With the Geneva summit of 1955 failing to produce results, the world once again plunged into the depths of cold war. The Russians' brutal invasion of Hungary in 1956 and the Suez crisis strained official nerves in both Washington and Moscow. On 4 October 1957, the Soviet launching of the Sputnik satellite induced panic anew in America and sidetracked negotiations on a nuclear testing moratorium. Democratic critics in the Senate who a year earlier had claimed a "bomber gap" with the Russians now claimed a "missile gap" as well.

Adding to the alarm were the recommendations contained in the Gaither Report, issued in November by the Security Resources Panel of the Office of Defense Mobilization Science Advisory Committee. The panel, chaired by Ford Foundation head H. Rowan Gaither, recommended reorganizing the Defense Department, dispersing the Strategic Air Command's North American bases and keeping more bombers on in-flight alert, placing intercontinental ballistic missiles in hardened silos, building an elaborate national fallout shelter system, and rapidly expanding American conventional forces. Although he rejected the last two costly items in the Gaither Report, Eisenhower did attempt to reassure the public of the adequacy of America's missile research by posing with a nose cone retrieved from an Atlantic missile test and by naming James R. Killian, the president of the Massachusetts Institute of Technology, as his new special assistant for science and technology. But his substantive attempts to shore up NATO's nuclear defenses were stymied by the reluctance of many European allies to accept new Jupiter and Thor intermediate-range missiles on their territory. Only the British, the Italians, and the Turks immediately accepted the new weapons when they became operational in 1958.[22]

Following a highly publicized Senate Armed Services subcommittee investigation of the U.S. government's missile and rocketry programs, spearheaded by Lyndon Johnson of Texas, and an embarrassing public failure of a Vanguard test rocket in December 1957, Eisenhower asked for additional money for missile research and testing. Congress gave him even more than he requested, helping to push the federal budget deficit during the recession of 1957–58 to a then whopping $12.5 billion. A principal spin-off of the "Sputnik syndrome" in America in 1958 was Eisenhower's request, under congressional pressure, for the separation of military and civilian missile programs and the creation of a new agency for civilian space research called the National Aeronautics and Space Administration (NASA). Within three months after his recommendation, on 29 July 1958, Eisenhower signed the bill into law. Intent on preserving the maximum "bang for the buck" while reasserting control over the budget, the president also tried to hold down military manpower costs by advocating the equipping of conventional forces with tactical nuclear-tipped weapons for prospective "limited wars" in Europe.[23]

Public fencing between the United States and the Russians on the nuclear testing issue resumed in early 1958, and both sides finally met again in Geneva in late October. Although no formal test ban was signed, after a two-month race of atomic testing both sides suspended tests indefinitely—a tacit agreement that lasted three years. Optimism generated by this informal agreement, however, failed to last long. In November, Soviet leader Khrushchev triggered a new Berlin crisis by announcing his intention to sign a separate peace treaty with East Germany. The action threatened to leave West Berlin territorially isolated within a formal partner of the Soviet Union, and it raised renewed concern over Western occupation and access rights to the city. Negotiations in Geneva again deadlocked, and tensions eased only after Eisenhower and Khrushchev agreed to confer at Camp David in the fall of 1959. Ironically, both the Camp David meeting and the Soviet leader's subsequent ten-day U.S. tour occurred because Undersecretary of State Robert Murphy misinterpreted the president's instructions to make any invitation conditional on further progress at Geneva. In addition, John Foster Dulles, who most likely would have worked to block the meeting, had died of cancer after a long battle with the disease the previous May.[24]

Despite the fact that initially he had not wanted the meeting, Eisenhower became a principal beneficiary of the "spirit of Camp David." Plans followed for a new and, it was hoped, more productive summit conference in Paris for May 1960. Lacking Dulles's militant presence and basking in the afterglow of Camp David, Eisenhower intended to demonstrate additional American patience in achieving a more lasting ban on nuclear tests. Hopes for a successful Paris meeting, however, shattered along with the wreckage of a downed U.S. spy plane in Soviet territory. High-altitude overflights of the Soviet Union by U-2 aircraft had begun back in 1956, and although the Russians had been aware by radar of their presence from the outset, their interceptors and surface-to-air missiles at the time had not been able to reach them. In spite of the information the missions provided, Eisenhower had worried for some time about the danger of losing a plane in Russia and about the public controversy such a discovery would arouse. Six months before the Paris summit he had suggested the overflights be halted, but because the CIA and the State and Defense departments had objected, he had reversed himself. Advisers sought to reassure him by insisting that plane and pilot would self-destruct in any emergency situation over Russia.[25]

Only fifteen days before the scheduled start of the Paris summit, Eisenhower learned that a U-2 flight piloted by Francis Gary Powers was overdue and presumed missing over Soviet territory. When the Russians announced on 5 May they had downed an American spy plane, Eisenhower, assuming Powers had been killed in the crash, authorized the State Department to affirm an earlier cover story that the plane was but a weather research craft that had lost its bearings. On 8 May a gloating Khrushchev revealed to the world that the Soviets had captured the pilot of the plane and the aircraft wreckage intact. In Washington, Eisenhower gloomily admitted, "We're going to take a beating on this." He was right. Following a State Department admission of the flight the next day and a presidential acknowledgement two days later, the Russians savored the propaganda triumph of catching American officials in an outright lie. The incident, coupled with Soviet demands for an apology and an end to U.S. overflights, dominated the Paris summit and doomed any hopes of agreements on a nuclear test ban or on a Berlin settlement.[26]

For the rest of his life Eisenhower found it difficult to admit to errors of judgement in the U-2 affair. Before the NSC he described the Powers mission as a "failure," but he became furious when an aide suggested that the embarrassment now required the United States to "regain" moral leadership in the cold war. In his later memoirs, Eisenhower did not even concede that he had been wrong in issuing "a premature and erroneous cover story." But the rhetorical sidestepping only partially cloaked his deep disappointment at an opportunity lost for serious negotiations with the Russians. To his science adviser George Kistiakowsky he lamented in July 1960 about "how he had concentrated his efforts for the last few years on ending the cold war, how he felt that he was making big progress, and how the stupid U-2 mess had ruined his efforts."[27]

Eisenhower's inability to lessen the high level of mistrust and militancy of the cold war doomed the chances for an early resolution of East-West issues or the early curbing of the nuclear arms race. Continued superpower confrontation, combined with the deemphasis on American unilateral use of conventional forces under the New Look, had one other major and unfortunate long-term consequence—the expanded use of covert action by the CIA in the Third World. In the absence of a meaningful U.S.-Soviet dialogue or a willingness of the superpowers to act in concert, either in showing restraint or in policing the globe, American policymakers, including Eisenhower, viewed revolutionary nationalism as the willing or unsuspecting ally of communism. Sometimes it was, but sometimes it was not, and the cold war assumptions of a bipolar world obscured Eisenhower's ability to tell the difference.

During the Eisenhower years, the U.S. government consistently found itself, whether for economic, political, or military reasons, fighting on the side of the status quo in the Third World and against an increasingly militant anti-Western and anticolonial nationalism. Committed to preventing any additional communist gains anywhere, the administration found the more conventional military methods of responding to localized wars and revolutionary upheavals limited by the New Look budgetary decisions and by the desire to avoid an unpopular troop intervention so soon after the Korean "police action." When combined with an unwillingness to scale down its cold war objectives, the administration found that such internal budgetary and manpower restraints led almost inevitably to the increased employment of the CIA. Agency projects required Eisenhower's overall verbal approval, and the earliest covert actions in the Third World during the Eisenhower administration were directed from the Oval Office.[28]

As early as 1953, Eisenhower first had ordered the CIA to organize and carry out a coup in the oil-rich nation of Iran. In 1951 Dr. Mohammed Mossadeq, an ardent nationalist, had become prime minister of the country and had nationalized Western oil holdings. Firms not directly affected in Britain and the United States nonetheless had responded by cooperating in an international boycott of Iranian oil. In May 1953 Mossadeq had paired an appeal for Eisenhower's help to break the boycott and for military aid with a veiled threat to seek Soviet assistance if the United States refused. Seeing Mossadeq's continued presence as head of government as an invitation to Soviet penetration, Eisenhower approved a plot to overthrow him, which was organized by the grandson of Theodore Roosevelt, Kermit. In what an operative later described as a "real James Bond operation," the CIA encouraged Iranian general Fazlollah Zahedi to seize the prime minister's office and prepare the way for the return of the previously deposed shah to power. The oil negotiations that followed, conducted by Herbert Hoover, Jr., ended in a new arrangement that brought American companies into the Iranian consortium and expanded American influence in the country. The resentment of militant religious and nationalist groups in the country would not disappear, however, but would resurface in more virulent form a quarter of a century later under the leadership of the Ayatollah Khomeini.[29]

The Iranian affair provided a warm-up for a second CIA covert operation in the Third World, this time in the Central American nation of Guatemala. As in Iran, economic incentive meshed neatly with the administration's determination to prevent communist penetration of the region. A leftist regime headed by President Jacobo Arbenz Guzman had initiated a land reform program in the country that expropriated some 234,000 uncultivated acres owned by the U.S.-based United Fruit Company. Despite the need for land reform in Guatemala, where 2 percent of the population owned 70 percent of the land, American officials saw in the redistribution program the first steps toward a complete Marxist takeover. Official perceptions of danger no doubt were sharpened by the facts that CIA Director Allen Dulles had served on United Fruit's board of directors and that Eisenhower's White House personal secretary, Ann Whitman, was married to United Fruit's vice-president for public relations.[30]

At the tenth conference of the Organization of American States in March 1954, Secretary of State Dulles obtained regional authorization to "take measures to eradicate and prevent subversive activities." The CIA immediately began training a band of Guatemalan mercenaries in Honduras and an offshore Nicaraguan island for an insurrection against Arbenz, to be led by Col. Carlos Castillo Armas of the Guatemalan army. When the Arbenz government, after being rebuffed by the West, purchased quantities of small arms from Czechoslovakia, the CIA stepped up its airborne drops of supplies to rebels inside the country. On 18 June 1954, Castillo Armas crossed the border from Honduras and marched his band of followers toward Guatemala City. U.S. representatives at the UN blocked international intervention, and CIA pilots in World War II–era planes bombed the capital city. Arbenz fled the country for Eastern Europe, and Castillo Armas formed a military junta to rule the country. American aid to Guatemala immediately shot up from $600,000 a year to $45 million, and a grateful junta restored United Fruit's lands and removed taxes on foreign investors' dividends. Despite Castillo Armas's own assassination three years later, the country remained in pro-American hands. But one of those in the capital at the time of the CIA bombing carried the memory, and an intense hatred of the United States, with him in the years ahead—an Argentinian Marxist revolutionary named Ernesto "Che" Guevara.[31]

The continuing threat of revolutionary, anti-Western insurgency in the Middle East and Latin America did have the effect of encouraging Eisenhower to modify his traditional resistance to foreign aid programs. In his new view, the effective use of American trade and government aid packages to the Third World could contribute to more stable economic and political relations and to a reduced need for covert operations. When he first had entered the White House in 1953, he had preferred to leave all assistance to underdeveloped countries up to the decisions of private investors. But early in his second term, in the spring of 1957, Eisenhower made a concerted effort to increase the amount of soft, long-term government loans to both pro-American and neutral nations. Even his proposal was modest by later standards, calling for a Development Loan Fund of $2 billion spread over three years and direct-aid packages and military assistance programs that would bring the overall total to $4 billion. But despite his lobbying of Congress, particularly of members of his own party with long-standing aversions to foreign aid, the legislators cut his request by nearly one-third and even more drastically scaled back aid to neutral nations in the Third World.[32]

Given Eisenhower's unwillingness to modify American global objectives, his failure to secure the effective use of foreign aid as a weapon against Third World subversion meant the continuing reliance on the CIA's covert activities. In Eisenhower's last years as president, a more formalized structure for authorizing CIA actions was instituted that better preserved his official "ignorance" of their activities. The CIA's counterrevolutionary activities continued at the very time that Eisenhower sought new ways to break the U.S.-Soviet impasse on nuclear arms and Berlin. In Southeast Asia, operatives commanded by Col. Edward G. Lansdale conducted illegal sabotage raids into North Vietnam. In Indonesia, the CIA airlifted supplies to rebels in an abortive attempt to overthrow President Achmed Sukarno in early

1958. Responding to Chinese pressure against neighboring Tibet, the agency established a secret training base for Tibetan guerrillas in the Colorado Rockies and organized a covert action to rescue the Dalai Lama in 1959. In the spring of 1960, Eisenhower himself authorized the secret training and equipping of Cuban exiles in Guatemala following the island's takeover by Fidel Castro and his followers. Training bases in Guatemala became staging points for the later, ill-fated Bay of Pigs invasion in the early months of the Kennedy administration. And in sub-Saharan Africa, a CIA-backed revolt against the leftist premier of the newly created Republic of the Congo, Patrice Lumumba, resulted in the seizure of power by Congolese chief of staff Joseph Mobutu and Lumumba's assassination. Although no direct evidence tied Eisenhower to the order to kill the premier, the president had previously indicated to aides that he wanted Lumumba somehow removed from the scene. The lid of secrecy was preserved on most of the CIA's activities during the administration's own lifetime, but its "unleashing" of the agency set the stage for the future embarrassments of the Bay of Pigs, assassination plots against Castro, and the Chilean "destabilization."[33]

By the end of the Eisenhower presidency, a decided gap had formed between the short-term successes of his foreign policy and its longer term drawbacks. Through the New Look, Eisenhower had exerted a successful temporary restraint upon the fiscal hunger of the "military-industrial complex." His unwillingness to undertake open unilateral military intervention in Vietnam in 1954 had postponed, at least, the commitment of American ground forces to the South. His strategy of nuclear bluff apparently had hastened the resolution of the Korean War, and his willingness to show restraint in the employment of force had prevented the triggering of atomic war over Quemoy and Matsu. Although lacking a formal agreement, he nonetheless had secured an informal pause in the atmospheric testing of nuclear weapons. But he had not rolled back communism where it already existed, and the rhetoric of liberation had not offered him any more clout to do so than had the doctrine of containment for Truman. No mutual basis for long-term coexistence between the United States and the Soviet Union had been found, and in its absence the race to develop superior intercontinental ballistic missiles continued and threatened to accelerate. In the Third World, perceived threats to American economic security and to global stability had been met through covert action, but at the cost of casting America as the new defender of Western colonial imperialism and political repression. A strange new world of emerging nations and complex economic and political arrangements was surfacing to challenge the old verities of a bipolar worldview. But recognition of the new realities, and the new limits they imposed on American power, would have to await subsequent presidents and their own foreign policy teams.

10

MANAGING THE AMERICAN COMMONWEALTH

Eisenhower's commitment to a democratic capitalist world safe from communist penetration was matched by a determination to restore America as a self-disciplined, cooperative society marked by enlightened corporate leadership, government-business partnership, and limited state power. Drawing upon his notions of the ideal family, which shared burdens and responsibilities for the common good, and the ideal army, driven more by self-discipline and common purpose than by coercion to serve the nation, Eisenhower disdained government "paternalism" and the factional clamor of "special interests." The conflicts and passions produced by individual or group shortsightedness could be resolved, he believed, but only through the leadership of national managers with a firm focus on the long view rather than on immediate gain. Societal discipline would be required, but such restraint would have to be the self-discipline of free individuals rather than the compulsion of a coercive statism. As he observed to Gen. Alfred M. Gruenther in 1953, "To induce people to do more, leadership has the chore of informing people and inspiring them to real sacrifice."[1]

The economic advances of postwar America, however, had made the task of encouraging personal sacrifice in the pursuit of long-term goals more difficult. After the breadlines of the Great Depression, the rationing of World War II, and the inflation of the early Truman years, Americans had had their fill of sacrifice and demanded the good life now. Eisenhower himself was hardly immune to the desire for material comfort, for he was an inveterate consumer who insisted on never wearing the same custom-fitted suits more than twice before discarding them. In addition, in his own philosophy of political economy it was "greed," or as Eisenhower preferred to call it, "dissatisfaction with the inadequate" that fueled the private sector to produce the new goods and services that raised living standards and, in his words, converted housework into "pleasure rather than drudgery." Because of the need to reconcile individual gain and collective sacrifice, he placed special emphasis on the need to promote "national morale." For as he had written years earlier in the military context, "Morale is born of loyalty, patriotism, discipline, and efficiency, all of which breed confidence in self and comrades. Most of all morale is promoted by unity—unity in service to the country and in the determination to attain the objective of national security." He had concluded, "Morale is at one and the same time the strongest, and the most delicate of growths. It withstands schocks [sic], even disasters of the battlefield, but can be destroyed utterly by favoritism, neglect, or injustice."[2]

Because boosting national morale for common purposes was so essential to Eisenhower's building of the cooperative national commonwealth, he paid particular attention to his public style and tactics of presidential leadership. He constantly emphasized his formal duties as chief of state instead of his role as partisan leader, despite whatever partisan strategies he might plan in private. His leadership was marked by public restraint, an absence of name-calling, and regular appeals for moderation and conciliation. He honored in textbook fashion the separation of powers doctrine, and he alternately charmed the Republican Old Guard and sought compromise with the Democrats in order to build a domestic political consensus. Often he had more luck with the Democrats than with his own party, for in his first year alone they provided winning margins for administration bills on fifty eight separate occasions. Although in private he despised the passionate demagoguery and partisan maneuverings of congressional rivals such as Joseph McCarthy and Lyndon Johnson, he kept his disgust to himself for the sake of his policies and his personal standing with the public. His ability to rein in his fury at Washington politicians was not always appreciated by his staff, who then had to face the full violence of the private "Eisenhower temper."[3]

Eisenhower's public self-control was a major part of a larger theme of his presidency—his preoccupation with, and skill at, public relations. He had risen to prominence in an era when the power and importance of public relations, electronic communication, and image management was just being fully discovered. During World War II, for example, General Marshall had been the first chief of staff to establish a formal public relations section within the War Department. If Eisenhower intended to sell the public on the need for national cooperation without resorting to statist coercion, he had to master the arts of public persuasion. Public relations techniques could encourage restraint among competing interests, could defuse divisive social issues that threatened national unity and morale, and could legitimize his vision of the efficiently managed voluntarist society. In 1953 he noted that his administration's task was "not unlike the advertising and sales activity of a great industrial organization." And besides having a policy "product" worth selling, he required "an effective and persuasive way of informing the public of the excellence of the product." In pursuit of that aim, he created a standing White House committee on public relations. He monitored the informational activities of the Republican party, directed special "sales" campaigns on various administration policies, and enlisted the support of public relations groups such as the Advertising Council to promote his program.[4]

Eisenhower was his administration's and his own best salesman. Often, however, his own popularity exceeded that of the program he sold. He was the first to employ effectively the new medium of television, marketing himself and his policies through campaign advertisements and formal presidential addresses to the nation. He pioneered the use, on a selective edited basis, of excerpts from presidential news conferences on television news programs. In the words of C. D. Jackson, himself a former executive of Time-Life publications, "We will merchandise the hell out of the Eisenhower program." Eisenhower was careful while doing so, however, to control his direct access to the public from the intrusions of reporters and other middlemen. Early television policies aided him in bypassing hostile commentators and in delivering his own message directly to the audiences at home. In a similar fashion, he maintained reasonably good treatment from the print media by disdaining, with a few select exceptions, extensive contacts with Washington reporters in favor of a wide correspondence with their editors and publishers. These behind-the-scenes brokers of the information establishment often were invited to the president's famous after-hours stag dinners at the White House.[5]

Because Eisenhower controlled access so skillfully, what the public saw of their president was a great national father figure or, for the younger generation of Americans, a genial grandfather. Although advisers worried that the president's oft-recorded vacations playing golf or fishing might suggest that he was a figurehead leader, he recognized that the sight of a president with time for relaxation tended to reassure a nervous cold war nation. In any case, his hatred of desk duty and his various health problems dictated frequent sabbaticals from the White House to Camp David and other retreats. Americans truly "liked Ike," and a major part of the reason was that he presented them with little cause not to. Even his illnesses (a heart attack in 1955, an intestinal operation for ileitis in 1956, and a stroke in late 1957), followed as they were by public reassurances of his rapid recovery, became less sources of national trepidation than occasions to close ranks behind the fallen but recuperating leader. Even his mangled syntax at press conferences, induced by his desire to maintain secrecy over administration policy deliberations, did not harm him but further cemented his popular image of the common man as leader.[6]

Eisenhower's management of the executive branch displayed a public collegiality and a respect for traditional policymaking institutions that concealed a more secretive informal side. Because of his lesser experience in domestic policy matters, he delegated much of their day-to-day management to his cabinet heads. He maintained overall control of broad policy objectives, however, and he made the key decisions when domestic crises arose that threatened national harmony and his political popularity. Despite the emphasis he placed publicly on scrapping Rooseveltian informality in executive management with a restored cabinet authority, the meetings of Eisenhower's cabinet were less often policy-initiating sessions than administration pep rallies. The president used the meetings to ensure internal harmony in the administration, to prevent policy surprises, and to serve as a personal "bully pulpit" for exhortations on national teamwork. Only a select number of cabinet officers and White House aides, such as Treasury Secretary George Humphrey and Press Secretary James Hagerty, enjoyed regular personal access to the president, and it was in such private sessions that much of the real business of policymaking was done. Chief of Staff Sherman Adams regulated personnel access to Eisenhower, but although Washington reporters misinterpreted his role as that of an assistant president, he actually served as a gatekeeper without a major policy voice. The supreme irony of Eisenhower's executive leadership style was that despite his well-publicized dread of statist dictatorship, he ran his administration with a firm, if hidden, hand, which even included a concealed taping system in the Oval Office.[7]

The president selected members of his cabinet largely on the basis that their experience as corporate executives had prepared them for the task of managing executive departments and, through them, the welter of interests that made up the country. In drawing primarily upon the corporate boardrooms for managerial talent, however, he also underscored his own class, racial, and sexual biases. Despite the managerial skills of such men, it remained an open question whether they could mediate honestly the interests of other groups such as organized labor, minorities, women, conservationists, the poor, and the elderly. Columnists lampooned the original Eisenhower cabinet as "eight millionaires and a plumber." Within a year the plumber, Labor Secretary Martin Durkin, had been replaced. Eisenhower's entire emphasis on making America a consensual society run by professional managers displayed both an acquired elitism and a distrust of the messiness of popular democracy at its most passionate and vigorous. He viewed Congress privately as an "occupational hazard" rather than as the people's representative. Fearing radical change from an irrational public will, he warned, "We can't let just a popular majority sweep us in one direction, because then you can't recover." He viewed the New Deal and Fair Deal as just such sweeping, shortsighted change, and in his first weeks as president he praised the Supreme Court as an institution that provided the "needed stability in a form of government where political expediency might at times carry parties and political leaders to extremes." Within months, the civil liberties and civil rights decisions of the Court under his own appointee, Earl Warren, would alter even that positive assessment.[8]

Eisenhower's hidden-hand style of presidential leadership, which sought a least-common-denominator version of public consensus and employed the concealed methods of bureaucratic politics to manage rather than confront controversial issues, was itself inherently conservative in its objectives. His initial test in building his conservative domestic consensus was provided by the anticommunist hysterics of Sen. Joseph McCarthy. Could internal security and hardheaded American vigilance against the communist threat be maintained, he asked, without the excesses, without the cost to innocent reputations and individual freedoms? His previous unwillingness to confront McCarthy during the 1952 campaign had not boded well for his capacity for decisive and fair leadership on the issue. He also had a number of reasons, some laudable, others less so, for wanting to avoid a showdown with the junior senator from Wisconsin. The reason he most often gave privately, expressed in a letter to Swede Hazlett, was that openly challenging McCarthy would only publicize him more and further polarize the country. "Whenever the President takes part in a newspaper trial of some individual of whom he disapproves," he wrote, "one thing is automatically accomplished. This is an increase in the headline value of the individual attacked." The less attractive reasons for his passivity included his hope that as a Republican president, his presence alone would remove the partisan motivation from McCarthy's attacks, and his awareness of the senator's support among conservative Republican congressmen whose cooperation he needed.[9]

For months Eisenhower chose to address the issue by appeasing McCarthy in various ways. He publicly cast himself as equally vigilant in matters of internal security, despite the risks that doing so posed to civil liberties and despite the danger that McCarthy's wild charges would gain even greater public credence. He supported legislation to remove the citizenship of those convicted of conspiring the violent overthrow of the government, to force witnesses to give up Fifth Amendment protections and testify in national security investigations, to legalize wiretap information in such cases, and to broaden espionage and sabotage laws. He created a new federal internal security review program, replacing the Truman one, which broadened employee requirements beyond loyalty to "suitability." Under the new rules, federal workers could be dismissed for such characteristics unrelated to their political beliefs as drinking, homosexuality, or even "blabbermouthing." He continued efforts to prosecute Communist party leaders under the Smith Act and approved the Federal Bureau of Investigation's COINTELPRO program to infiltrate and disrupt party activities. Aware of the FBI's "custodial detention" program, he approved plans for rounding up suspected subversives without charges in event of national emergency. He endorsed the decision to remove physicist J. Robert Oppenheimer's security clearance, despite admitting privately that little evidence existed to justify the action. And he declined to commute the death sentences of Julius and Ethel Rosenberg for espionage, not because he necessarily believed they had received a fair trial, but because "the exemplary feature of the punishment, the hope that it would deter others, is something that cannot be ignored.[10]

With his initial actions failing to defuse McCarthy, Eisenhower permitted the appointment of Scott McLeod, a McCarthy ally, as the State Department's chief of security and consular affairs. Within weeks the chaos caused by McLeod's accusations against career Foreign Service professionals brought department morale to a new low. Undeterred by Eisenhower's conciliatory deeds, McCarthy unsuccessfully tried to pressure the White House into withdrawing the nomination of Charles E. Bohlen (Roosevelt's interpreter at Yalta) as ambassador to Moscow, and he did succeed in forcing the dismissal of the State Department's remaining China hands. Two directors of the International Information Administration also resigned in protest after McCarthy attacked them for maintaining books by such "subversives" as mystery writer Dashiell Hammett in libraries abroad. After issuing a vague denunciation of book burners at Dartmough College in June 1953, Eisenhower immediately backed off from any specific criticism of the senator or his methods. When Press Secretary Hagerty announced that 1,456 employees had been dropped from the federal payroll, McCarthy seized upon the statement to claim that all those dismissed had been "security risks" and that many more remained in the government.[11]

Eisenhower did not even challenge McCarthy through covert means until the winter of 1953–54, nearly a year into his presidency, and only then after McCarthy's attacks had clearly shifted from Truman holdovers and career diplomats to Eisenhower's own appointees. Aware since the summer that McCarthy planned a headline-hunting investigation of the United States Army, only on 21 January 1954 did the president directly lend his private backing to army countercharges against the senator. During the subsequent army-McCarthy hearings, he attempted to discredit McCarthy by having Hagerty leak negative information and plant anti-McCarthy questions with the press corps. He also ordered Vice-President Nixon into the fray in order to challenge the Wisconsin senator for television coverage, but he refrained from a personal public denunciation of the senator. His most visible stand against McCarthy came in May 1954, when on grounds of executive privilege he refused to turn over notes of private strategy sessions between administration and army officials.[12]

The army-McCarthy hearings served their desired purpose of publicly humiliating the Wisconsin senator. But it was less the president's covert actions than army counsel Joseph Welch's televised plea— "Have you no sense of decency, sir, at long last?"—that finally brought McCarthy down. Once McCarthy's popularity had peaked and he found himself hounded by a growing legion of critics, Eisenhower helped hasten the destruction process by encouraging Republican senators such as Vermont's Ralph E. Flanders to push for a censure resolution. Eisenhower associate Paul Hoffman also aided the effort by organizing a private anti-McCarthy committee. In Hoffman's words, the events of 1954 did result in "replacing, in the public mind, the disuniting symbol of McCarthyism with the unifying image of the President as the effective instrument of anti-subversion." But it is worth considering if the excesses of McCarthyism might have been curbed sooner if Eisenhower had been willing to put his personal prestige and his own anticommunist credentials on the line by openly challenging McCarthy, instead of delaying a year and then only exercising hidden-hand leadership.[13]

In addition to his goal of substituting a more hardheaded vigilance at home for the emotionalism of McCarthyism, Eisenhower was intent on restraining federal regulation of, and competition with, the nation's private economy. He lowered tax burdens for industry and capital. He lifted Korean War wage and price controls and pursued policies intended to eliminate public forms of competition with the private sector. He carried out his campaign promise to turn over control of tideland undersea oil reserves to the states and private industry, and he pushed for the deregulation of natural gas. He reversed previous federal policy by withdrawing official obstacles to private hydroelectric power projects in Idaho and California, while placing obstacles in the path of any expansion of the Tennessee Valley Authority. And under Eisenhower, the federal government enacted legislation that marked the end of the public monopoly of nuclear energy development in the country.[14]

The actions of Eisenhower administration officials in the energy development field in relinquishing more responsibility to the private sector soon led to charges of conflict of interest. Following an administration-sponsored report that urged the private development of any future power needs in the Tennessee Valley, President Edgar Dixon of the Middle South Utilities Corporation and President Eugene Yates of the Southern Company formed a combine to seek governmental approval for a steam electrical generation plant at West Memphis, Arkansas. Under the terms of the proposal, the new plant would supply power both to the city of Memphis and to Atomic Energy Commission (AEC) facilities in the area. However, the author of the administration's report, Adolph Wenzell, turned out to be not only a government consultant but also a consultant to the firm underwriting the Dixon-Yates enterprise. After Memphis city officials announced plans for their own generating plant, Eisenhower in 1955 canceled the Dixon-Yates contract with the AEC. Advocates of public power development charged similar irregularities the same year in the federal licensing of a private dam and generating complex at Hell's Canyon to the Idaho Power Company. But despite their attempts to block the dam's authorization, after court appeals were exhausted the Snake River project went ahead.[15]

Eisenhower's opposition to the intrusions of the federal state in the energy field, and to statist "paternalism" generally, did not lead him to attempt the repeal of popular and broad-based government income support programs such as Social Security and the minimum wage. These programs, which filled gaps in the private economy and sustained national purchasing power in slow growth times, he conceded were a "floor that covers the pit of disaster." In any event, as he told brother Milton Eisenhower, "should any political party attempt to abolish Social Security, unemployment insurance, and eliminate labor laws and farm programs, you would not hear of that party again in our political history." Although he tried to hold down the rate of increase in individual benefits, Eisenhower actually endorsed the expansion of Social Security coverage in 1954 to an additional 7.5 million workers, or five-sixths of the nation's paid work force. This expansion of the "welfare state," however, was noteworthy for being exceptional in the

Eisenhower years. During his presidency, the volume of federal transfer payments, a handy gauge of the welfare state, remained unchanged as a percentage of the federal budget.[16]

The centerpiece of the Eisenhower domestic program was the promotion of new and stronger forms of government-business cooperation—an approach that hearkened back to the trade association concepts of Herbert Hoover in the 1920s. The president's cabinet itself was a prime example of a cooperative attitude toward business, but additionally Eisenhower appointed business representatives in huge numbers to government regulatory boards and commissions, and he expanded the number and role of industrial advisory committees. Existing groups such as the Business Advisory Council and the National Petroleum Council grew in power, while Commerce Secretary Sinclair Weeks created a Business and Services Administration, which presided over a network of defense and atomic energy advisory committees. Businessmen also were the most frequent invitees to Eisenhower's stag dinners, and his message to them rarely varied—to think and act in broad cooperative national terms rather than just in accordance with immediate profitability.[17]

Eisenhower's belief in shared stewardship with the private sector also influenced his macroeconomic policies. Like most business leaders in the 1950s, he feared the ravages of inflation far more than those of unemployment, and he accepted slow growth and periodic recessions as preferable alternatives to government spending increases and deliberate budget unbalancing. When his fiscal and monetary policies produced economic slowdowns, he encouraged the private sector to assume a greater self-responsibility for business revival. During the 1954 recession, he privately urged bankers to lower their interest rates and to loosen credit, and the following year he pressed for price restraint on the part of the major automobile manufacturers. He also was not above employing the services of business groups to promote the positive message of American abundance for his and their mutual benefit, for in both 1954 and 1958 he enlisted the Advertising Council in a campaign to promote "Confidence in Growing America."[18]

Although Eisenhower consistently maintained his belief in preserving the avenues of individual opportunity, he viewed the state as a far greater danger to personal opportunity than the corporation and saw no contradiction between his homilies to personal initiative and his acceptance, even promotion, of corporatism. His administration's view of bigness in business as both inevitable and good manifested itself in his antitrust policy, which opted for cooperative arrangements such as prefiling conferences, consent decrees, and premerger clearances over open confrontations in federal courts. When executives complained that even such mild tactics were intrusive and involved "petty" matters, the president ordered Attorney General Herbert Brownell to reassure them of the administration's supportive attitude. Even flagrant examples of what Eisenhower viewed as shortsighted business greed seldom brought more than private denunciations. When steel executives in 1955 announced price increases of seven dollars a ton, for example, he declared to his secretary that he was "pretty disgusted with businessmen and didn't know when he would get over it." But the disappointment did not last long, and he viewed an open airing of such critical opinions of the business community as counterproductive both to himself and to national harmony.[19]

In policy fields where Eisenhower secured the private cooperation he sought, the results were beneficial both to industry and to the administration. In addressing the national housing shortage, for example, he created a national advisory committee to study the problem and to issue legislative recommendations. The panel consisted almost exclusively of realtors, builders, bankers and proadministration politicians hostile to the competition of federal public housing. The administration-backed Housing Act of 1954 consequently did little to alleviate the housing shortage of low-income Americans, and federal policies consistently accelerated the displacement of poor and minority urban dwellers through slum clearance schemes that failed to replace destroyed dwellings with equal numbers of new units. In the atomic energy field, the proindustry Atomic Energy Act of 1954 authorized the licensing of private power companies to produce and market nuclear power while explicitly prohibiting the Atomic Energy Commission from doing likewise. As a result, the development of nuclear power fell to the decisions of large private utilities, with significant long-range consequences for consumer rate structures, plant locations, and safety and health regulation.[20]

Perhaps the most far-reaching example of Eisenhower's concept of public-private partnership, however, came in the field of national transportation policy. For over three decades, presidents had attempted to launch a joint U.S.-Canadian project converting the St. Lawrence River into an inland waterway connecting the Great Lakes with the Atlantic Ocean. With American iron ore supplies running out in the Great Lakes region by the early 1950s, the project had gained new urgency. After soliciting the advice of the major interested parties, Eisenhower endorsed the creation of the St. Lawrence Seaway Development Corporation in 1954 to build the deep-water navigation channel. Overcoming the long-standing objections of American mining and railroad interests, Eisenhower saw the project completed in 1959, with part of the costs to taxpayers defrayed through users' fees. Underscoring the president's desire to decentralize government functions to the states and the private sector, he granted approval for the state of New York to develop electric power sites on the U.S. side of the seaway.[21]

Problems in the nation's overland transportation system presented an even greater opportunity for Eisenhower to apply his version of cooperative national stewardship. With America's railroads in financial straits and service cutbacks proliferating, and with the existing network of federal highways growing more and more inadequate to national needs, Eisenhower appointed an advisory committee, headed by longtime associate Lucius Clay, to develop policy recommendations for a sweeping increase in the federal highway system. Eisenhower intended to remove highway policy considerations from the separate group interests of truckers, auto clubs, state engineers, the auto industry, and oil companies; but nonetheless the committee's report reflected the viewpoints of the most powerful groups at the expense of other unorganized but affected parties. The subsequent Interstate Highway Act, which authorized construction of some 42,000 miles of controlled-access, four-to-eight-lane roads linking major cities, assisted enormously the movement of goods and people across the country, but it failed to anticipate the social problems posed by expressway construction, erosion of urban tax bases through suburban sprawl, disincentives to mass transit and energy conservation, and increases in automobile air pollution. Despite the imposition or increase of federal taxes on fuels, tires, and commercial vehicles to pay for the new roads, only 7,500 miles of interstate highways were open to traffic when Eisenhower left office, and costs had skyrocketed far beyond original estimates.[22]

Despite the long-term shortcomings of Eisenhower's approach to domestic problems, by the end of his first term, with the McCarthy threat defused and the nation enjoying both peace and prosperity, his triumphant reelection seemed reassured. Following the health scare generated by his heart attack in 1955, Eisenhower's announcement of his candidacy in February 1956 was met with open sighs of relief by Republican leaders, party rank and file, and a strong majority of the American public. Most Americans seemed basically satisfied with their country and their leader. In the words of administration spokesman Arthur Larson, Eisenhower had placed himself at the "authentic American center" as the symbol of the "American consensus." Within Republican party ranks, about the only source of disquiet in early 1956 stemmed from the president's unwillingness to publicly endorse his vice-president's renomination. The distance of the Eisenhower-Nixon relationship had led to renewed speculation about the Californian's place on the ticket, and the president's former Mutual Security administrator, Harold Stassen, went public with a "dump Nixon" effort. Privately Eisenhower believed that, despite the vice-president's service to the administration and the GOP, Nixon remained too rash and immature to possibly succeed to the nation's highest office and required additional executive seasoning, perhaps in a cabinet post. After months of ambiguous silence, however, GOP support for Nixon forced Eisenhower to reindorse the vice-president as his running mate shortly before the Republican convention in San Francisco.[23]

An attack of ileitis (a severe inflammation of the lower intestine) Eisenhower suffered in early June caused a temporary renewal of concern for his health and for GOP presidential prospects within Republican ranks, but upon his recovery the outcome of his rematch with Adlai Stevenson was never in serious doubt. Stevenson's efforts to make Eisenhower's age and health an issue in the campaign backfired, and no other issues raised by the Democrats dented the president's overall popularity, either. Nixon, for his part, cultivated a more restrained, moderate image in the campaign, which also reassured voters. Although farmers were upset at administration attempts to reduce government price supports, Stevenson could not capitalize upon the discontent. Foreign crises in Suez and Hungary late in the campaign only reinforced the popular desire to keep the trusted Ike at the tiller of the ship of state. Given his unique personal ability to appeal across class, regional, ethnic, and even party lines, his margin of 10 million popular votes over Stevenson on 6 November surprised no one. But, even more than in 1952, the triumph was limited to Eisenhower alone. Congress, which had been recaptured by the Democrats in the off-year elections of 1954, remained in their hands despite the president's own impressive reelection victory.[24]

The election results boded ill for Eisenhower's second term, for they suggested not the prospect of continued consensus building but instead heightened partisanship in preparation for 1960. Because of the Twenty-second Amendment, which prohibited a third term, the lame-duck president's bargaining leverage immediately was reduced. Already in policy fields in which a national consensus had been more difficult to forge, fragmenting interests were fighting for control. In farm policy, the administration's effort to reduce price supports, spearheaded by Agriculture Secretary Ezra Taft Benson, encountered stiff resistance from farmers and their organizational representatives in Washington. Having pledged to seek changes in the Taft-Hartley Act, Eisenhower now found himself caught between unions wanting the act weakened and businessmen urging even greater restrictions on union organizing and striking rights. Aided by bipartisan revelations of scandals and organized crime influence in several major unions, including the Teamsters, the president did manage to win a minor victory—passage of the Landrum-Griffin Act in 1959. The new law's antiunion provisions pleased corporate lobbyists, while the administration's accompanying restraint in invoking injunction powers against strikes helped to pacify labor.[25]

The biggest challenge to Eisenhower's consensus leadership, however, was the issue of civil rights. During the first term, he had tried to defuse the issue and win cold war propaganda points by implementing armed forces desegregation and integrating public facilites in the national capital. Intent on avoiding southern wrath, however, he had ordered the drafting of a noncommittal Justice Department brief in the *Brown* school segregation cases being argued before the Supreme Court in 1953. The Court had ruled in May 1954 that the state-sponsored segregation of public schools violated the Constitution, but privately the president had confessed to aides that while he believed in legal and economic equality of opportunity, he opposed "social mingling" or the notion "that a Negro should court my daughter." He maintained public silence on his opinion of the *Brown* verdict and at the same time urged private efforts at racial cooperation and the prevention of antiintegration violence. But it was less his public and private jawboning than the waiting of both sides for the Supreme Court's 1955 implementation ruling for the *Brown* case that had postponed more serious racial showdowns in the South during the administration's first two years.[26]

Hoping to relieve his administration from the need to intervene, while still offering southern blacks some form of self-protection, Eisenhower hesitantly supported civil rights legislation authored by the Justice Department in 1956. After much watering down by Congress, and waffling by the president on major portions, the bill, designed to strengthen black claims to voting rights, passed in mid-1957. But the action proved both too late and too weak to head off a showdown between the federal courts and the state of Arkansas over the integration of Little Rock's Central High School in September. Required by law to enforce a desegregation order he personally questioned, Eisenhower dispatched army paratroopers and National Guardsmen to the school to escort the black students and protect them from segregationist violence. A majority of Americans approved of his action, as well as his delay in taking it. But the controversy had torn at his image as a symbol of national unity and common purpose, particularly in the eyes of the white South.[27]

Following the Little Rock crisis, Eisenhower backed away almost completely from the continuing civil rights struggle in the South. Refusing public comment on the problem, he even declined to tell reporters whether he agreed with the intent of the initial *Brown* decision. Two years later, prodded by the U.S. Commission on Civil Rights his 1957 legislation had created, he sought and obtained additional voting rights legislation in 1960. But he could never bring himself to recognize that civil rights represented a cause on which delay, compromise, and accommodation with the racial segregationists was neither morally right nor politically possible in the long run. Instead, he privately maintained to aides that the *Brown* decision had been a mistake that had seriously set back the cause of racial desegregation. The objective of school integration, he insisted, would require at least thirty to forty years to complete even in the more moderate Upper South and border states.[28]

On the heels of the Little Rock crisis followed the Soviet Sputnik launch of October 1957, and with it an additional round of domestic political controversy over the adequacy of federal aid to education. Congressional Democrats attacked Eisenhower's opposition to direct grants to states and school districts, and they condemned his resistance to college student aid programs beyond minimal amounts to financially hard-pressed science and mathematics students. Eisenhower resisted the effort to increase federal education funding, citing budgetary reasons and the danger that new programs signaled a move toward the federal takeover of public education. After a year of wrangling on the issue with Congress, Eisenhower reluctantly signed the National Defense Education Act (NDEA) on 2 September 1958. The legislation offered long-term, low-interest loans to college students, retained federally financed graduate fellowships, and authorized grants to improve science, mathematics, and, to a lesser extent, foreign language instruction. Despite Eisenhower's fears of the financial cost of the program, NDEA actually made little impact on either the cost or the quality of American education, given its modest $1 billion price tag spread over seven years.[29]

As if his political agonies over civil rights and federal aid to education were not enough, in 1958 Eisenhower also witnessed the tainting of a member of the White House inner circle by charges of financial scandal. Chief of Staff Sherman Adams, accused of influence peddling in behalf of a New England textile manufacturer in exchange for personal gifts, bowed to congressional pressure and resigned in September. Not surprisingly, given Eisenhower's growing list of political headaches, in that fall's congressional elections the Democrats amassed majorities of 75 to 34 in the Senate and 282 to 154 in the House of Representatives. During the next two years, Eisenhower struggled successfully to rebuild his own high standing with the American public. But his fragile political consensus had irreparably fragmented beneath the weight of recession, escalating popular expectations, and renewed special interest demands. By 1960 the nation was headed into yet another recession, this time more severe than previous ones, and Eisenhower found it doubly difficult to hold back the budgetary demands of domestic interests and the armed services in the name of fiscal restraint. Class, race, and youth tensions, never that far from the surface during the best of Eisenhower's days in the White House, now demanded hearing and response anew.[30]

It was the ultimate irony of the Eisenhower presidency that his own policies had contained within them the seeds of social discord and the demise of consensus. Part of the restlessness and alienation of white youths, for example, stemmed from the very tranquility and comfort of the 1950s that his policies had sought. America's general affluence made more obvious the blots of "pockets of poverty," which liberals cited as the nation's duty to eradicate. The promises of America in the 1950s of democratic freedoms and individual opportunity, free from statist oppression, had helped underscore the black demand for civil rights. And Eisenhower's own promotion of the material as well as spiritual benefits of the cooperative society, his encouragements to Americans to seek private answers to their dreams, ultimately had undercut his own capacity to employ the legal tools of the state to promote individual sacrifice and discipline. His leadership had provided Americans one of the most prosperous and tranquil decades of the century, but he had not built the institutional foundation capable of maintaining those assets. In a turbulent, diverse society, no single individual or administration could.

11

RETIREMENT AND RETROSPECTION

Dwight D. Eisenhower's last year in the White House was marked by a single striking contradiction. While his policies were increasingly assailed by the press critics and presidential hopefuls of both parties, his personal popularity with the American public rebounded completely from a mid-1958 low. He remained at his tenure's end, as he had been at its outset, the country's most constant symbol of unity and domestic tranquility. For Eisenhower, a man who prided himself on his capacity to manage events, 1960 seemed to unleash ever more uncontrollable national and international forces, turning him into less their master than their captive. But none of the turmoil seriously damaged his continuing popular reputation as America's greatest soldier-statesman.

The public remained so satisfied with him that it probably would have voted him a third term if it had been possible. But growing numbers of politicians, intellectuals, and even business leaders disagreed with the popular verdict. A recession was deepening, civil rights sit-in demonstrations had erupted across the South, diplomatic relations with Castro's Cuba had fallen apart, nationalist upheaval shook the African continent, and communist advances in Vietnam and a failed right-wing coup in Laos threatened additional American entanglement in Indochina. Critics at home blamed the president for a "flabbiness" and "softness" in the country. Intellectuals complained of a dearth of popular commitment to public affairs and an unhealthy national preoccupation with materialism. Even Eisenhower's own Commission on National Goals, containing notables from government, industry, education, and labor, implicitly criticized his policies. The commission's report, entitled *Goals for Americans,* included such recommendations as an increase in defense spending for the next decade, economic stimulus programs to promote faster growth, additional assistance to the Third World, greater federal promotion of public education, the fine arts, and scientific research, and an end to voting discrimination throughout the nation.[1]

The Commission on National Goals report could have served as an issues summary sheet for the Democratic presidential nominee in 1960, Sen. John F. Kennedy. Kennedy maintained that Eisenhower's massive retaliation doctrine had hampered American response to communist-inspired "brushfire wars" in the Third World, and his advisers backed large new increases in conventional spending to finance "counterinsurgency." In the nuclear weapons field, the Massachusetts senator attacked the administration from both sides, criticizing the president for failing to obtain a testing agreement with the Soviets, while insisting that current procurement policies had permitted the creation of a "missile gap." Kennedy's domestic program also advocated new approaches, including tax cuts and targeted spending for depressed economic areas of the country, to stimulate economic growth and end the 1960 recession.[2]

As important as the issue differences between them, however, was the leadership image Kennedy sought to cast in contrast to Eisenhower's. Kennedy based his campaign effort on the idea of presenting a vigorous new vision of leadership, while refraining from direct attacks on the popular incumbent. To Kennedy and his advisers, Eisenhower's stewardship had been a triumph of the "bland leading the bland." If the outgoing president's style emphasized restraint, moderation, dignity, and tranquility, Kennedy would offer something more exciting, glamorous, vigorous, even risque. The heroic standard of Eisenhower's generation was the quiet courage of a Gary Cooper in *High Noon* (one of the president's favorite movies)—the modest, dutiful service of a brave commoner. But for Kennedy's postwar generation of eager followers, the preferred image was that of the flashy, sexy James Bond, motivated by duty, but certain to take the most adventurous path to accomplish his mission.[3]

Eisenhower's surrogate in the 1960 campaign, Republican presidential nominee Richard Nixon, found it necessary to bend with the winds of change and to accept implicit criticisms of the administration in the party platform, while he defended its record on the stump. Nixon's willingness to promote party unity by incorporating the views of his rival in the primaries, Nelson Rockefeller, for increasing domestic and military spending did not sit well with his mentor in the White House. Eisenhower had never been very enthusiastic about Nixon, having tried to maneuver him off of the ticket in 1956 with the offer of a cabinet post. But if he privately doubted Nixon, the thought of a Kennedy victory in November horrified him, symbolizing as it would a direct repudiation of his leadership and policies. He wanted the chance to take on the Democratic nominee personally, but Nixon refused to give him the opportunity until the general election campaign's eleventh hour.[4]

For Nixon, the campaign represented a precious chance to escape the Eisenhower shadow. Nursing long-standing resentment over his treatment by the president in the Checkers incident and over the relatively minor role he had been granted in administration policymaking, he was determined to win the presidency on his own. Soon after the Republican convention, a Nixon aide expressed the sentiment that all his candidate wanted from Eisenhower was for him to prevent the eruption of an international crisis before election day. Unfortunately for Nixon, a presidential slip of the tongue did equally as much harm. When asked by a reporter at a White House news conference, "What major decisions of your Administration has the Vice President participated in?," Eisenhower, appearing flustered, replied, "If you give me a week, I might think of one." Although he later tried to explain the comment away as a joke, Eisenhower's remark undercut one of Nixon's most potent arguments against Kennedy—that his experience as vice-president made him better prepared to be president than the young Massachusetts senator. Whatever vestiges of the experience issue remained in voters' minds were shattered permanently by Kennedy's performance against Nixon in their series of televised campaign debates.[5]

By the last week of October, with only eight days of campaigning left and his candidacy floundering, Nixon finally asked Eisenhower to deliver a series of speeches on the stump. The president answered by working vigorously for the Nixon-Lodge ticket, even giving a nationally televised address on election eve. His late participation contributed to the closest presidential contest of the twentieth century, but it could not overcome Kennedy's debate performances, Lyndon Johnson's presence on the Democratic ticket, and the political gains among blacks produced by Kennedy's intercession on behalf of the jailed civil rights leader Martin Luther King, Jr. Kennedy held on to win the White House, but if Eisenhower's push had begun but days earlier, the outcome might well have been reversed. As the results stood, a shift of only twelve thousand votes in five states would have made Nixon president. Nixon gained the late momentum in the campaign, thanks to Eisenhower, and with a record voter turnout of 69 million the Democrat's popular margin nationwide was but 118,000 votes, or a fourth of a percentage point. To Eisenhower the close results underlined Nixon's mistake in not calling upon him earlier, and they encouraged his belief that the American people had not been so eager to repudiate his leadership as the Kennedy campaign and press pundits had asserted.[6]

His remaining duties as president included arranging a smooth transition of power, keeping a close watch on continuing global trouble spots, and delivering his own farewell address to the nation. He insisted on retaining complete control of the executive branch until inauguration day, but he provided extensive briefings with CIA director Dulles and other officials for the president-elect. In those sessions Kennedy learned for the first time of the advance preparations for the anti-Castro invasion of Cuba. Soon, of course, such responsibilities would pass from Eisenhower's hands to his successor's. In the afterglow of postelection national unity, Gallop poll ratings fixed the outgoing Eisenhower's public approval rating at at 59 percent, a far cry from his predecessor's 30 percent figure of January 1953. Despite his enduring popularity, however, he sought one last opportunity to address the nation. Because he felt a special kinship with another president who had endured increasing criticism in his final days in office, George

Washington, he chose to deliver his own version of a formal farewell address.[7]

On the evening of 17 January 1961, three days before his presidency ended, he spoke to the nation for fifteen minutes. Like Washington's own farewell address, his speech consisted of a series of cautions to the nation. Some were predictable, such as his warning against the "hostile ideology—global in scope, atheistic in character, ruthless in purpose, and insidious in method"—of communism. In turn, he argued against budget-busting to meet the Soviet threat, arguing against "a huge increase in newer elements of our defense." He issued a jeremiad against excessive materialism, urging his countrymen to "avoid the impulse to live only for today, plundering, for our own ease and convenience, the precious resources of tomorrow." But his most memorable words sought to warn the public and the government against "the acquisition of unwarranted influence, whether sought or unsought, by the military-industrial complex." He cautioned that government interconnection with the scientific and educational communities could bring about either the statist domination of research and scholarship or the "opposite danger that public policy could itself become captive of a scientific-technological elite."[8]

His countrymen would have many occasions to consider his words during the decade of the 1960s. John F. Kennedy's call for a "new generation of leadership," summoning the "best and brightest" of the universities and think tanks to Washington and demanding the citizenry to "pay any price, bear any burden" in the defense of liberty, foundered on revolutionary shoals in Latin America, Africa, and Southeast Asia. The new administration raised the 1962 defense budget 27 percent above the Eisenhower figure, seeking overwhelming superiority in long-range missiles and a buildup in conventional forces. But only nine months after taking office, Kennedy's Defense Department reluctantly conceded that no missile gap had ever existed. Under Eisenhower, the United States had enjoyed a two-to-one margin in operational intercontinental missiles and clear overall nuclear superiority. Lacking either the former president's inbred caution or his military judgment, Kennedy proceeded to dismantle his predecessor's NSC policymaking apparatus, and he authorized the ill-fated Bay of Pigs invasion of Cuba without the umbrella of accompanying American air strikes. Ironically, in giving the go-ahead for the Cuban operation, Kennedy accepted without hesitation the advice of the hawkish Joint Chiefs of Staff and of CIA Director Dulles, both Eisenhower administration holdovers.[9]

Publicly Eisenhower gave a dutiful show of support for the beleaguered young president and his foreign policy, although privately he referred to the Cuban fiasco as a "profile in timidity." Ever the good soldier for bipartisanship and internationalism in foreign policy, he also endorsed the growing American involvement in South Vietnam, despite his earlier reluctance to become involved in an Asian land war. After the assassination of President Kennedy in November 1963, he lent his counsel and his voice of national unity behind the foreign policy objectives of the Johnson administration. He publicly backed the U.S. military intervention in the Dominican Republic in 1965, as well as the massive troop escalation in South Vietnam that commenced in 1965. Reflecting his own preference not to undertake overt military interventions without formal Allied and congressional approval, however, in July 1967, he called for a formal American declaration of war against North Vietnam and a push for complete military victory.[10]

He gave advice to his successors when they asked for it, but he did not play a major formulating role in the foreign policy of the Kennedy and the Johnson administrations. Instead, he spent the bulk of his time in retirement and reflection, either at his home near Gettysburg, Pennsylvania, or on vacation in southern California. He had purchased the Gettysburg farm with the help of his neighbor George Allen back in 1950, and in addition to the obvious Civil War symbolism of the location, it represented his homecoming to the land of his family ancestors. Making the farm doubly attractive was Eisenhower's belief that it marked the site where the Marquis de Lafayette had squelched the Conway cabal and had preserved George Washington as commander of the Continental Army in 1778.[11]

From the seclusion of his own Mount Vernon, he continued to defend his reputation and his popularity from any challengers. Following his retirement he agreed to a series of television documentaries, the most famous being a CBS production of his recollections of D day filmed at the historic locations with correspondent Walter Cronkite. As he had done in the years immediately after World War II, he also produced memoirs, this time in two volumes covering his presidential years. This time, however, the guardedness of his recollections and the controversial events they discussed brought a less worshipful public and critical response. Sensitive as ever to criticism of his actions or motives, he initiated steps to prevent the publication of more critical administration memoirs by former White House aides Emmet Hughes and E. Frederic Morrow. He released a more modest, freewheeling literary effort, entitled *At Ease: Stories I Tell to Friends*, in 1967, and its tales of personal experiences in a long and fruitful life proved enormously successful with the public.[12]

Like many well-to-do Americans of his age, Eisenhower spiced his retirement with stays in the sun and on the golf courses of southern California, with Palm Desert a particular favorite of his. Occasionally he punctuated his schedule with speeches, banquets, or partisan ceremonies as the Republican party's elder statesman. But he displayed only an infrequent interest in the direction of his party, usually preferring to remain above the fray. In 1964 he witnessed the Republican march to certain defeat with Barry Goldwater, but he refused to back Nelson Rockefeller, whom he had come to despise, and he made no public effort to enhance the chances of other moderate Republicans he preferred, such as Governor William Scranton of Pennsylvania or Henry Cabot Lodge of Massachusetts.[12]

Although his lukewarm efforts in behalf of his party did not demonstrate it, he was increasingly alarmed at the developments in American society under Democratic party stewardship. Horrifying to an American of his generation, traditional moral standards and apparently even a basic reverence for law and order were disintegrating in an orgy of rioting, antiwar protest, and changing sexual mores. Having once resisted an official commitment to a manned lunar landing program on the grounds that "I'm not about to hock my jewels," he expressed shock at the Democrats' doubling of federal government costs in a decade. Tax cuts and deliberate deficits had triggered an impressive economic boom by mid-decade, but the escalating fiscal demands of the Vietnam conflict and the Great Society threatened to reignite inflation and already had generated, to his alarm, renewed special interest fighting over government spoils.[14]

He had witnessed many changes during his lifetime, many good in his estimation, others more ominous. He had risen to fame at the same time that the nation had become the world's dominant economic and military power, a power that offered an even higher standard of living for its citizens, but at the cost of morally ambiguous commitments around the globe. He had emerged from outside the normal breeding grounds of American leadership to master the bureaucratic politics of the modern military and then of the presidency. He had employed the tools of organization to achieve a hero's status second to none in his country and in the world. His life, as he looked back on it, had been the triumph of the individual, both in mastering the arts of modern national management and in protecting and promoting in the nation the old-fashioned values of duty, individual responsibility, frugality, cooperation, and honor.

But would such values persist past his own lifetime, or would the centrifugal forces pulling at modern America shatter his dream—the dream of a society where leaders still could mold disparate social elements and institutions in service to a larger shared national purpose without resorting to statist tyranny? Those who had hailed the end of the "dull tranquility" of the Eisenhower years, who had yearned for Kennedy's Camelot, had viewed his blending of the older individualist values with the new national institutions of corporate organization as the real threat to freedom. They had seen as the product of Eisenhower's America the unquestioning, unimaginative "organization man," with an "other-directed" personality that craved the security and approval of conformity. One of the critics, the author Norman Mailer, had assailed Eisenhower's era as the unimaginative triumph of the small-town mind, asserting, "The small-town mind is rooted—it is rooted in the small-town—and when it attempts to direct history the results are disastrously colorless because the instrument of world power which is used by the small-town mind is the committee. Committees do not create, they merely proliferate, and the incredible dullness wreaked upon the landscape in Eisenhower's eight years has been the triumph of the corporation."[15]

Eisenhower vehemently disagreed with such scathing dismissals of his national leadership. In his view, the rise of larger and more complex systems of organization in business, the media, the military, and government did not mean the inevitable loss of individual freedom, opportunity, and creativity. If properly channeled by wise leadership in both the public and the private spheres, modern bureaucracy actually could help provide the advanced material standards of life basic to the realization of broader creative human pursuits and aspirations. That remaining sense of hope for his nation led him in 1965, despite the turmoil around him, to predict that "the ideals and the way of life that Western civilization has cherished . . . will flourish everywhere to the infinite benefit of mankind." He concluded, "At home . . . our level of education constantly rises. . . . Opportunity for the properly ambitious boy or girl increases daily. Prospects for the good life were never better, provided only that each continues to feel that he, himself, must earn and deserve these advantages."[16]

By the end of the 1960s, many of those who had dismissed such statements as outdated homilies would look upon his years as president with a growing nostalgia. Appreciation for his "negative" accomplishments of avoiding war and major domestic unrest would spring from liberal disillusionment with the Vietnam debacle, the stubborn persistence of poverty, and the spectacle of riots in American streets. Such sentiments would blossom into a full-blown "Eisenhower revisionism," which would transform the previous scholarly portrait of the former president from that of a naive bumbler in the White House to that of a skillful manipulator of the hidden levers of power. Eisenhower himself likely would have been only partly pleased at the belated reassessment of his leadership, however. For while he would have approved of the improved estimations of his operational skills, he would never have divorced an analysis of his methods from a consideration of the policy ends he sought. He would have wanted a genuine revival of the values and political ideals he had promoted, not merely a preoccupation with management technique or a vague nostalgia among intellectuals for the tranquility of an era they believed could not be recaptured.

In his last years, he predicted that his place in American history would be determined eventually by whether his countrymen continued to turn to the federal government as the paternalistic broker of special interests or returned to an earlier, homogeneous ideal of a nation bound together as one by the values of personal initiative, individual responsibility, and voluntary cooperation for the common good. If the country repudiated the "statist" legacy of the New Deal and its followers, he believed, "then the future would hold encomiums for my administration as the first great break with the political philosophy of the decade beginning in 1933. The years of my two terms would be counted as some of the most meaningful during our national existence." If it did not, he predicted, "the growth of paternalism to the point of virtual regimentation would so condition the attitude of future historians that our time in office would be represented as only a slight impediment to the trend begun in 1933 under the New Deal."[18]

He would not live to hear the verdict of his nation and of history. Already in 1965 he had suffered two heart attacks, and during the turbulent year of 1968, he suffered four more within three and a half months, again rallying afterward. But at the age of seventy-eight, on 28 March 1969, having witnessed the presidential inauguration of his former vice-president, Richard Nixon, he finally succumbed. True to the identity he had forged through a lifetime, he declared on his deathbed, "I've always loved my wife. I've always loved my children. I've always loved my grandchildren. I've always loved my country."[19] Dressed in the famous Eisenhower jacket he had made famous in World War II, his body was placed in an eighty-dollar army coffin and was borne by train back to Abilene. Attended by military and family pallbearers, he was buried in the Place of Meditation on the grounds of the Eisenhower Presidential Library and Museum. The hero had earned his final rest.

CHRONOLOGY

14 October 1890	Dwight David Eisenhower born, Denison, Texas.
14 June 1911	Joins U.S. Military Academy, West Point.
July 1915	Graduates from West Point, commissioned second lieutenant.
1 July 1916	Marries Mamie Geneva Doud.
6 April 1917	United States enters World War I.
24 September 1917	Birth of son, Doud Dwight (dies of scarlet fever 2 January 1921).
March 1918	Eisenhower commands tank training detachment, Camp Colt, Pennsylvania.
11 November 1918	Armistice with Germany.

January 1922	Named Brig. Gen. Fox Conner's staff officer, Panama Canal Zone.
3 August 1922	Birth of son, John Sheldon Doud.
August 1925–June 1926	Student at Command and General Staff School, Fort Leavenworth, Kansas.
26 December 1926	Joins staff, War Monuments Commission.
August 1927–June 1928	Student at War College, Washington, D.C.
June 1928–July 1929	Revises, in Paris, War Monuments guidebook of World War I battle sites.
October 1929	Stock market crash, beginning of Great Depression.
October 1929–December 1932	On staff of Maj. Gen. George Van Horn Mosely, deputy secretary of war.
1 January 1933	Appointed personal military assistant to Army Chief of Staff Douglas MacArthur.
October 1935	Accompanies MacArthur to Philippines.
December 1939	Returns to United States.
August 1941	Named chief of staff to Third Army (becomes publicized during Louisiana maneuvers).
7 December 1941	Japanese attack Pearl Harbor; United States declares war on Japan on 8 December, Germany and Italy on 11 December.
14 December 1941	Joins War Plan Division, Washington, D.C.
16 February 1942	Appointed chief of War Plans.
11 June 1942	Named to command U.S. forces, European theater of operations.

6 August 1942	Nominated to head Allied Expeditionary Force for Torch landings in North Africa, 7–8 November 1942.
12 May 1943	German surrender in North Africa.
10 July 1943	Allied landings in Sicily (island captured 17 August).
8–9 September 1943	Landings on Italian mainland.
7 December 1943	Named to command Overlord, Allied invasion of France.
6 June 1944	D day, Normandy invasion of France.
25 July 1944	Opening of Cobra offensive in northern France (leads to Battle of the Falaise Gap, 13–21 August).
25 August 1944	Liberation of Paris.
17–26 September 1944	Battle of Arnhem.
16 December 1944–17 January 1945	Battle of the Bulge.
4–10 February 1945	Yalta Conference.
12 April 1945	Death of Franklin D. Roosevelt; Harry S Truman becomes commander in chief.
8 May 1945	V-E Day.
6 August 1945	A-bomb dropped on Hiroshima (second bomb dropped on Nagasaki 9 August).
2 September 1945	V-J Day, World War II ends.
November 1945–May 1948	Army chief of staff.
May 1948–January 1953	President of Columbia University.
25 June 1950	Korean War begins.
19 December 1950	Appointed supreme Allied commander, Europe.

July 1952	Retires from United States Army, launches presidential campaign.
4 November 1952	Elected president of the United States (visits Korea 29 November–5 December).
20 January 1953	Inaugurated president.
26 July 1953	Korean armistice signed.
August 1953	USSR tests hydrogen warhead (United States follows suit in March 1954). CIA-backed coup reinstates shah in Iran.
8 December 1953	Delivers "Atoms for Peace" address to United Nations.
April–June 1954	Anti-McCarthy hearings.
26 April—21 July 1954	Geneva Conference on Indochina (7 May, French surrender at Dien Bien Phu; 8 September, SEATO alliance announced).
17 May 1954	*Brown* school desegregation decision announced by United States Supreme Court.
June 1954	CIA-backed coup overthrows Arbenz regime in Guatemala.
18–24 July 1955	Attends Geneva disarmament conference, offers Open Skies proposal.
24 September 1955	Suffers heart attack.
7 June 1956	Ileitis attack.
October–November 1956	Hungarian, Suez crises.
6 November 1956	Reelected president.
5 January 1957	Announces Eisenhower Doctrine for Middle East.
9 September 1957	Signs Civil Rights Act of 1957.
24 September 1957	Federal troops intervene in Little Rock school desegregation crisis.
4 October 1957	USSR launches Sputnik satellite.

25 November 1957	Suffers stroke.
31 January 1958	Explorer I satellite launched (NASA created in July 1958).
15 July 1958	Marine landings in Lebanon.
August–September 1958	Quemoy-Matsu crisis.
1 January 1959	Batista flees Cuba, Castro enters Havana.
3 January 1959	Alaska becomes 49th state.
21 January 1959	Hawaii becomes 50th state.
September 1959	Khrushchev tours United States, Camp David summit.
1 February 1960	Sit-ins begin in Greensboro, North Carolina.
1 May 1960	U-2 incident, subsequent Paris summit fails.
6 May 1960	Signs Civil Rights Act of 1960.
8 November 1960	John F. Kennedy elected president.
17 January 1961	Delivers Farewell Address, "military-industrial complex" warning.
20 January 1961	Retires to Gettysburg, Pennsylvania.
17 April 1961	Bay of Pigs invasion of Cuba.
22 November 1963	President Kennedy assassinated in Dallas.
August 1964	President Johnson proposes Tonkin Gulf Resolution (American troop role in Vietnam expanded, 1965–1969).
28 March 1969	Dies at Walter Reed Army Hospital following series of heart attacks.

NOTES AND REFERENCES

I. AMBITION WITHOUT ARROGANCE

1. Quoted in Stephen E. Ambrose, *Eisenhower: Soldier, General of the Army, President-Elect, 1890–1952* (New York: Simon and Schuster, 1983), 27.

2. Ibid., 26.

3. Bela Kornitzer, *The Great American Heritage: The Story of the Five Eisenhower Brothers* (New York: Farrar, Straus and Cudahy, 1955), 52; Dwight D. Eisenhower, *At Ease: Stories I Tell to Friends* (Garden City, N.Y.: Doubleday & Co., 1967), 31–32, 51–53, 74.

4. Eisenhower, *At Ease*, 56–63.

5. Ibid., 31; Peter Lyon, *Eisenhower: Portrait of the Hero* (Boston: Little, Brown and Co., 1974), 34–35; Kenneth S. Davis, *Soldier of Democracy: A Biography of Dwight Eisenhower* (Garden City, N.Y.: Doubleday, Doran & Co., 1945), 27–34.

6. Lyon, *Eisenhower*, 35; Davis, *Soldier of Democracy*, 35–43, 65.

7. Davis, *Soldier of Democracy*, 37; Lyon, *Eisenhower*, 35–36.

8. Eisenhower, *At Ease,* 71–72; Lyon, *Eisenhower,* 39; Davis, *Soldier of Democracy,* 49.

9. Eisenhower, *At Ease,* 31–32, 70–71, 80.

10. Ibid., 31, 37, 76.

11. Ibid., 32, 76–78.

12. Ibid., 32–35.

13. Davis, *Soldier of Democracy,* 37–38.

14. Eisemhower, *At Ease,* 33–34, 83–85, 96–97.

15. Ibid., 33–34, 37, 79, 97.

16. Ibid., 39–41, 88–89; Davis, *Soldier of Democracy,* 94.

17. Eisenhower, *At Ease,* 42, 101; Davis, *Soldier of Democracy,* 73–80.

18. Eisenhower, *At Ease,* 97–98; Davis, *Soldier of Democracy,* 97.

19. Eisenhower, *At Ease,* 37, 102–3; Davis, *Soldier of Democracy,* 99–101.

20. Eisenhower, *At Ease,* 104; Davis, *Soldier of Democracy,* 106–7.

21. Eisenhower, *At Ease,* 105–6; Davis, *Soldier of Democracy,* 108–10.

22. Eisenhower, *At Ease,* 106; Davis, *Soldier of Democracy,* 110–13.

23. Eisenhower, *At Ease,* 106.

24. Ibid., 106–8.

2. WEST POINT, WAR, AND FRUSTRATION

1. Eisenhower, *At Ease,* 4–6; Ambrose, *Duty, Honor, Country: A History of West Point* (Baltimore: Johns Hopkins Press, 1966), 223–26.

2. Ambrose, *Duty, Honor, Country,* 250–51.

3. Davis, *Soldier of Democracy,* 134.

4. Eisenhower, *At Ease,* 12–14.

5. Ibid., 14–15; Steve Neal, *The Eisenhowers: Reluctant Dynasty* (Garden City, N.Y.: Doubleday & Co., 1978), 25; Davis, *Soldier of Democracy,* 135.

6. Eisenhower, *At Ease,* 16; Davis, *Soldier of Democracy,* 140–141; Lyon, *Eisenhower,* 45.

7. Eisenhower, *At Ease,* 16; Neal, *The Eisenhowers,* 29–30.

8. Eisenhower, *At Ease,* 17.

9. Ibid., 8, 12; Neal, *The Eisenhowers,* 30.

10. Ambrose, *Duty, Honor, Country,* 330–33; Ambrose, *Eisenhower,* 1:52–53.

11. Eisenhower, *At Ease,* 119–25, 129.

12. Ibid., 132–33; Neal, *The Eisenhowers,* 43; Lyon, *Eisenhower,* 50–51; Davis, *Soldier of Democracy,* 174–75.

13. Eisenhower, *At Ease*, 137–152; Davis, *Soldier of Democracy*, 177–78; Neal, *The Eisenhowers*, 45.

14. Eisenhower, *At Ease*, 157–67.

15. Ibid., 168–70; Davis, *Soldier of Democracy*, 187; Lyon, *Eisenhower*, 55; Eisenhower, "A Tank Discussion," *Infantry Journal*, November 1920.

16. Eisenhower, *At Ease*, 173–74.

17. Ibid., 113–18; Alden Hatch, *Red Carpet for Mamie* (New York: Henry Holt and Co., 1954), 69–73, 83, 97–98, 114; Dorothy Brandon, *Mamie Doud Eisenhower* (New York: Charles Scribner's Sons, 1954), 42–43, 72; Neal, *The Eisenhowers*, 38–43.

18. Neal, *The Eisenhowers*, 64–65.

19. Eisenhower, *At Ease*, 155, 181; Russell Weigley, *History of the United States Army* (New York: Macmillan Co., 1967), 396, 403.

3. APPRENTICESHIP

1. Eisenhower, *At Ease*, 178–82; Lyon, *Eisenhower*, 56; Davis, *Soldier of Democracy*, 188.

2. Eisenhower, *At Ease*, 185–87; Davis, *Soldier of Democracy*, 196–97.

3. Eisenhower, *At Ease*, 195.

4. Brandon, *Mamie Doud Eisenhower*, 141; John S. D. Eisenhower, *Strictly Personal* (Garden City, N.Y.: Doubleday and Co., 1974), 9–10.

5. Davis, *Soldier of Democracy*, 202–3; Eisenhower, *At Ease*, 200.

6. Eisenhower, *At Ease*, 201.

7. Ibid., 202.

8. Ibid., 203.

9. Davis, *Soldier of Democracy*, 205; Patton quoted in Ambrose, *Eisenhower*, 1:83.

10. Eisenhower, *At Ease*, 204–7.

11. Ibid., 207–9.

12. Lyon, *Eisenhower*, 63; Davis, *Soldier of Democracy*, 225.

13. Ambrose, *Eisenhower*, 1:88.

14. Lyon, *Eisenhower*, 65–68, 75; Eisenhower, *At Ease*, 213; Eisenhower, "War Policies," *Cavalry Journal*, November–December 1931.

15. D. Clayton James, *The Years of MacArthur*, vol. 1, 1880–1941 (Boston: Houghton Mifflin, 1970), 343, 461–67.

16. Ibid., 564; Eisenhower, *At Ease*, 214; Lyon, *Eisenhower*, 69.

17. Eisenhower, *At Ease*, 215–217.

18. Ibid., 217–18.

19. James, *Years of MacArthur*, 1:403–4; Robert H. Ferrell, ed., *The Eisenhower Diaries* (New York: W. W. Norton & Co., 1981), 21–22.

20. Lyon, *Eisenhower*, 73–74.

21. Ibid., 75; Davis, *Soldier of Democracy*, 242.
22. James, *Years of MacArthur*, 1:485–530.
23. Eisenhower, *At Ease*, 219–21.
24. Ibid., 223–24.
25. Ibid., 221–22, 224, 228–229.
26. Lyon, *Eisenhower*, 77–78.
27. Eisenhower, *At Ease*, 229–30.
28. Quoted in Ambrose, *Eisenhower*, 1:115–16.

4. WAR AND OPPORTUNITY

1. Eisenhower, *At Ease*, 235–37.
2. Ibid., 240–41; Ambrose, *Eisenhower*, 1:121–22.
3. Eisenhower, *At Ease*, 237–39.
4. Ibid., 242; Davis, *Soldier of Democracy*, 263; Lyon, *Eisenhower*, 82–83.
5. Eisenhower, *At Ease*, 242–43.
6. *New York Times*, 17 September 1940; Davis, *Soldier of Democracy*, 269–272.
7. Lyon, *Eisenhower*, 83; Davis, *Soldier of Democracy*, 272.
8. Davis, *Soldier of Democracy*, 273.
9. Ambrose, *The Supreme Commander: The War Years of General Dwight D. Eisenhower* (Garden City, N.Y.: Doubleday & Co., 1970), 3.
10. Eisenhower, *At Ease*, 246–48.
11. Forrest C. Pogue, *George C. Marshall: Ordeal and Hope, 1939–42* (New York: Viking Press, 1966), 237–39; Eisenhower, *Crusade in Europe* (Garden City, N.Y.: Doubleday & Co., 1948), 14–22.
12. Ambrose, *Supreme Commander*, 9–18.
13. Ferrell, ed., *Eisenhower Diaries*, 51–54.
14. Michael McKeogh and Richard Lockridge, *Sergeant Mickey and General Ike* (New York: G. P. Putnam's Sons, 1946), 21; Ferrell, ed., *Eisenhower Diaries*, 50–51; Eisenhower, *At Ease*, 248–49.
15. Eisenhower, *At Ease*, 250; Eisenhower, *Crusade*, 32–38.
16. Ferrell, ed., *Eisenhower Diaries*, 48–49.
17. Eisenhower, *At Ease*, 103–4, 109–10.
18. Ibid., 115–16.
19. Ferrell, ed., *Eisenhower Diaries*, 48.
20. Eisenhower, *At Ease*, 121.
21. Ibid., 122–23.
22. Ferrell, ed., *Eisenhower Diaries*, 58–62.
23. Ibid., 62.

5. TIME OF TESTING

1. Davis, *Soldier of Democracy*, 317–22.

2. Quoted in Ambrose, *Eisenhower*, 1:176.

3. Ferrell, ed., *Eisenhower Diaries*, 76.

4. Eisenhower, *At Ease*, 252; Pogue, *Ordeal and Hope*, 348; Eisenhower, *Crusade*, 71.

5. See Alan F. Wilt, *The Atlantic Wall: Hitler's Defenses in the West, 1941–1944* (Ames, Iowa: Iowa State University Press, 1975).

6. Ambrose, *Supreme Commander*, 76–77.

7. Ferrell, ed., *Eisenhower Diaries*, 76–78.

8. Ambrose, *Supreme Commander*, 96–99.

9. Ibid., 100.

10. Mark Wayne Clark, *Calculated Risk* (New York: Harper & Bros., 1950), 67–72, 90; Eisenhower, *Crusade*, 88.

11. Eisenhower, *Crusade*, 101–7.

12. Harold Macmillan, *The Blast of War, 1939–1945* (New York: Harper & Row, 1968), 174.

13. Ambrose, *Supreme Commander*, 130–34; Robert Murphy, *Diplomat among Warriors* (Garden City, N.Y.: Doubleday & Co., 1964), 150–51.

14. Clark, *Calculated Risk*, 128–31.

15. Sir Arthur Bryant, *The Turn of the Tide* (New York: Doubleday & Co., 1957), 430; John S. D. Eisenhower, ed., *Letters to Mamie* (Garden City, N.Y.: Doubleday & Co., 1978), 88.

16. Bryant, *Turn of the Tide*, 452–55; Eisenhower, ed., *Letters to Mamie*, 94–95.

17. Martin Blumenson, *Kasserine Pass* (Boston: Houghton Mifflin, 1967), 86–95, 278–83; Omar N. Bradley and Clay Blair, *A General's Life* (New York: Simon and Schuster, 1983), 133–34; Eisenhower quoted in Ambrose, *Supreme Commander*, 176.

18. Quoted in Ambrose, *Eisenhower*, 1:235.

19. Lyon, *Eisenhower*, 204–5.

20. Eisenhower, *At Ease*, 263–64; Lyon, *Eisenhower*, 206–9.

21. Eisenhower, *At Ease*, 265; Bradley, *A General's Life*, 159–63.

22. Bradley, *A General's Life*, 164; Hanson W. Baldwin, *Battles Lost and Won: Great Campaigns of World War II* (New York: Harper & Row, 1966), 460–61.

23. Lyon, *Eisenhower*, 229–34; Ambrose, *Supreme Commander*, 230; Eisenhower, *At Ease*, 261.

24. Albert N. Garland and Howard McGaw Smyth, *Sicily and the Surrender of Italy* (Washington, D.C.: U.S. Department of the Army, 1965), 474–505.

25. Ibid., 506–9.
26. Lyon, *Eisenhower*, 247–50.
27. Ibid., 250.
28. Ibid., 250–52; Bradley, *A General's Life*, 213.
29. Ambrose, *Supreme Commander*, 296–97.
30. Lyon, *Eisenhower*, 253–54; Eisenhower, *At Ease*, 266.
31. Lyon, *Eisenhower*, 255; Ambrose, *Supreme Commander*, 302–6.

6. CRUSADE IN EUROPE

1. See Gordon A. Harrison, *Cross-Channel Attack* (Washington, D.C.: U.S. Department of the Army, 1951).
2. Lyon, *Eisenhower*, 257–58.
3. Ibid., 267.
4. Ibid., 259, 269.
5. Bradley, *A General's Life*, 240–41; Lyon, *Eisenhower*, 275.
6. Lyon, *Eisenhower*, 263.
7. Ibid., 272; Harrison, *Cross-Channel Attack*, 219.
8. Sir Arthur Tedder, *With Prejudice* (London: Cassell, 1966), 510–33.
9. Weigley, in *Eisenhower's Lieutenants: The Campaigns of France and Germany, 1944–1945* (Bloomington, Ind.: Indiana University Press, 1981), 58–64, criticizes the Transportation Plan, as have official United States Army Air Force historians. See also Lyon, *Eisenhower*, 274.
10. Eisenhower, *Crusade*, 238; Eisenhower, *At Ease*, 273–75.
11. Harrison, *Cross-Channel Attack*, 272; Tedder, *With Prejudice*, 545; Eisenhower, *Crusade*, 249.
12. Sir Francis de Guingand, *Operation Victory* (New York: Charles Scribner's Sons, 1947), 302; Pogue, *The Supreme Command* (Washington, D.C.: U.S. Department of the Army, 1954), 170; Harrison, *Cross-Channel Attack*, 274; Eisenhower, *Crusade*, 250.
13. Eisenhower, *Crusade*, 251–52.
14. Kay Summersby Morgan, *Past Forgetting: My Love Affair with Dwight D. Eisenhower* (New York: Simon & Schuster, 1976), 216; Harrison, *Cross-Channel Attack*, 302–6; Eisenhower, ed., *Letters to Mamie*, 189–90.
15. Quoted in Ambrose, *Eisenhower*, 1:312.
16. Bernard Law Montgomery, *Memoirs* (Cleveland: World Publishing Co., 1958), 43; Bryant, *Triumph in the West* (London: Collins, 1959), 178.
17. Bradley, *A Soldier's Story* (New York: Henry Holt and Co., 1951), 350–77; Pogue, *Supreme Command*, 200–33; Eisenhower, *Crusade*, 272–83.
18. Eisenhower, *Crusade*, 279.
19. Pogue, *Supreme Command*, 245–64; Montgomery, *Memoirs*, 240.

20. Montgomery, *Memoirs*, 243; David Irving, *The War between the Generals* (New York: Congdon & Lattès, 1981), 250–51.

21. Lyon, *Eisenhower*, 307, 310; Tedder, *With Prejudice*, 590–91; Ambrose, *Supreme Commander*, 518.

22. Chester Wilmot, *Struggle for Europe* (New York: Harper, 1952), 573–74.

23. Lyon, *Eisenhower*, 315; Weigley, *Eisenhower's Lieutenants*, 574.

24. Pogue, *Supreme Command*, 376–77; Eisenhower, *Crusade*, 350; Bradley, *A Soldier's Story*, 470–76.

25. Eisenhower, *Crusade*, 360–63; Tedder, *With Prejudice*, 631–33; Montgomery, *Memoirs*, 284–89; de Guingand, *Operation Victory*, 348; Weigley, *Eisenhower's Lieutenants*, 572, 605; Lyon, *Eisenhower*, 325.

26. Bradley, *A General's Life*, 396; Lyon, *Eisenhower*, 326.

27. Ambrose, *Supreme Commander*, 629–30.

28. Wilmot, *Struggle for Europe*, 690; Bradley, *A General's Life*, 410; Cornelius Ryan, *The Last Battle* (New York: Simon and Schuster, 1966), 241; Lyon, *Eisenhower*, 333–35.

29. Weigley, *Eisenhower's Lieutenants*, 698; Winston S. Churchill, *Triumph and Tragedy* (Boston: Houghton Mifflin, 1953), 515–16.

30. Lyon, *Eisenhower*, 338–39.

31. Ibid., 3–13.

7. RETURN OF THE HERO

1. Eisenhower, *At Ease*, 298–300; Morgan, *Past Forgetting*, 257.

2. Ambrose, *Eisenhower*, 1:412–13; Neal, *The Eisenhowers*, 224.

3. Quoted in Ambrose, *Eisenhower*, 1:455.

4. Ibid., 416–18; Morgan, *Past Forgetting*, 277.

5. Ambrose, *Eisenhower*, 1:418–19.

6. Eisenhower, ed., *Letters to Mamie*, 209–10; Eisenhower, *Crusade*, 287; Eisenhower, *At Ease*, 324–28.

7. Lyon, *Eisenhower*, 346–48.

8. Eisenhower, *At Ease*, 307.

9. Ibid., 311; Lyon, *Eisenhower*, 349–52.

10. Lyon, *Eisenhower*, 354–58.

11. Ibid., 356.

12. Ibid., 367.

13. Eisenhower, *At Ease*, 315–21.

14. Lyon, *Eisenhower*, 382.

15. Ambrose, *Eisenhower*, 1:436–37.

16. Ibid., 437–38.

17. Lyon, *Eisenhower*, 383–84.

18. Ibid., 373–74.

19. Eisenhower, *At Ease*, 339–41.

20. Herbert S. Parmet, *Eisenhower and the American Crusades* (New York: Macmillan Co., 1972), 15; Lyon, *Eisenhower*, 383; Eisenhower, *At Ease*, 55.

21. Neal, *The Eisenhowers*, 249–51; Eisenhower, *At Ease*, 349–50; Ira H. Freeman, "Eisenhower of Columbia," *New York Times Magazine*, 7 November 1948.

22. Eisenhower, *At Ease*, 343, 346–48, 351.

23. Ibid., 352–55.

24. Ibid., 355.

8. CINCINNATUS IN POLITICS

1. Bradley, *A General's Life*, 444; Lyon, *Eisenhower*, 348; Eisenhower, *Crusade*, 444.

2. Kevin McCann, *Man from Abilene* (Garden City, N.Y.: Doubleday & Co., 1952), 140–41.

3. Eisenhower, *At Ease*, 333–34; Eisenhower quoted in Ambrose, *Eisenhower*, 1:462.

4. Lyon, *Eisenhower*, 378.

5. Ibid., 386–87, 390.

6. Ambrose, *Eisenhower*, 1:489–90.

7. Lyon, *Eisenhower*, 378, 396.

8. Ibid., 390–92.

9. Ibid., 396–97; Kelland quoted in Ambrose, *Eisenhower*, 1:491–92.

10. Ferrell, ed., *Eisenhower Diaries*, 161; Lyon, *Eisenhower*, 407; Parmet, *Eisenhower*, 36.

11. Lyon, *Eisenhower*, 410; Ambrose, *Eisenhower*, 1:493–94.

12. Ambrose, *Eisenhower*, 1:495–96.

13. Lyon, *Eisenhower*, 413.

14. Eisenhower, *At Ease*, 361–63; Ferrell, ed., *Eisenhower Diaries*, 178–80; Ambrose, *Eisenhower*, 1:496.

15. Lyon, *Eisenhower*, 416–17; Eisenhower, *At Ease*, 371–72; Eisenhower, *Mandate for Change* (Garden City, N.Y.: Doubleday & Co., 1963), 14.

16. Ferrell, ed., *Eisenhower Diaries*, 193, 195.

17. Ambrose, *Eisenhower*, 1:514–15.

18. Ibid., 491; Arthur Krock, *In the Nation: 1932–1966* (New York: McGraw-Hill, 1966), 194–95; Krock, *Memoirs: Sixty Years on the Firing Line* (New York: Funk & Wagnalls, 1968), 267–69.

19. Eisenhower, *Mandate*, 18; *New York Herald-Tribune*, 25 October 1951.

20. Richard Norton Smith, *Thomas E. Dewey and His Times* (New York: Simon and Schuster, 1982), 579.

21. Quoted in Ambrose, *Eisenhower*, 1:521.

22. Ibid., 523–24; Lyon, *Eisenhower*, 432–33.

23. Ambrose, *Eisenhower*, 1:524–35; Lyon, *Eisenhower*, 434–42.

24. Lyon, *Eisenhower*, 442–44.

25. Ibid., 445; Ambrose, *Eisenhower*, 1:537–41; Parmet, *Eisenhower*, 99–100.

26. Eisenhower, *Mandate*, 45–46; Smith, *Dewey*, 596–97; Parmet, *Eisenhower*, 97–101; Richard M. Nixon, *The Memoirs of Richard M. Nixon* (New York: Grosset & Dunlap, 1978), 87–90.

27. Eisenhower, *Mandate*, 54–55; Athan G. Theoharris, *The Yalta Myths: An Issue in U.S. Politics, 1945–1955* (Columbia, Mo.: University of Missouri Press, 1970), 145; Parmet, *Eisenhower*, 127–28; Emmet John Hughes, *The Ordeal of Power* (New York: Atheneum, 1963), 41; *New York Times*, 13 September 1952.

28. Ambrose, *Eisenhower*, 1:553–54.

29. Eisenhower, *Mandate*, 69; William Bragg Ewald, *Eisenhower the President* (Englewood Cliffs, N.J.: Prentice-Hall, 1981), 51–57; Nixon, *Memoirs*, 97–106.

30. Quoted in Ambrose, *Eisenhower*, 1:561–62.

31. Hughes, *Ordeal*, 41–42; Ewald, *Eisenhower*, 60–63; Eisenhower, *Mandate*, 318–19; Thomas C. Reeves, *The Life and Times of Joe McCarthy* (New York: Stein and Day, 1982), 438–40; Robert Griffith, "The General and the Senator," *Wisconsin Magazine of History*, Autumn 1970, 27; John Bartlow Martin, *Adlai Stevenson of Illinois* (Garden City, N.Y.: Doubleday & Co., 1976), 713.

32. Ewald, *Eisenhower*, 61; Eisenhower, *Mandate*, 73.

33. Lyon, *Eisenhower*, 464; Ambrose, *Eisenhower*, 1:571; Ferrell, ed., *Eisenhower Diaries*, 225.

9. OLD ASSUMPTIONS AND A NEW LOOK

1. Nixon quoted in Fred I. Greenstein, *The Hidden-Hand Presidency: Eisenhower as Leader* (New York: Basic Books, 1982), 9.

2. Robert A. Divine, *Eisenhower and the Cold War* (New York: Oxford University Press, 1981), 23–25; Lyon, *Eisenhower*, 503–4.

3. Lyon, *Eisenhower*, 511; Eisenhower, *Mandate*, 142; Richard H. Im-

merman, "Eisenhower and Dulles: Who Made the Decisions?" *Political Psychology* 1 (Autumn 1979):3–20.

4. Charles C. Alexander, *Holding the Line: The Eisenhower Era, 1952–1961* (Bloomington, Ind.: Indiana University Press, 1975), 44–45.

5. Ibid., 71–72.

6. Divine, *Eisenhower and the Cold War*, 33–37.

7. Ibid., 38–39, 44–51.

8. Alexander, *Holding the Line*, 178–81.

9. Divine, *Eisenhower and the Cold War*, 27–31.

10. Eisenhower, *Mandate*, 345–47; Divine, *Eisenhower and the Cold War*, 40–41.

11. George Herring, *America's Longest War* (New York: John Wiley and Sons, 1979), 33; Eisenhower, *Mandate*, 354; Townsend Hoopes, *The Devil and John Foster Dulles* (Boston: Little, Brown and Co., 1973), 230.

12. Eisenhower, *Mandate*, 372; Herring, *America's Longest War*, 36–42; Divine, *Eisenhower and the Cold War*, 51–55.

13. Divine, *Eisenhower and the Cold War*, 79–96.

14. Ibid., 97–104; Eisenhower, *Waging Peace* (Garden City, N.Y.: Doubleday & Co., 1965), 265–74; Ambrose, *Eisenhower: The President* (New York: Simon and Schuster, 1984), 462–67; Alexander, *Holding the Line*, 230–34.

15. Eisenhower, *Mandate*, 460–72; Lyon, *Eisenhower*, 635–38; Divine, *Eisenhower and the Cold War*, 55–61.

16. Eisenhower, *Mandate*, 476–83; Eisenhower, *Waging Peace*, 292–99; Divine, *Eisenhower and the Cold War*, 61–68.

17. Divine, *Eisenhower and the Cold War*, 68–70; Eisenhower, *Waging Peace*, 302–4.

18. Divine, *Eisenhower and the Cold War*, 106–10; Robert J. Donovan, *Eisenhower: The Inside Story* (New York: Harper & Bros., 1956), 41, 72; Parmet, *Eisenhower*, 279–82; Eisenhower, *Mandate*, 145–47; Hughes, *Ordeal*, 113.

19. Donovan, *Eisenhower*, 184–85, 190–97; Eisenhower, *Mandate*, 252–54; Divine, *Eisenhower and the Cold War*, 110–14.

20. Hoopes, *Devil and John Foster Dulles*, 295.

21. Divine, *Eisenhower and the Cold War*, 114–22; Parmet, *Eisenhower*, 406; Ewald, *Eisenhower*, 103.

22. Alexander, *Holding the Line*, 214–17.

23. Ibid., 217–24.

24. Divine, *Eisenhower and the Cold War*, 127–46; Alexander, *Holding the Line*, 239–40; Eisenhower, *Waging Peace*, 337–42, 354–55, 432–35, 449.

25. Divine, *Eisenhower and the Cold War*, 146–48; Parmet, *Eisenhower*, 528; Eisenhower, *Waging Peace*, 544–49.

26. David Wise, *The Politics of Lying: Government Deception, Secrecy, and Power* (New York: Vintage Books, 1973), 47–50; Eisenhower, *Waging Peace*, 552–56; Lyon, *Eisenhower*, 811.

27. George B. Kistiakowsky, *A Scientist at the White House* (Cambridge, Mass.: Harvard University Press, 1976), 335–36, 375; Eisenhower, *Waging Peace*, 558.

28. Ewald, *Eisenhower*, 265–67. For overviews of covert operations during the Eisenhower years, see Ambrose, *Ike's Spies: Eisenhower and the Espionage Establishment* (Garden City, N.Y.: Doubleday & Co., 1981) and Blanche Wiesen Cook, *The Declassified Eisenhower* (Garden City, N.Y.: Doubleday & Co., 1981).

29. Lyon, *Eisenhower*, 544–53; Divine, *Eisenhower and the Cold War*, 71–79.

30. Lyon, *Eisenhower*, 588–92; Wise, *Politics of Lying*, 51; Alexander, *Holding the Line*, 74–77; Ambrose, *Eisenhower*, 2:193–97. For a comprehensive account of the Guatemalan operation, see Immerman, *The CIA in Guatemala: The Foreign Policy of Intervention* (Austin: University of Texas Press, 1982).

31. Immerman, *CIA in Guatemala*, 168–72.

32. For an overview of the foreign trade issue in the Eisenhower administration, see Burton I. Kaufman, *Trade and Aid: Eisenhower's Foreign Economic Policy* (Baltimore: Johns Hopkins University Press, 1982).

33. Ewald, *Eisenhower*, 267, 277; Wise, *Politics of Lying*, 244–55; Lyon, *Eisenhower*, 816–20.

10. MANAGING THE AMERICAN COMMONWEALTH

1. Eisenhower quoted in Robert Griffith, "Dwight D. Eisenhower and the Corporate Commonwealth," *American Historical Review* 87 (February 1982):93.

2. Ambrose, *Eisenhower*, 2:27; Eisenhower, *At Ease*, 42, 383.

3. Griffith, "Eisenhower and the Corporate Commonwealth," 109–10; Greenstein, *Hidden-Hand Presidency*, 36–37, 61; Lyon, *Eisenhower*, 500–501.

4. Eisenhower, *At Ease*, 320; Griffith, "Eisenhower and the Corporate Commonwealth," 111.

5. Lyon, *Eisenhower*, 483, 511.

6. Greenstein, *Hidden-Hand Presidency*, 92–95.

7. Ibid., 83–87, 102–4.

8. Lyon, *Eisenhower*, 467–68, 507; Griffith, "Eisenhower and the Corporate Commonwealth," 110.

9. Griffith, "Eisenhower and the Corporate Commonwealth," 114; Greenstein, *Hidden-Hand Presidency*, 161–64.

10. Griffith, "Eisenhower and the Corporate Commonwealth," 112–13; Lyon, *Eisenhower*, 491–96, 573; Greenstein, *Hidden-Hand Presidency*, 169.

11. Greenstein, *Hidden-Hand Presidency*, 164–81.

12. Ewald, *Eisenhower*, 122–23; Lyon, *Eisenhower*, 593, 598–600; Greenstein, *Hidden-Hand Presidency*, 182–209.

13. Greenstein, *Hidden-Hand Presidency*, 210–17; Lyon, *Eisenhower*, 618.

14. Griffith, "Eisenhower and the Corporate Commonwealth," 100, 106.

15. Alexander, *Holding the Line*, 161–63.

16. Griffith, "Eisenhower and the Corporate Commonwealth," 102.

17. Ibid., 103.

18. Ibid., 104.

19. Ibid., 104–5.

20. Ibid., 106.

21. Ambrose, *Eisenhower*, 1:80, 158; Alexander, *Holding the Line*, 40–41.

22. Ambrose, *Eisenhower*, 2:250–51, 527–28, 547–48; Alexander, *Holding the Line*, 41–42.

23. Alexander, *Holding the Line*, 160, 165–67; Ewald, *Eisenhower*, 200; Lyon, *Eisenhower*, 670–77.

24. Alexander, *Holding the Line*, 167–71.

25. Griffith, "Eisenhower and the Corporate Commonwealth," 107–9.

26. For a closer analysis of the Eisenhower administration's civil rights policies, see Robert F. Burk, *The Eisenhower Administration and Black Civil Rights* (Knoxville: University of Tennessee Press, 1984).

27. Ambrose, *Eisenhower*, 2:304, 307–8, 326–27, 406–26.

28. Ibid., 497–99.

29. Ibid., 459–60.

30. Alexander, *Holding the Line*, 242–43.

11. RETIREMENT AND RETROSPECTION

1. Lyon, *Eisenhower*, 823–25.

2. Alexander, *Holding the Line*, 269–71.

3. Ewald, *Eisenhower*, 167; Alexander, *Holding the Line*, 271, 273.

4. Ambrose, *Eisenhower*, 2:593–94.

5. Ibid., 600–601.

6. Alexander, *Holding the Line*, 278–79.

7. Lyon, *Eisenhower*, 828–29.

8. Alexander, *Holding the Line*, 288–91; Ambrose, *Eisenhower*, 2:611–13.

9. Ambrose, *Eisenhower*, 2:608–10, 637–38.

10. Lyon, *Eisenhower*, 842–43.

11. Eisenhower, *At Ease*, 49–50, 358–60.

12. Ambrose, *Eisenhower*, 2:632–35.

13. Lyon, *Eisenhower*, 833–39.

14. Alexander, *Holding the Line*, 291–92.

15. Mailer quoted in Garry Wills, *The Kennedy Imprisonment* (Boston: Little, Brown and Co., 1981), 145.

16. Eisenhower quoted in Richard Rovere, "Eisenhower Revisited—A Political Genius? A Brilliant Man?" *New York Times Magazine*, 7 February 1971, 62.

17. One of the earliest and most enthusiastic of the revisionist assessments of the Eisenhower stewardship was offered by Murray Kempton, "The Underestimation of Dwight D. Eisenhower," *Esquire* 72 (September 1967). The most important scholarly revisionist treatment of the Eisenhower leadership is Greenstein, *Hidden-Hand Presidency*.

18. Eisenhower, *Waging Peace*, 654.

19. R. Alton Lee, *Dwight D. Eisenhower: Soldier and Statesman* (Chicago: Nelson-Hall, 1981), 330.

BIBLIOGRAPHIC ESSAY

The essential primary sources for the study of Dwight D. Eisenhower's life are *The Papers of Dwight D. Eisenhower*, vols. 1–5, ed. Alfred D. Chandler, Jr., et al.; vols. 6–9, ed. Louis Galambos et al. (Baltimore: Johns Hopkins University Press, 1970, 1978) and the Eisenhower Papers at the Eisenhower Library in Abilene, Kansas. To date *The Papers of Dwight D. Eisenhower* cover the period from December 1941 to February 1948. The Eisenhower Library holdings document Eisenhower's entire life, with special emphasis on the presidential years. A portion of Eisenhower's military and presidential writings from the Eisenhower Library has been published as *The Eisenhower Diaries*, ed. Robert H. Ferrell (New York: W. W. Norton & Co., 1981). Eisenhower's own published writings include *At Ease: Stories I Tell to Friends* (Garden City, N.Y.: Doubleday & Co., 1967); his memoir of World War II, *Crusade in Europe* (Garden City, N.Y.: Doubleday & Co., 1948); and his two volumes of presidential memoirs, *Mandate for Change* and *Waging Peace* (Garden City, N.Y.: Doubleday & Co., 1965). Accounts by other family members are John S. D. Eisenhower, *Strictly Personal* (Garden City, N.Y.: Doubleday & Co., 1974) and Milton S. Eisenhower, *The President Is Calling* (Garden

City, N.Y.: Doubleday & Co., 1974) and *The Wine Is Bitter* (Garden City, N.Y.: Doubleday & Co., 1963).

Published biographies of Dwight D. Eisenhower, written at varying times during his life and after his death in 1969 include Stephen E. Ambrose, *Eisenhower: Soldier, General of the Army, President-Elect. 1890–1952* and *Eisenhower: The President* (New York: Simon and Schuster, 1983, 1984); Kenneth S. Davis, *Soldier of Democracy: A Biography of Dwight Eisenhower* (New York: Doubleday, Doran & Co., 1945); John Gunther, *Eisenhower: The Man and the Symbol* (New York: Harper & Bros., 1952); R. Alton Lee, *Dwight D. Eisenhower: Soldier and Statesman* (Chicago: Nelson-Hall, 1981); Peter Lyon, *Eisenhower: Portrait of the Hero* (Boston: Little, Brown and Co., 1974); Kevin McCann, *Man from Abilene* (New York: Doubleday & Co., 1952); and Francis Trevelyan Miller, *Eisenhower: Man and Soldier* (Philadelphia: John C. Winston Co., 1944). Of these, Ambrose is the most comprehensive while generally sympathetic to his subject, Lyon the most critical, and Davis the best for information on Eisenhower's early life. For additional material on Eisenhower's boyhood years, see Bela Kornitzer, *The Great American Heritage: The Story of the Five Eisenhower Brothers* (New York: Farrar, Straus and Cudahy, 1955) and Steve Neal, *The Eisenhowers: Reluctant Dynasty* (Garden City, N.Y.: Doubleday & Co., 1978). For information on Mamie Eisenhower and her marriage to Dwight, the reader should consult Dwight D. Eisenhower, *Letters to Mamie* ed. John S. D. Eisenhower (Garden City, N.Y.: Doubleday & Co., 1978), and two biographies of Mamie Eisenhower—Dorothy Brandon, *Mamie Doud Eisenhower* (New York: Charles Scribner's Sons, 1954) and Alden Hatch, *Red Carpet for Mamie* (New York: Henry Holt and Co., 1954).

For Eisenhower's early career in the United States Army, the previously cited memoirs and biographies constitute the principal sources. For additional insights into the history of the twentieth-century American army, see Ambrose, *Duty, Honor, Country: A History of West Point* (Baltimore: Johns Hopkins Press, 1966); Samuel Huntington, *The Soldier and the State* (Cambridge, Mass.: Harvard University Press, 1957); Morris Janowitz, *The Professional Soldier: A Social and Political Portrait* (New York: Free Press of Glencoe, 1960); and Russell Weigley, *The History of the United States Army* (New York: Macmillan Co., 1967). Eisenhower's early views on tank warfare are outlined in "A Tank Discussion," *Infantry Journal*, November 1920. His depression-era plans for war mobilization are detailed in "War Policies," *Cavalry Journal*, November-December 1931. Memoirs and papers of colleagues in the prewar and wartime United States Army in the 1920s, 1930s, and 1940s include Martin Blumenson, *The Patton Papers*, 2 vols. (Boston: Houghton Mifflin Co., 1972, 1974); Omar Bradley, *A Soldier's Story* (New York; Henry Holt and Co., 1951) and, with Clay Blair, *A General's Life* (New York: Simon and

Schuster, 1983); Mark Wayne Clark, *Calculated Risk* (New York: Harper & Bros., 1950); Douglas MacArthur, *Reminiscences* (New York: McGraw-Hill, 1964); George S. Patton, Jr., *War as I Knew It* (Boston: Houghton Mifflin Co., 1947); Walter Bedell Smith, *Eisenhower's Six Great Decisions* (New York: Longmans, Green and Co., 1956); and Lucian K. Truscott, Jr., *Command Missions* (New York: E. P. Dutton and Co., 1954).

Some of the most revealing personal insights into Eisenhower's military command style during World War II come from the memoirs of Eisenhower's personal staff. They include Harry Butcher, *My Three Years with Eisenhower* (New York: Simon and Schuster, 1946); Michael McKeogh and Richard Lockridge, *Sergeant Mickey and General Ike* (New York: G. P. Putnam's Sons, 1946); and Kay Summersby, *Eisenhower Was my Boss* (New York: Prentice-Hall, 1948) and, under her married name, Kay Summersby Morgan, *Past Forgetting: My Love Affair with Dwight D. Eisenhower* (New York: Simon and Schuster, 1976). The latter volume's assertions of a relationship between Summersby and Eisenhower must be read with both skepticism and caution. For wartime accounts of Eisenhower's leadership as a supreme commander by his American colleagues, see the previously cited works. Other participant accounts by wartime diplomats and politicians and by British and French military leaders are Lewis H. Brereton, *The Brereton Diaries* (New York: William Morrow and Co., 1946); Winston S. Churchill, *The Second World War*, 6 vols. (Boston: Houghton Mifflin Co., 1948–53); Viscount Cunningham of Hyndhope *A Soldier's Odyssey* (London: Hutchinson & Co., 1951); Charles de Gaulle, *The War Memoirs of Charles de Gaulle*, vol. 2, *Unity* (New York: Simon and Schuster, 1959); Sir Francis de Guingand, *Operation Victory* (New York: Charles Scribner's Sons, 1947); Hastings L. Ismay, *The Memoirs of General Lord Ismay* (New York: Viking Press, 1960); Harold Macmillan, *The Blast of War: 1939–1945* (New York: Harper & Row, 1968); Bernard Law Montgomery, *Memoirs* (Cleveland: World Publishing Co., 1958); Robert Murphy. *Diplomat among Warriors* (Garden City, N.Y.: Doubleday & Co., 1964); and Sir Arthur Tedder, *With Prejudice* (London: Cassell, 1966).

The best published assessment of Eisenhower's performance as a supreme commander in World War II is Ambrose, *The Supreme Commander: The War Years of General Dwight D. Eisenhower* (Garden City, N.Y.: Doubleday & Co., 1970). The British view of Eisenhower's strengths and weaknesses is presented in E. K. G. Sixsmith, *Eisenhower as Military Commander* (New York: Stein and Day, 1972). Biographies of key American commanders include Ladislas Farago, *Patton: Ordeal and Triumph* (New York: Astor-Honor, Inc., 1964); D. Clayton James, *The Years of MacArthur*, vol. 1, *1880–1941* (Boston: Houghton Mifflin Co., 1970); and Forrest C. Pogue's magnificent multivolume biography of George C. Marshall, especially *Ordeal and Hope, 1939–1942* (New York: Viking Press, 1966) and *Organizer of Victory, 1943–*

1945 (New York: Viking Press, 1973). Among the flood of studies of particular campaigns and incidents are Ambrose, *Eisenhower and Berlin, 1945: The Decision to Halt at the Elbe* (New York: W.W. Norton & Co., 1967); Hanson W. Baldwin, *Battles Lost and Won: Great Campaigns of World War II* (New York: Harper & Row, 1966); Martin Blumenson, *Breakout and Pursuit* (Washington, D.C.: U.S. Department of the Army, 1961) and *Kasserine Pass* (Boston: Houghton Mifflin Co., 1967); Sir Arthur Bryant, *Triumph in the West* (London: Collins, 1959) and *The Turn of the Tide* (New York: Doubleday & Co., 1957); Albert N. Garland and Howard McGaw Smyth, *Sicily and the Surrender of Italy* (Washington, D.C.: U.S. Department of the Army, 1965); Gordon A. Harrison, *Cross-Channel Attack* (Washington, D.C.: U.S. Department of the Army, 1951); David Irving, *The War between the Generals* (New York: Congdon & Lattès, 1981); W. G. F. Jackson, *The North African Campaign, 1940–1943* (London: Batsford, 1975); Charles MacDonald, *Siegfried Line Campaign* (Washington, D.C.: U.S. Department of the Army, 1963); Pogue, *The Supreme Command* (Washington, D.C.: U.S. Department of the Army, 1954); Russell Weigley, *Eisenhower's Lieutenants: The Campaigns of France and Germany, 1944–1945* (Bloomington, Ind.: Indiana University Press, 1981); Chester Wilmot, *Struggle in Europe* (New York: Harper, 1952); and Alan F. Wilt, *The Atlantic Wall: Hilter's Defenses in the West, 1941–1944* (Ames, Iowa: Iowa State University Press, 1975).

Overviews of the early cold war years include such works as Ambrose, *Rise to Globalism: American Foreign Policy Since 1938* (New York: Penguin, 1972); John Lewis Gaddis, *The United States and the Origins of the Cold War, 1941–1947* (New York: Columbia University Press, 1972); and Walter LaFeber, *America, Russia, and the Cold War, 1945–1975* (New York: John Wiley and Sons, 1976). For discussion of Eisenhower's own postwar duties in occupied Germany, see Lucius Clay, *Decision in Germany* (New York: Doubleday & Co., 1950); Beate Ruhm von Oppen, ed., *Documents on Germany under Occupation* (London: Oxford University Press, 1955); and Harold Zink, *The United States in Germany, 1944–1955* (Princeton, N.J.: D. Van Nostrand Co., 1957). Memoirs of Truman administration foreign policy officials include Dean Acheson, *Present at the Creation* (New York: W.W. Norton & Co., 1969); William C. Bullitt, *The Great Globe Itself: A Preface to World Affairs* (New York: Charles Scribner's Sons, 1946); and David E. Lilienthal, *The Journals of David E. Lilienthal*, vol. 2, *The Atomic Energy Years, 1945–1950* (New York: Harper & Row, 1964). For Truman's own views see his *Memoirs*, vol. 1, *Year of Decisions* (Garden City, N.Y.: Doubleday & Co., 1955) and vol. 2, *Years of Trial and Hope* (Garden City, N.Y.: Doubleday & Co., 1956), and also Merle Miller, *Plain Speaking: An Oral Biography of Harry S. Truman* (New York: Berkley Publishing Co., 1973). For a study of the Joint Chiefs of Staff and Eisenhower's service on it in the late 1940s, consult *His-*

tory of the Joint Chiefs of Staff, 4 vols., (Washington, D.C.: Government Printing Office, 1982). Eisenhower's uneasy tenure at Columbia Univeristy is discussed in Ira H. Freeman, "Eisenhower of Columbia," *New York Times Magazine*, 7 November 1948. The early history of the NATO alliance, including Eisenhower's service as supreme commander, is chronicled in Robert E. Osgood, *NATO: The Entangling Alliance* (Chicago: University of Chicago Press, 1962).

Eisenhower's growing interest in the presidency, and the growing popular speculation about his political intentions, is noted in the memoirs of such journalists as Arthur Krock, *In the Nation: 1932–1966* (New York: McGraw-Hill, 1966) and *Memoirs: Sixty Years on the Firing Line* (New York: Funk and Wagnalls, 1968); and C. L. Sultzberger, *A Long Row of Candles* (New York: Macmillan, 1969). Insights from two close business friends of Eisenhower are offered in Clifford Roberts, *The Story of the Augusta National Golf Club* (Garden City, N.Y.: Doubleday & Co., 1976), and Ellis D. Slater, *The Ike I Knew* (New York: privately printed, 1980). Thomas E. Dewey's role in encouraging an Eisenhower presidential candidacy in 1952 is analyzed in Richard Norton Smith, *Thomas E. Dewey and His Times* (New York: Simon and Schuster, 1982). The opening chapters of Herbert S. Parmet, *Eisenhower and the American Crusades* (New York: Macmillan Co., 1972) offer an overview of Eisenhower's 1952 campaign. For the "liberation," McCarthyism, and internal security issues of cold war politics and their treatment in 1952, see Robert Griffith, "The General and the Senator," *Wisconsin Magazine of History*, Autumn 1970; Thomas C. Reeves, *The Life and Times of Joe McCarthy* (New York: Stein and Day, 1982); and Athan G. Theoharris, *The Yalta Myths: An Issue in U.S. Politics, 1945–1955* (Columbia, Mo.: University of Missouri Press, 1970). The best biography of Eisenhower's general election opponent in both 1952 and 1956, Adlai E. Stevenson, is John Bartlow Martin, *Adlai Stevenson of Illinois* (Garden City, New York: Doubleday & Co., 1976). For insider accounts of the Eisenhower campaign of 1952, including the Checkers incident, see Sherman Adams, *Firsthand Report* (New York: Harper & Bros., 1961); Emmet John Hughes, *The Ordeal of Power: A Political Memoir of the Eisenhower Years* (New York: Atheneum, 1963); Henry Cabot Lodge, Jr., *As It Was: An Inside View of Politics and Power in the '50s and '60s* (New York: W.W. Norton & Co., 1976); and Richard M. Nixon, *The Memoirs of Richard M. Nixon* (New York: Grosset & Dunlap, 1978) and *Six Crises* (Garden City, N.Y.: Doubleday & Co., 1962).

In addition to Eisenhower's own papers and published memoirs, insider accounts of the Eisenhower White House provide useful insights into the president's methods and policies. In addition to the Adams, Hughes, Lodge, and Nixon accounts listed above, see also Ezra Taft Benson, *Cross Fire: The Eight Years with Eisenhower* (Garden City, N.Y.: Doubleday & Co., 1962);

Robert Cutler, *No Time for Rest* (Boston: Little, Brown and Co., 1966); William Bragg Ewald, *Eisenhower the President: Crucial Days, 1951–1960* (Englewood Cliffs, N.J.: Prentice-Hall, 1981); Robert H. Ferrell, ed., *The Diary of James C. Hagerty: Eisenhower in Mid-Course, 1954–1955* (Bloomington, Ind.: Indiana University Press, 1983); George B. Kistiakowsky, *A Scientist at the White House* (Cambridge, Mass.: Harvard University Press, 1976); Arthur Larson, *The President Nobody Knew* (New York: Charles Scribner's Sons, 1968); E. Frederic Morrow, *Black Man in the White House* (New York: Coward-McCann, 1963) and *Forty Years a Guinea Pig* (New York: Pilgrim Press, 1980); and Lewis Strauss, *Men and Decisions* (Garden City, N.Y.: Doubleday & Co., 1962). An early assessment by a journalist with special access to the White House in the administrator's early months is Robert J. Donovan, *Eisenhower: The Inside Story* (New York: Harper & Bros., 1956). Participant recollections of foreign policy events and crises include William Colby, *Honorable Men: My Life in the CIA* (New York: Simon and Schuster, 1978); Kermit Roosevelt, *Countercoup: The Struggle for the Control of Iran* (New York: McGraw-Hill, 1979); and Vernon Walters, *Silent Missions* (Garden City, N.Y.: Doubleday & Co., 1978). For a view from a major Allied leader, see Anthony Eden, *Full Circle* (Boston: Houghton Mifflin Co., 1960).

Published overviews of the Eisenhower administration, in addition to the Ambrose, Lee, Lyon, and Parmet books previously cited, include Charles C. Alexander, *Holding the Line: The Eisenhower Era, 1952–1961* (Bloomington, Ind.: Indiana University Press, 1975); Robert Griffith, "Dwight D. Eisenhower and the Corporate Commonwealth," *American Historical Review* 87 (February 1982); and Elmo Richardson, *The Presidency of Dwight D. Eisenhower* (Lawrence: Regents Press of Kansas, 1979). For analyses of electoral politics in the 1950s, see Barton J. Bernstein, "Election of 1952" and Theodore C. Sorenson, "Election of 1960," in Arthur M. Schlesinger, Jr., and Fred L. Israel, eds., *The Coming to Power: Critical Presidential Elections in American History* (New York: Chelsea House. 1972), 385–457; two studies by Angus Campbell, Philip Converse, Warren Miller, and Donald Stokes, *The Voter Decides* (Evanston, Ill.: Row Peterson, 1954) and *The American Voter* (New York: John Wiley and Sons, 1960), which examined the 1952 and 1956 elections; Heinz Eulau, *Class and Party in the Eisenhower Years: Class Roles and Perspectives in the 1952 and 1956 Elections* (New York: Free Press of Glencoe, 1962); and Charles A. H. Thomson, *Television and Presidential Politics: The Experience in 1952 and the Problems Ahead* (Washington, D.C.: Brookings Institution, 1956). Eisenhower's early legislative performance is assessed in Gary W. Reichard, *The Reaffirmation of Republicanism* (Knoxville: University of Tennessee Press, 1975).

Overviews of Eisenhower foreign policy include Blanche Wiesen Cook, *The Declassified Eisenhower: A Divided Legacy of Peace and Political Warfare*

(Garden City, N.Y.: Doubleday & Co., 1981); Robert A. Divine, *Eisenhower and the Cold War* (New York: Oxford University Press, 1981); and Douglas Kinnard, *President Eisenhower and Stategy Management* (Lexington: University Press of Kentucky, 1977). On the relationship between Secretary of State John Foster Dulles and Eisenhower, the reader should consult Townsend Hoopes, *The Devil and John Foster Dulles* (Boston: Little Brown and Co., 1973), and Richard Immerman, "Eisenhower and Dulles: Who Made the Decisions?" *Political Psychology* 1 (1979). The New Look is examined in the Brookings Institution, *Force without War: U.S. Armed Forces as a Political Instrument* (Washington, D.C., 1978) and E. Bruce Geelhoed, *Charles E. Wilson and Controversy at the Pentagon, 1953 to 1957* (Detroit: Wayne State University Press, 1979). The Suez crisis is detailed in Donald Neff, *Warriors at Suez: Eisenhower Takes America into the Middle East* (New York: Simon and Schuster, 1981). The best study of the nuclear testing issue is Divine, *Blowing on the Wind: The Nuclear Test Ban Debate* (New York: Oxford University Press, 1978). Eisenhower's foreign aid policies are covered in Burton I. Kaufman, *Trade and Aid: Eisenhower's Foreign Economic Policy* (Baltimore: John Hopkins University Press, 1982). In addition to the Cook study, other accounts of CIA operations during the Eisenhower years include Ambrose, *Ike's Spies: Eisenhower and the Espionage Establishment* (Garden City, N.Y.: Doubleday & Co., 1981); Immerman, *The CIA in Guatemala: The Foreign Policy of Intervention* (Austin: University of Texas Press, 1982); David Wise, *The Politics of Lying: Government Deception, Secrecy, and Power* (New York: Vintage Books, 1973); and Peter Wynden, *Bay of Pigs: The Untold Story* (London: Jonathan Cape, 1979).

Numerous monographs analyzing Eisenhower administration domestic policies have been produced in recent years. The subject of McCarthyism and Eisenhower's official response to it has been examined in Ewald, previously cited; and Fred I Greenstein, *The Hidden-Hand Presidency: Eisenhower as Leader* (New York: Basic Books, 1982), tries to build a case for the effectiveness of Eisenhower's strategy against McCarthy. Robert Griffith, *The Politics of Fear: Joseph McCarthy and the Senate* (Lexington: University Press of Kentucky, 1970) and Thomas C. Reeves, previously cited, are also valuable for their insights into the political dangers of challenging McCarthy. For analyses of transportation policies during the Eisenhower years, see Richard O. Davies, *The Age of Asphalt: The Automobile, the Freeway, and the Condition of Metropolitan America* (Philadelphia: J.B. Lippincott Co., 1975); Mark Rose, *Interstate: Express Highway Politics* (Lawrence: Regents Press of Kansas, 1979); and Gary T. Schwartz, "Urban Freeways and the Interstate System," *Southern California Law Review* 49 (March 1976). For additional insights on the effects of the Interstate Highway program and other policies on American cities, see Mark I. Gelfand, *A Nation of Cities: The Federal Government and Urban Amer-*

ica, 1933–1965 (New York: Oxford University Press, 1975). On the St. Lawrence Seaway project, see William R. Willoughby, *The St. Lawrence Seaway: A Study in Politics and Diplomacy* (Madison: University of Wisconsin Press, 1961).

On public power and environmental issues, see Elmo Richardson, *Dams, Parks, and Politics: Resource Development and Preservation in the Truman-Eisenhower Era* (Lexington: University Press of Kentucky, 1973) and Aaron Wildavsky, *Dixon-Yates: A Study in Power Politics* (New Haven, Conn.: Yale University Press, 1962). Charges of administration-business collusion are examined in David A. Frier, *Conflict of Interest in The Eisenhower Administration* (Ames: Iowa State University Press, 1969). Sympathetic treatments of the administration's antitrust and farm policies are offered in Theodore P. Kovaleff, *Business and Government during the Eisenhower Administration: A Study of the Antitrust Division of the Justice Department* (Athens: Ohio University Press, 1980) and Edward L. and Frank H. Schapsmeier, *Ezra Taft Benson and the Politics of Agriculture: The Eisenhower Years, 1953–1961* (Danville, Ill.: Interstate, 1975). Labor law developments are covered in Alan K. McAdams, *Power and Politics in Labor Legislation* (New York: Columbia University Press, 1964). The Eisenhower record in social policies is contrasted with his successors by James L. Sundquist in *Politics and Policy: The Eisenhower, Kennedy, and Johnson Years* (Washington, D.C.: Brookings Institution, 1968). On civil rights, the best treatment is Robert F. Burk, *The Eisenhower Administration and Black Civil Rights* (Knoxville: University of Tennessee Press, 1984). Barbara Barksdale Clowse, *Brainpower for the Cold War: The Sputnik Crisis and the National Defense Education Act of 1958* (Westport, Conn.: Greenwood Press, 1981) charts the debate over federal aid to education in the second term.

The earliest attempts at long-term assessments of Dwight Eisenhower's success or failure as a national leader were offered by journalists and political scientists in the 1950s and early 1960s, and most tended to offer negative evaluations. For examples, see Marquis Childs, *Eisenhower: Captive Hero* (New York: Harcourt, Brace and Co., 1958); Richard Neustadt, *Presidential Power: The Politics of Leadership* (New York: John Wiley, 1960); Richard Rovere, *Affairs of State: The Eisenhower Years* (New York: Farrar, Straus and Cudahy, 1956); William V. Shannon, "Eisenhower as President," *Commentary* 26 (November 1958); and Norman A. Graebner, "Eisenhower's Popular Leadership," *Current History* 39 (October 1960). The first major reassessment of Eisenhower by a liberal journalist in the 1960s was Murray Kempton's "The Underestimation of Dwight D. Eisenhower," *Esquire* 68 (September 1967). Since the late 1960s, the tide of critical opinion has been moving steadily toward more favorable assessments of Eisenhower's leadership. Among the many articles and books containing such reassessments are Ambrose, "The Ike Age," *New Republic* 9 May 1981; Vincent P. DeSantis, "Eisenhower Revisionism," *Journal of Politics* 38 (September 1976); Gary W. Reichard, "Eisenhower as President: The Changing View," *South Atlantic Quarterly* 77 (Summer 1978); Richard Rhodes, "Ike: An Artist in Iron," *Harper's* 241 (July 1970); and Garry Wills, *The Kennedy Imprisonment: A Meditation on Power* (Boston: Little, Brown and Co., 1981), which draws contrasts between Kennedy recklessness and Eisenhower restraint. By far the most important revisionist, however, has been Fred I. Greenstein, who has stressed Eisenhower's presidential activism and effectiveness in "Eisenhower as an Activist President," *Political Science Quarterly* 94 (Winter 1979–80) and *The Hidden-Hand Presidency,* previously cited. Critics of this revisionism have either reasserted Eisenhower's passivity as a leader, as does Richard Rovere in "Eisenhower Revisited—A Political Genius? A Brilliant Man?" *New York Times Magazine,* 7 February 1971, or have noted that whatever activism Eisenhower displayed was for decidedly conservative ends, as does William E. Leuchtenberg in *In the Shadow of FDR: From Harry Truman to Ronald Reagan* (Ithaca, N.Y.: Cornell University Press, 1983).

INDEX

ABOUT THE AUTHOR

Robert Fredrick Burk was born in Topeka, Kansas, in 1955 and grew up in the town of Scranton. He attended the University of Kansas as a National Merit Scholar from 1973 to 1977, where he received his B.A. degree. From 1977 to December 1982, he pursued graduate studies at the University of Wisconsin—Madison, from which he obtained his M.A. and Ph.D. degrees. He was chosen as the first Merle Curti Lecturer at the University of Wisconsin in the spring semester of 1983, and became visiting assistant professor of history at the University of Cincinnati for the 1983–84 academic year. In the fall of 1984 he assumed duties as assistant professor of U.S. history at Muskingum College, in New Concord, Ohio, where he presently teaches. Dr. Burk is the author of various articles on race relations and the Eisenhower presidency, as well as *The Eisenhower Administration and Black Civil Rights*, published in 1984 by the University of Tennessee Press.